Insights to Performance Excellence 2000

Also Available from ASQ Quality Press

From Baldrige to the Bottom Line: A Road Map for Organizational Change and Improvement
David W. Hutton

Principles and Practices of Organizational Performance Excellence
Thomas J. Cartin

The Certified Quality Manager Handbook
Quality Management Division of ASQ

Critical SHIFT: The Future of Quality in Organizational Performance
Lori Silverman with Annabeth L. Propst

Business Process Improvement Toolbox
Bjørn Andersen

Managing Change: Practical Strategies for Competitive Advantage
Kari Tuominen

Success through Quality: Support Guide for the Journey to Continuous Improvement
Timothy J. Clark

101 Good Ideas: How to Improve Just About Any Process
Karen Bemowski and Brad Stratton, editors

Principles of Quality Costs: Principles, Implementation and Use, Third Edition
ASQ Quality Costs Committee—Jack Campanella, editor

Managing Quality Fads: How American Business Learned to Play the Quality Game
Robert Cole

Statistical Quality Control Using Excel (with software)
Steven M. Zimmerman, Ph.D. and Marjorie L. Icenogle, Ph.D.

Root Cause Analysis: Simplified Tools and Techniques
Bjørn Andersen and Tom Fagerhaug

To request a complimentary catalog of ASQ Quality Press publications, call 800-248-1946, or visit our online bookstore at http://qualitypress.asq.org.

Insights to Performance Excellence 2000

An Inside Look at the 2000 Baldrige Award Criteria

Mark L. Blazey

ASQ Quality Press
Milwaukee, Wisconsin

Insights to Performance Excellence 2000: An Inside Look at the 2000 Baldrige Award Criteria
Mark L. Blazey

ISBN 0-87389-483-9

Acquisitions Editor: Ken Zielske
Project Editor: Annemieke Koudstaal
Production Administrator: Shawn Dohogne
Special Marketing Representative: David Luth

ASQ Mission: The American Society for Quality advances individual and organizational performance excellence worldwide by providing opportunities for learning, quality improvement, and knowledge exchange.

Attention: Bookstores, Wholesalers, Schools and Corporations: ASQ Quality Press books, videotapes, audiotapes, and software are available at quantity discounts with bulk purchases for business, educational, or instructional use. For information, please contact ASQ Quality Press at 800-248-1946, or write to ASQ Quality Press, P.O. Box 3005, Milwaukee, WI 53201-3005.

To place orders or to request a free copy of the ASQ Quality Press Publications Catalog, including ASQ membership information, call 800-248-1946. Visit our web site at www.asq.org. or http://qualitypress.asq.org.

Printed in the United States of America

 Printed on acid-free paper

American Society for Quality

Quality Press
611 East Wisconsin Avenue
Milwaukee, Wisconsin 53202
Call toll free 800-248-1946
www.asq.org
http://qualitypress.asq.org
http://standardsgroup.asq.org

This book is dedicated to the memory of my father,
who taught me the value of continuous improvement,
and to my family, who provide support for the continuous search for quality: my mother, Ann Marrer Blazey;
my brothers Scott, Brian, and Brent; my children
Elizabeth and Mark; and most of all, my lifelong
partner and loving wife Karen.

Contents

Foreword

LEADERSHIP CHALLENGES

Today's business leaders find themselves at a critical historical juncture. They find themselves having to change and often reinvent the way business is run. The old way of doing it just doesn't get it done any longer. Successfully leading a business today demands virtually all of a leader's attention and energy. It used to be that change involved leading the organization across a chasm from one steady state to another steady state. In the middle was the chasm of chaos we call "change." The change portion of the journey was treated as a temporary state. Change was something to be dealt with, attacked, and put behind you—the quicker the better.

Today's leader is faced with a constant state of change. This constant change demands a different kind of organization and a different kind of focus. In the emerging economy, it's the excellence of the system and its ability to very quickly bring value to the marketplace that makes the difference. This difference demands a major change in the way we think. We have come to think of our organizations as machine-like. That thinking is an outgrowth of the Industrial Revolution. It even dominates our language. I recently heard someone talking about "driving" their organization—driving people. They were referring to motivating and inspiring people (not transporting). Have you "driven" your children lately? Have you "driven" your spouse lately? As much as we admire the organizational forms we have invented, they are by and large not systems, and they are not efficient. More importantly, they are not getting the job done.

Leaders today are confronted with this challenge—harness the energy of the organization and its people to very quickly bring value to the marketplace. The tools to help leaders make these types of changes are few and far between. A partial list includes the systematic approach of the Baldrige criteria, literature on some of the breakthrough thinking around learning organizations, and the move toward knowledge management and knowledge sharing. This book by Dr. Blazey is one of those tools. Mark Blazey's work provides important insights into practices that can be used to understand your business and help begin the continuous improvements that lead to business excellence. In a world of constant change, this is the kind of assistance business leaders look for to help move the ball forward.

—John Lawrence
Vice President of Quality, Xerox

Acknowledgments

Curt Reimann, Harry Hertz, and the dedicated staff of the Malcolm Baldrige National Quality Award office have provided long-standing support and guidance in promoting quality excellence. The book would not be possible in a timely fashion without the design and layout expertise, dedication, and commitment of Enterprise Design and Publishing. In addition, several others have helped shape my thinking about Performance Excellence and refined this book, including John Lawrence, Mary Gamble, Karen Davison, Orland Pitts, Jeff Martin, Sharon Miletich, Maryann Brennan, John A. Pieno, Jr., Dione Geiger, Ed Hare, April Mitchell, George Bureau, Debra Danziger-Barron, Skip Coggins, Jim Shipley, Karen Hoffman, Michael Chapman, Sheryl Billups, Tom Kubiak, Pat Billings, Wendy Brennan, Gerald Brown, Anne O'Brien, Wendy Steager, Steve Hoisington, Gary Floss, Jack Evans, Arnie Weimerskirch, Paul Grizzell, Olga Striltschuk, Dale Misczynski, Don Anderson, Dennis Sester, Greg Feldman, George Raemore, and Kasuko Nishizaki. I also appreciate the typing assistance and proofreading of Jessica Ayers. The chapter on site visits, the criteria model, the Pilot survey, the supplemental scoring guidelines, and some of the information pertaining to changes from the 1999 Criteria are used with permission of Quantum Performance Group, Inc. The core values, Criteria, selected glossary terms, and background information in this book are drawn from the *Malcolm Baldrige National Quality Award 2000 Criteria for Performance Excellence.* Kevin Hendricks and Vinod Singhal provided research results that were used in this book from their extensive study of financial performance. Data from the Foundation for the Malcolm Baldrige National Quality Award regarding the perception of chief executive officers from over 300 U.S. organizations were also included in this book.

—*Mark Blazey*

Preface

A substantial portion of my professional life has been spent helping people understand the power and benefits of this integrated management system and become quality award examiners. These people come from all types of organizations and from all levels within those organizations. Participants include corporate quality directors, state organization chiefs, small business owners, heads of hospitals, and school superintendents, to name a few. This book was originally developed for them. It was used as a teaching text to guide their decisions and deliberations as they provided feedback to organizations that documented their continuous improvement efforts using Baldrige Award-type management systems. Many examiners who used this text asked me to publish it in a stand-alone format. They wanted to use it to help their own organizations, customers, and suppliers guide and assess their continuous improvement efforts.

These two groups of readers—examiners of quality systems and leaders of high-performing organizations—can gain a competitive edge by understanding not only the parts of a high-performance management system, but how these parts connect and align. My goal for this book is that readers will understand fully what each area of the quality system means for organizations and find the synergy within the seven major parts of the system: leadership, strategic planning, customer and market focus, information and analysis, human resource focus, process management, and business results.

Organization leaders have reported that this book has been valuable as a step-by-step approach to help identify and put in place continuous improvement systems. As this progresses, improvement efforts in one area will lead to improvements in other areas. This process is similar to experiences we have all encountered as we carry out home improvement: Improve one area, and many other areas needing improvement become apparent. This book will help identify areas that need immediate improvement, as well as areas that are less urgent but, nevertheless, vitally linked to overall improvement.

Introduction

The *Malcolm Baldrige National Quality Award 2000 Criteria for Performance Excellence* and scoring guidelines are powerful assessment instruments that help leaders identify organizational strengths and key areas for improvement. The primary task of leaders is then to use the information to achieve higher levels of performance.

Building an effective management system capable of driving performance improvement is an ongoing challenge because of the intricate web of complex relationships among management, labor, customers, stakeholders, partners, and suppliers. The best organizations have a management system that improves its work processes continually. They measure every key facet of business activity and closely monitor organizational performance. Leaders of these organizations set high expectations, value employees and their input, communicate clear directions, and align the work of everyone to achieve organizational goals and optimize performance.

Unfortunately, because of the complexity of modern management systems, the criteria used to examine them are also complex and difficult to understand. *Insights to Performance Excellence 2000* helps Performance Excellence examiners and organization improvement practitioners clearly understand the 2000 Baldrige Performance Excellence Criteria and the linkages and relationships between the Items.

Five types of information are provided in this book for each of the 19 Items that comprise the Criteria:
- **The actual language of each Item, including notes.**
- **A *plain English* explanation of the essence of the Item** with some suggestions about meeting key requirements.
- **A summary of the requirements of the Item in flowchart form.** The flowcharts capture the essence of each Item and isolate the requirements of each Item to help organizations focus on the key points the Item is assessing. Note that most boxes in the flowcharts contain an Item reference in brackets [ ]. This indicates that the Criteria require the action. If there is no Item reference in brackets, it means the action is suggested but not required. Occasionally a reference to "[scoring guidelines]" is included in a box. This means that, according to the scoring guidelines, the requirement to evaluate and refine a process is required to score above the 50 percent level.

- **The key linkages between each Item and the other Items.** The major or primary linkages are designated using a solid arrow (———►). The secondary linkages are designated using a dashed arrow (- - - - ►).
- **Examples of effective practices that some organizations have developed and followed.** These samples present some ideas about how to meet requirements. Examiners should not take these sample effective practices and convert them into requirements for organizations they are examining.

Several changes have been made to this 2000 edition:
- Changes have been made in some of the linkages between the Items.
- An explanation of the changes in the core values and concepts between 1999 and 2000 is provided in this edition.
- A more indepth explanation of the Criteria requirements has been added.
- Minor changes in the scoring guidelines have been identified.
- A revised section has been added to guide organizations through a streamlined self-assessment process. In addition, a short organizational self-assessment has been provided with the permission of Quantum Performance Group, Inc.

Taken together, *Insights to Performance Excellence 2000* will strengthen your understanding of the Criteria and provide insight on analyzing your organization, improving performance, and applying for the award.

Insights to Performance Excellence

This section provides information for leaders who are transforming their organizations to achieve Performance Excellence. This section:
- Presents a business case for using the Baldrige Criteria to improve organizational performance;
- Describes the core values that drive organizational change to high levels of performance and underlie the Baldrige Criteria; and
- Provides practical insights and lessons learned—ideas on transition strategies to put high-performance systems in place and promote organizational learning.

This section emphasizes themes driven by the 2000 Criteria and core values. It also includes suggestions about how to start down the path to systematic organizational improvement, as well as lessons learned from those who chose paths that led nowhere or proved futile despite their best efforts.

The Business Case for Using the Baldrige Performance Excellence Criteria

All leaders know that change is not easy. They will be asked and perhaps tempted to turn back many times. They may not even be aware of these temptations or of the backsliding that occurs when their peers and subordinates sense their commitment is wavering. Those leaders who are dedicated to achieving high performance appreciate examples of success from organizations that are ahead of them on the journey. These are organizations that have held the course despite nagging doubts, organizational turbulence, and attempts at sabotage.

The following section of the book:
- Summarizes perceptions and predictions about business trends and the value of the Malcolm Baldrige Award, based on survey responses of chief executive officers (CEOs) from 308 major U.S. organizations. This survey was conducted by the Foundation for the Malcolm Baldrige National Quality Award, April 1998.
- Summarizes research on financial performance of approximately 400 firms that were recognized by local, state, or national award for quality management practices. (Research results are reported with permission of Dr. Vinod R. Singhal. Research was conducted by Kevin B. Hendricks and Vinod R. Singhal.)

- Describes public and private sector organizations that have made rapid strides forward on their journeys, having achieved recognition as winners of the Malcolm Baldrige National Quality Award. It then identifies the core values that have guided these organizations to achieve high levels of Performance Excellence.

Value of Baldrige Criteria and Awards

In a report entitled The Nation's CEOs Look to the Future,[1] 308 CEOs from large, small, and several noncorporate organizations described what they believe lies ahead for business in the United States and the value of the Baldrige Criteria and Award. These trends relate in many ways to the 1999 Criteria and will be considered each year as the Criteria are revised to reflect the current business environment and the most effective management practices for that environment.

The vast majority (67 percent to 79 percent) of the CEOs believe that the Baldrige Criteria and Awards are very or extremely valuable in stimulating improvements in quality and competitiveness in U.S. businesses. Given the trends and business environment they describe in the survey and how they see U.S. businesses keeping pace, the Criteria provide a valuable competitive advantage.

Major Trends

More than 70 percent of the CEOs reported the following trends as major ones that will be likely to effect the business environment significantly in the coming years:

- **Globalization.** This trend, identified as critical by 94 percent of respondents, has implications for all Categories, but particularly strategic planning, where global competition and alliances must be included in planning and for customer and market focus where building and maintaining customer relationships is critical;
- **Improving knowledge management.** This trend, identified as critical by 88 percent of respondents, means that knowledge acquisition management is and will continue to be a significant competitive advantage. How information and analysis, as well as training, education and sharing of best practices is managed will be key to Performance Excellence.
- **Cost and cycle time reduction.** This trend, identified as critical by 79 percent of respondents, is particularly relevant to process management. Organizations that effectively manage key product and service design

---

[1]"The Nation's CEOs Look to the Future: A Survey Conducted for the Foundation for the Malcolm Baldrige National Quality Award." Data collection: February–April 1998. Results tabulated and analyzed by Louis Harris & Associates, Inc.

and delivery processes will have a competitive edge in the global marketplace.

- **Improving supply chains globally.** This trend, identified as critical by 78 percent of respondents, is a companion to the trend already described as globalization. As business is increasingly taking place on the global stage, supply chain management needs to improve—either with direct suppliers and partners or beyond to partnerships and alliances. These requirements are particularly important to process management.

- **Manufacturing at multiple locations in many countries.** This trend, identified as critical by 76 percent of respondents, again relates to globalization and also to improving supply chain management. To be successful at multiple country manufacturing, one needs to use a systems approach involving all Categories from strategic planning to process management with a strong focus on customers and markets, as well as human resources.

- **Managing the use of more part-time, temporary and contract workers.** This trend, identified as critical by 71 percent of respondents, reflects the rapidly changing environment that businesses operate within. The "hot" skills and technologies of today become out of date quickly. The product and service focus of today is tomorrow's throwaway. Organizations must manage successfully with a more flexible and contingent work force, yet they must still manage that workforce effectively; they still need the right skills and knowledge, motivation and incentives, and satisfaction from work. This trend is a major challenge particularly relevant to the human resource focus category.

Other Major Trends

More than 51 percent of the CEOs reported the following trends as major ones that will be likely to affect business in the years ahead. These include (from most-cited 69 percent to least-cited 52 percent):

- Developing new employee relationships based on performance;
- Improving human resources management;
- Improving the execution of strategic plans;
- Developing more appropriate strategic plans;
- Ongoing measurement and analysis of organizational processes;
- Developing a consistent global corporate culture;
- Outsourcing of manufacturing; and
- Creating a learning organization.

These trends, together with the ones previously listed, present a picture of what CEOs predict will be major business trends in the coming decade. The case for using the Baldrige Criteria as a way to manage effectively is validated and strengthened by the specific trends, their close relationship to the Criteria, and the next section in which the same CEOs rate the competencies major U.S. industries must possess to take advantage of these trends as a competitive advantage. CEOs report a huge gap between current state competency and future/desired state competency for many major trends. For example:

- Almost all of the CEOs report globalization as a major trend, but only 18 percent rate major U.S. organization competency as excellent. Seventy percent rated the competency as only fair.
- Improving knowledge management was cited by 88 percent of CEO respondents as a major trend, but only 23 percent see U.S. organization competency as excellent. Fifty-five percent rate the competency level as only fair.
- Competency in cost and cycle time reduction was rated as excellent by 31 percent and only fair by 52 percent.

These are a sample of competency gaps cited by CEOs in the survey. They reiterate the need to use proven management practices to close these gaps and ensure that U.S. organizations remain or become leaders in the global marketplace to sustain our quality of life.

CEO Skills Needing Improvement

CEOs were asked as part of the survey to reflect on their skills and their peer group's skills and to report on which skills were most in need of improvement. The following skills were thought by more than 50 percent to need "a great deal" of improvement. They are key to addressing the major business trends reported earlier in this section. The skills include:

- The ability to think globally and execute strategies successfully;
- Flexibility in a changing world;
- The ability to develop appropriate strategies and rapidly redefine their business; and
- The understanding of new technologies.

Another 40 to 50 percent of CEOs believe that these skills also need to improve "a great deal." Skills needing improvement include the ability to:

- Work well with different stakeholders;
- Create a learning organization;
- Make the right bets about the future;
- Be a visible, articulate, charismatic leader; and
- Be a strong enough leader to overcome opposition.

Stakeholders and Interests that Are Becoming More Important

The majority of CEOs (75 percent or more) think that international customers, consumers and employees are becoming more important to business success. Over 60 percent believe that suppliers, outside board directors and institutional shareholders are also becoming more important. Addressing requirements of the Customer and Market Focus category and Employee Focus categories is increasing in importance according to the CEOs surveyed.

Execution of Strategies Is Critical

When asked which required more improvement—the development or execution of appropriate strategies, CEOs selected "execution" by about a three-to-one margin. This means that alignment and realistic action plans need to be improved along with accountability. If the organization is pulling in different directions to accomplish individual unit or division priorities, energies and resources are being drained. Execution is flawed and results are suboptimized.

Expanding Market Size Is Critical

When asked which is more important to increase market share or expand market size, CEOs selected "expanding market size" by over a four-to-one margin. This will require improved leadership, strategic planning, and customer and market focus, particularly in the global economy. It will also require a more skilled and diverse workforce and more effective work processes.

The Competition Ahead

CEOs had various ideas about where the most serious competition to their businesses will come from in the next decade. Only a small number (12 percent) thought the toughest competition would come from other Fortune 500 companies. About 33 percent thought it was most likely to come from U.S. companies not yet on the Fortune 500 list. About 30 percent thought their toughest competitors were most likely to be foreign companies. Some saw start-up, entrepreneurial businesses as being the most serious competition. Comparing services and products to the competition and determining what the competition is doing to satisfy its customers is central to Baldrige-based assessments.

It is interesting though that most CEOs did not see the most serious competitors as being the major Fortune 500 companies of today. Perhaps this, more than any other CEO opinion, presents a compelling case for using the Baldrige Criteria—the fast and relentless pace of business change where companies on top today are not likely to be on top tomorrow without corresponding changes and improvements in their business.

Research Supports the Business Case

Two researchers were interested in quality award winners and to what extent (if any) quality management affected financial performance. The research of Dr. Kevin B. Hendricks from the College of William and Mary, School of Business and Vinod R. Singhal from the Georgia Institute of Technology, Dupree College of Management is the basis for the following piece of evidence that supports the use of the Baldrige Criteria.[2]

Their research looked beyond "hype and the popular press" to the real impact of quality management and examined the facts surrounding Performance Excellence. The research was based on about 600 recipients of various quality awards and similar recognition. The recognition provided to these organizations was based upon similar core values and concepts. Companies were mostly manufacturing firms (75 percent). All were publicly traded companies. Although they did not find that quality management turned "straw into gold," their research added significantly to the business case for using the Criteria as a tool to enhance performance.

Hendricks and Singhal examined the following efficiency or growth measures to examine:
- Percent change in sales;
- Stock price performance;
- Percent change in total assets;
- Percent change in number of employees;
- Percent change in return on sales; and
- Percent change in return on assets.

[2]This research is described in the following papers: K. B. Hendricks and V. R. Singhal, "Quality Awards and the Market Value of the Firm; An Empirical Investigation," *Management Science* 42, no. 3 (1996): 415-436; K. B. Hendricks and V. R. Singhal, "Does Implementing an Effective TQM Program Actually Improve Operating Performance? Empirical Evidence from Firms that Have Won Quality Awards," *Management Science* 43, no. 9 (1997): 1258-1274; K. B. Hendricks and V. R. Singhal, "The Long-Run Stock Price Performance of Firms with Effective TQM Programs," working paper, Georgia Institute of Technology and the College of William and Mary, 1998.

Implementation Costs Do Not Negatively Affect the Bottom Line

The research examined two five-year periods during the quality management implementation cycle. The first period can be called beginning implementation. This period started six years before and ended one year before the receipt of their first award. During this period, organizations are implementing quality management and incurring associated costs of implementation, such as training, communications and production, and design changes. The researchers found no significant differences in financial measures between these companies (winners) and the control group of companies (nonwinners but similar in other respects) for this period. This is important because of both direct and indirect costs associated with implementing quality management systems. The research suggests that the significant cost savings identified during this period of intensified focus on cycle time, time to market, and other factors pay for the implementation costs.

Improved Financial Results Can Be Expected with Successful Implementation

The study then examined results of companies from one year before winning the award to four years after the award was given. This period can be called mature implementation, and it is in this period that one would expect the improved management to bear fruit. This was the case with this research. There were significant differences in financial performance between award winners and controls (nonwinners). For example, the growth in operating income averaged 91 percent for winners contrasted to 43 percent for non-award winners. Award winning companies reported 69 percent growth in sales compared with 32 percent for the control group. The total assets of the winning companies increased 79 percent compared to 37 percent for the controls. Winners had significantly better results than the control group.

Stock Price Performance of Winners Is Significantly Better

Consistent with other efficiency and financial findings, the winners outperformed the S&P 500 Index by 115 percent to 80 percent. In actual dollars, the better performance would be worth $669 million for the average award winner. They also outperformed other benchmark composites from the New York, American, and NASDAQ stock exchanges. It is important to note here that most of the "winners" did not also win the Baldrige Award. Baldrige recipients performed two to three times better than the S&P 500 index (460 percent to 147 percent).

Quality Management Is a Long-Term Solution

Companies that expect immediate gains from quality management systems are likely to be disappointed. It took years to create the culture you have today; it can take years to change it. Nevertheless, this research, combined with other results makes a solid business case for using Baldrige-based management criteria as the way to run the successful business of the future.

High Performing Organizations

High-performing organizations outrun their competition by delivering value to stakeholders through an unwavering focus on customers and improved organizational capabilities. Examples of improved capabilities have occurred in all sectors of the economy, not just the private sector. These results range from time and cost savings to customer retention and loyalty.

Many examples of significant improvements are evident from using the Baldrige-based management system:

- BI, a 1999 Baldrige recipient, is a training organization that helps the performance of people. In this way, it helps its customers achieve their business goals. BI designs and delivers performance improvement programs that integrate communications, training, measurement, and rewards. These programs benefit customers' distributors, employees, and consumers. BI designs training, and it helps customers with organizational change and strategic planning, customer loyalty programs, and sales incentive programs. Over five years, BI's revenue has grown 47 percent. Its successful strategy has been to target strategic accounts to create a much higher rate of customer satisfaction in these accounts rather than target growth in overall market share. Its products and services have resulted in customer loyalty that outperforms its top two competitors. It has retained an average of 73 percent of customers and an average of 96.3 percent of revenue.
- STMicroelectronics, Inc. designs, develops, manufactures, and markets semiconductor integrated circuits for consumer electronics and automotive, medical, telecommunications, and computer applications in the United States and around the world.
- ST has earned a "Best in Class" measured against major semiconductor companies, based on 19 standard benchmark areas in the most recent industry report. It has performed better than key competitors in many financial and growth areas during a very volatile decade in its market. Its revenue has grown from $493 million to $937 million from 1994 to 1998, which exceeded the average of seven competitors. Its market share has increased from 1.88 percent in 1991 to 2.36 percent in 1998. Employee empowerment is widespread. Its employee satisfaction survey results exceeded the industry composite in 8 of 10 factors.

- The Ritz-Carlton Hotel Company, L.L.C. manages 36 luxury hotels worldwide. It is the only service company to receive a Baldrige Award twice. The Ritz-Carlton holds the top position in complete satisfaction with a score of 70 percent compared to 56 percent for its closest competitor on a recent nationwide survey. Since 1995, pretax return on investment has nearly doubled. Training is key to employee retention and the company's customer-focused culture. First year managers and employees receive 250 to 310 hours of training. It has developed an innovative customer database to record guests' preferences and customize services to meet these preferences.

- Sunny Fresh Foods is the first food manufacturer to receive the Baldrige Award. It manufactures further processed egg products, including pasteurized, refrigerated, and frozen egg products; fat-free products; peeled hard-cooked eggs; and such precooked egg products as omelets, french toast, and frozen scrambled eggs. This company has increased market share in U.S. markets from fourteenth in 1988 to second in 1999. It has received numerous awards from its customers. Its return on gross investment has tripled in the last several years. All of Sunny Fresh Foods' facilities score in the excellent range on sanitation. It has many innovative work system designs that create a safe facility and minimize injuries.

- Boeing Airlift and Tanker, a 1998 Baldrige winner, designs, develops, and produces military transport aircraft. They targeted 50 key processes for improvement and cut cycle time by over 80 percent. Return on net assets is seven times greater than the next best competitor. Net asset turnover improved sevenfold since 1994, while the return on sales improved threefold. Empowered employee teams have produced a 60 percent improvement in productivity.

- Texas Nameplate Company, Inc., a 1998 winner, makes identification labels. Their market share in Texas increased from 69 to 93 percent and almost doubled nationally. A gain-sharing program augments wages by 11 percent and has helped double net profit as a percent of sales in the last four years. Gross profit as a percent of sales is 59 percent.

- Xerox Business Services (XBS), a 1997 Baldrige winner, provides document services throughout the world. XBS increased revenues more than 30 percent annually, growing into a $6 billion business in less than 10 years.

- ADAC Laboratories of California, a 1996 Baldrige Award winner, designs, manufactures, markets and supports products for health-care customers. Customer retention increased from 70 to 90 percent during the past five years. Since 1990, average cycle time declined from 56 hours to 17 hours and revenue tripled.

- For the past two years, Trident Precision Manufacturing, another 1996 Baldrige Award winner, has experienced zero defects in its custom products. Trident's quality rating for its major customers (based on customer reports) is higher than 99.8 percent.
- Wainwright Industries, a 1994 Baldrige Award winner, cut the time for making one of its principal extruded products from 8.75 days to 15 minutes and reduced defect rates tenfold.
- Cadillac, a 1990 Baldrige Award winner, reduced the time for die changes in its stamping plant from 8 hours to 4 minutes by redesigning the entire process.
- Corning Telecommunications Products Division, a 1995 Baldrige Award winner, has become the world market leader and the low-cost provider, and has earned the highest customer satisfaction ratings in the industry by far.
- In five years, Solectron Corporation, a 1991 and 1997 Baldrige Award winner, experienced a sales increase from $130 million to $3.7 billion, representing a 2800 percent improvement. Net profits soared more than tenfold. Market share doubled since 1992. The stock price went up sixtyfold since 1989.
- At Federal Express, a 1989 Baldrige Award winner, cost per package was cut by more than 40 percent.
- Globe Metallurgical, Inc., a 1988 Baldrige Award winner, experienced a 60 percent increase in revenues and a 40 percent increase in profits since 1992.
- Ames Rubber Corporation, a 1993 Baldrige Award winner, achieved a 99.9 percent quality and on-time delivery status through sharing quality techniques with suppliers.
- AT&T Consumer Communications, a 1994 Baldrige Award winner, listened to its customers and received its largest customer response ever in a short time frame to its "true" marketing program.
- AT&T Transmission Sales Business Unit, a 1992 Baldrige Award winner, achieved a tenfold improvement in equipment quality and a 50 percent reduction in cycle time that saved $400 million over six years.

Similar findings are appearing throughout the world as organizations use the Baldrige Performance Excellence Criteria to manage their businesses. The fact that more companies are using the Criteria should both threaten and comfort. They are more formidable competitors as a result. However, leaders contemplating the use of the Criteria should be comforted by the knowledge that so many others have found it valuable.

In summary, as expected, organizations using the Baldrige Criteria to enhance performance do better on the stock market—a lot better! The

Baldrige Award office in the U.S. Department of Commerce found similar results in recent studies:

- They "invested" a hypothetical sum of money in each of the publicly traded whole companies that won the Baldrige Award since 1988. They tracked the investment from the first business day of the month following the announcement of the Baldrige winners' award, or the date they began trading publicly, to December 1998. Adjustments were made for stock splits. The results continue to show that the publicly traded Baldrige-winning companies outperformed the S&P 500 by a substantial margin, achieving a 460 percent return on investment compared to 175 percent for the S&P 500.

The Core Values to Achieve Performance Excellence

Summary of Changes in Core Values and Concepts from 1999

The Criteria are built upon a set of core values and concepts. These values and concepts are the foundation for integrating key business requirements within a results-oriented framework. These values and concepts are the embedded behaviors found in high-performing organizations.

Many of the core values and concepts have been changed to better describe the foundation for the Performance Excellence Criteria. The number of core values and concepts remains constant at 11.

Seven Core Values and Concepts have been revised:
- **Visionary leadership** (formerly Leadership). Essentially the same, more emphasis on coaching and developing future leaders.
- **Customer driven** (formerly Customer-driven quality). Essentially the same with more emphasis on meeting performance requirements, enhancing referrals, and anticipating future customer desires.
- **Organizational and personal learning** (formerly Continuous improvement and learning). Expanded to emphasize not only process improvement, but also the need to invest in employee development to enhance motivation, value, and innovation.
- **Valuing employees and partners** (formerly Valuing employees and partnership development). Challenges include demonstrating leader commitment to employees, providing recognition beyond normal compensation, opportunities for growth and development, sharing knowledge to help employees contribute, and environment to encourage risk taking.

- **Agility** (elements of Fast response and design quality and prevention). Sets expectations for faster, more flexible, customized service and shorter cycle times for new and improved products and services.
- **Focus on the future** (same as Long-range view of the future). Future orientation to achieve sustainable growth and market leadership.
- **Focus on results and creating value** (formerly results focus). Create and balance value for all stakeholders—use balanced scorecard to focus and communicate.

The seven revised Core values and concepts are intended to provide a more holistic and current view of organizational Performance Excellence.

Two of the 1999 Core Values and Concepts have been incorporated into the 2000 Core Values and Concepts and eliminated as free-standing core values:
- Design quality and prevention
- Partnership development

Two new core values and concepts that underpin the Performance Excellence Criteria have been added:
- **Managing for innovation.** New—goes beyond traditional research and development (R&D). Need to make meaningful change to improve products, programs, processes, and value for stakeholders.
- **Systems perspective.** New core value but a long-time theme. Systems include core values, criteria, scoring guidelines; successful management requires *synthesis* of management system elements. *Alignment* links strategy, processes, and resources throughout organization.

Two 1999 Core Values and Concepts remain essentially the same:
- **Management by fact.** Essentially the same as 1999—measures and analysis aligned to strategy to focus work, decision making, and operational improvement.
- **Public responsibility and citizenship.** The same as 1999 plus elements of design and prevention—need to ensure product/program/service designs meet public responsibilities.

The 2000 Core Values and Concepts Are Visionary Leadership and Customer Driven

Visionary Leadership *(Formerly Leadership)*

Every system, strategy, and method for achieving excellence must be guided by **visionary leadership:**

- Effective leaders convey a strong sense of urgency to counter the natural resistance to change that can prevent the organization from taking the steps that these core values for success demand.
- Such leaders serve as enthusiastic role models, reinforcing and communicating the core values by their words and actions. Words alone are not enough.

Visionary Leadership

An organization's senior leaders need to set direction and create a customer focus, clear and visible values, and high expectations. The directions, values, and expectations should balance the needs of all your stakeholders. Your leaders need to ensure the creation of strategies, systems, and methods for achieving excellence, stimulating innovation, and building knowledge and capabilities. The values and strategies should help guide all activities and decisions of your organization. Senior leaders should inspire and motivate your entire work force and should encourage involvement, development and learning, innovation, and creativity by all employees.

Through their ethical behavior and personal roles in planning, communications, coaching, developing future leaders, review of organizational performance, and employee recognition, your senior leaders should serve as role models, reinforcing values and expectations and building leadership, commitment, and initiative throughout your organization.

Customer Driven *(Formerly Customer-Driven Quality)*

This value demonstrates a passion for making the organization **customer driven.** Without this, little else matters. Customers are the final judges of how well the organization did its job, and what they say counts. It is their perception of the service and product that will determine whether they remain loyal or constantly seek better providers. The following elements are important to consider in building a customer driven organization:

- The organization must focus on systematically listening to customers and acting quickly on what they say.
- The organization must build positive relationships with its customers through focusing on accessibility and management of complaints.
- Dissatisfied customers must be heeded, for they often deliver the most valuable information.
- If only satisfied and loyal customers (those who continue to do business with us no matter what) are paid attention, the organization will be led astray. The most successful organizations pay attention to customers who are not satisfied and work to understand their preferences and meet their demands.

Customer Driven

Quality and performance are judged by an organization's customers. Thus, your organization must take into account all product and service features and characteristics that contribute value to your customers and lead to customer satisfaction, preference, referral, and loyalty. Being customer driven has both current and future components—understanding today's customer desires and anticipating future customer desires and marketplace offerings.

Value and satisfaction may be influenced by many factors throughout your customer's overall purchase, ownership, and service experiences. These factors include your organization's relationship with customers that helps build trust, confidence, and loyalty.

Being customer driven means much more than defect and error reduction, merely meeting specifications, or reducing complaints. Nevertheless, defect and error reduction and elimination of causes of dissatisfaction contribute to your customers' view of your organization and are thus also important parts of being customer driven. In addition, your organization's success in recovering from defects and mistakes ("making things right for your customer") is crucial to retaining customers and building customer relationships.

Customer-driven organizations address not only the product and service characteristics that meet basic customer requirements, but also address those features and characteristics that differentiate products and services from competing offerings. Such differentiation may be based upon new or modified offerings, combinations of product and service offerings, customization of offerings, rapid response, or special relationships.

Being customer driven is thus a strategic concept. It is directed toward customer retention, market share gain, and growth. It demands constant sensitivity to changing and emerging customer and market requirements, and the factors that drive customer satisfaction and retention. It demands anticipating changes in the marketplace. Being customer driven thus demands awareness of developments in technology and competitors' offerings, and rapid and flexible response to customer and market requirements.

Organizational and Personal Learning *(Formerly Continuous Improvement and Learning)*

The most potent value is **organizational and personal learning.** High-performing organizations are learning organizations—they create a culture of seeking to evaluate and improve everything they do. They strive to get better at getting better:

- A culture of continuous improvement is essential to maintaining and sustaining true competitive advantage.
- Without systematic improvement and ongoing learning, organizations will ultimately face extinction.
- With systematic continuous improvement, time becomes a powerful ally. As time passes, the organization grows stronger and smarter.

Organizational and Personal Learning

Achieving the highest levels of performance requires a well-executed approach to organizational and personal learning. Organizational and personal learning is a goal of visionary leaders. The term *organizational learning* refers to continuous improvement of existing approaches and processes and adaptation to change, leading to new goals and/or approaches. Learning needs to be embedded in the way your organization operates. The term *embedded* means that learning (1) is a regular part of daily work; (2) is practiced at personal, work-unit, and organizational levels; (3) results in solving problems at their source; (4) is focused on sharing knowledge throughout your organization; and (5) is driven by opportunities to affect significant change and do better. Sources for learning include employee ideas, R&D, customer input, best practice sharing, and benchmarking.

Organizational learning can result in (1) enhancing value to customers through new and improved products and services; (2) developing new business opportunities; (3) reducing errors, defects, waste, and related costs; (4) improving responsiveness and cycle time performance; (5) increasing productivity and effectiveness in the use of all resources throughout your organization; and (6) enhancing your organization's performance in fulfilling its public responsibilities and service as a good citizen.

Employee success depends increasingly on having opportunities for personal learning and practicing new skills. Organizations invest in employee personal learning through education, training, and opportunities for continuing growth. Opportunities might include job rotation and increased pay for demonstrated knowledge and skills. On-the-job training offers a cost-effective way to train and to better link training to your organizational needs. Education and training programs may benefit from advanced technologies, such as computer-based learning and satellite broadcasts.

Personal learning can result in (1) more satisfied and versatile employees; (2) greater opportunity for organizational cross-functional learning; and (3) an improved environment for innovation.

Thus, learning is directed not only toward better products and services, but also toward being more responsive, adaptive, and efficient—giving the organization and your employees marketplace sustainability and performance advantages.

Valuing Employees and Partners *(Formerly Valuing Employees and Partnership Development)*

Organizations must invest in their people to ensure they have the skills for today and for the future. This core value has broadened from employee participation and development to **valuing employees and partners.** In high-performing organizations, the people who do the work of the organization should make most of the decisions about how the work is done. However, a significant barrier exists that limits employee decision making—access to data and poor data-based decision-making skills.

- As previously mentioned, leaders are unwilling to let subordinates make decisions based on intuition. They reserve that type of decision for themselves.
- Therefore, access to data and developing skills to manage by fact is a prerequisite for optimizing employee contributions to the organization's success.
- Organizations cannot effectively push decision making down to the level where most of the work is done unless those doing the work have access to the necessary data and are skilled at making fact-based decisions.

Valuing Employees and Partners

An organization's success depends increasingly on the knowledge, skills, innovative creativity, and motivation of its employees and partners.

Valuing employees means committing to their satisfaction, development, and well-being. Increasingly, this involves more flexible, high-performance work practices tailored to employees with diverse workplace and home life needs. Major challenges in the area of valuing employees include (1) demonstrating your leaders' commitment to your employees; (2) providing recognition opportunities that go beyond the normal compensation system; (3) providing opportunities for development and growth within your organization; (4) sharing your organization's knowledge so your employees can better serve your customers and contribute to achieving your strategic objectives; and (5) creating an environment that encourages risk taking.

Organizations need to build internal and external partnerships to better accomplish overall goals.

Internal partnerships might include labor-management cooperation, such as agreements with your unions. Partnerships with employees might entail employee development, cross-training, or new work organizations, such as high-performance work teams. Internal partnerships also might involve creating network relationships among your work units to improve flexibility, responsiveness, and knowledge sharing.

External partnerships might be with customers, suppliers, and education organizations. Strategic partnerships or alliances are increasingly important kinds of external partnerships. Such partnerships might offer entry into new markets or a basis for new products or services. Also, partnerships might permit the blending of your organization's core competencies or leadership capabilities with the complementary strengths and capabilities of partners, thereby enhancing overall capability, including speed and flexibility.

Successful internal and external partnerships develop longer-term objectives, thereby creating a basis for mutual investments and respect. Partners should address the key requirements for success, means of regular communication, approaches to evaluating progress, and means for adapting to changing conditions. In some cases, joint education and training could offer a cost-effective method of developing employees.

Agility *(Formerly Fast Response and Elements of Design Quality and Prevention)*

Agility is a value usually driven by customer requirements and the desire to improve operating efficiency and lower costs. The following elements are important to consider in developing a more agile organization:

- Except for a few pleasurable experiences, everyone wants things faster.
- Organizations that develop the capacity to respond faster by eliminating activities and tasks that do not add value, find that productivity increases, costs decrease, and customers are more loyal.
- Analyzing and improving work processes enables organizations to perform better, faster, and cheaper.
- To improve work processes, organizations need to focus on improving design quality and preventing problems. The cost of preventing problems and building quality into products and services is significantly less than the cost of taking corrective action later.
- It is critical to emphasize capturing learning from other design projects.
- Use information concerning customer preference, competitors products, cost and pricing, marketplace profiles, and R&D to optimize the process from the start.
- Public responsibility issues and factors including environmental demands must be included in the design stage.

Agility

Success in globally competitive markets demands creating a capacity for rapid change and flexibility. All aspects of electronic commerce require more rapid, flexible, and customized responses. Businesses face ever-shorter cycles for introductions of new or improved products and services. Faster and more flexible response to customers is now a more critical requirement. Major improvements in response time often require simplification of work units and processes and/or the ability for rapid changeover from one process to another. Cross-trained employees are vital assets in such a demanding environment.

A major success factor in meeting competitive challenges is the design-to-introduction (product generation) cycle time. To meet the demands of rapidly changing global markets, organizations need to carry out stage-to-stage integration (concurrent engineering) of activities from research to commercialization.

All aspects of time performance are becoming increasingly important and should be among your key process measures. Other important benefits can be derived from this focus on time; time improvements often drive simultaneous improvements in organization, quality, cost, and productivity measures.

Focus on the Future *(Formerly Long-Range View of the Future)*

To remain competitive, every organization must be guided by a common set of measurable goals and **a focus on the future.**

- These measurable goals, which emerge from the strategic planning process, align the work of everyone in the organization.
- Measurable goals allow everyone to know where they are going and when they deviate from their path.
- Without measurable goals, everyone still works hard, but they go in different directions—suboptimizing the success of the organization.
- Focusing on the future requires the organization's leaders to consider new, even revolutionary, ideas. Strategic objectives should reflect this future focus.

Focus on the Future

Pursuit of sustainable growth and market leadership requires a strong future orientation and a willingness to make long-term commitments to key stakeholders—your customers, employees, suppliers, stockholders, the public, and your community. Your organization should anticipate many factors in your strategic planning efforts, such as customers' expectations, new business and partnering opportunities, the increasingly global marketplace, technological developments, new customer and market segments, evolving regulatory requirements, community/societal expectations, and strategic changes by competitors. Short- and long-term plans, strategic objectives, and resource allocations need to reflect these influences. Major components of a future focus include developing employees and suppliers, seeking opportunities for innovation, and fulfilling public responsibilities.

Managing for Innovation (New)

The accelerating speed of change today demands ever-increasing **innovation**. Such innovation cannot be random. It must be focused. To be focused, it must be managed. Innovation should focus on changing products, services, and processes to create more value for the organization's stakeholders, employees, and customers. The winners in a highly charged race to innovate will be the organizations that uncover new paradigms of breakthrough performance. To begin to optimize this breakthrough capacity, EVERYONE in the organization needs to be involved. The more brainpower, the better. Requirements for innovation should be a part of every employee and managerial performance plan and appraisal. Just like continuous improvement, innovation must be imbedded in the culture and fabric of daily work. The best organizations are not satisfied to just "improve" or "innovate." The best organizations work hard at improving the speed at which they improve and innovate. To do less allows competitors to overtake them. To do less allows customer expectations to exceed the speed of change, causing the customers to look elsewhere.

Managing for Innovation

Innovation is making meaningful change to improve an organization's products, services, and processes and create new value for the organization's stakeholders. Innovation should focus on leading your organization to new dimensions of performance. Innovation is no longer strictly the purview of research and development departments. Innovation is important for key product and service processes and for support processes. Organizations should be structured in such a way that innovation becomes part of the culture and daily work.

Management by Fact *(Essentially the Same as 1999)*

Management by fact is the cornerstone value for effective planning, operational decision making at all levels, employee involvement and empowerment, and leadership.

- Everyone makes decisions every day. However, without data, the basis for decision making is intuition—gut feel. Although intuition can be valuable at times, it is not consistent from person to person or time to time. It is also difficult to explain the rationale for decisions based on intuition. That makes communication more difficult within the organization. Finally, if the decision must be made on the basis of intuition, it is usually the bosses' intuition that drives the decision. Because of this phenomenon, excessive reliance on intuition tends to minimize employee empowerment.

- Most drivers decide when to fill their fuel tanks based on data from the fuel gauge and get very uncomfortable if the gauge is broken. People, however, routinely make decisions of enormous consequence about customers, strategies, goals, and employees with little or no data. This is a recipe for disaster and not one designed to ensure optimization.

Management by Fact

Organizations depend upon the measurement and analysis of performance. Such measurements must derive from your organization's strategy and provide critical data and information about key processes, outputs, and results. Many types of data and information are needed for performance measurement, management, and improvement. Performance measurement areas include customer, product, and service; operations, market, and competitive comparisons; and supplier, employee, and cost and financial. Analysis refers to extracting larger meaning from data and information to support evaluation, decision making, and operational improvement within your organization.

Analysis entails using data to determine trends, projections, and cause and effect that might not be evident without analysis. Data and analysis support a variety of purposes, such as planning, reviewing your overall performance, improving operations, and comparing your performance with competitors or with "best practices" benchmarks.

A major consideration in performance improvement involves the selection and use of performance measures or indicators. The measures or indicators you select should best represent the factors that lead to improved customer, operational, and financial performance. A comprehensive set of measures or indicators tied to customer and/or organizational performance requirements represents a clear basis for aligning all activities with your organization's goals. Through the analysis of data from the tracking processes, the measures or indicators themselves may be evaluated and changed to better support such goals.

Public Responsibility and Citizenship *(Essentially the Same as 1999 with Some Elements of Design Quality and Prevention)*

Every high-performing organization practices good **public responsibility and citizenship.** The following elements are important to consider in promoting public responsibility and citizenship:

- Organizations must determine and anticipate any adverse effects to the public of their products, services, and operations. Failure to do so can undermine public trust and distract workers, and also adversely affect the bottom line. This is true of both private and public organizations.
- Safety and legal requirements need to be met beyond mere compliance.
- Strong community relationships also help enhance employee pride, morale, and productivity.

Public Responsibility and Citizenship

An organization's leadership needs to stress its responsibilities to the public and needs to practice good citizenship. These responsibilities refer to basic expectations of your organization—business ethics and protection of public health, safety, and the environment. Health, safety, and the environment include your organization's operations, as well as the life cycles of your products and services. Also, organizations need to emphasize resource conservation and waste reduction at the source. Planning should anticipate adverse impacts from production, distribution, transportation, use, and disposal of your products. Plans should seek to prevent problems, to provide a forthright response if problems occur, and to make available information and support needed to maintain public awareness, safety, and confidence.

For many organizations, the product design stage is critical from the point of view of public responsibility. Design decisions affect your production process and the content of municipal and industrial wastes. Effective design strategies should anticipate growing environmental demands and related factors.

Organizations should not only meet all local, state, and federal laws and regulatory requirements, they should treat these and related requirements as opportunities for continuous improvement "beyond mere compliance." This requires the use of appropriate measures in managing performance.

Practicing good citizenship refers to leadership and support—within the limits of your organization's resources—of publicly important purposes. Such purposes might include improving education, health care in the community, environmental excellence, resource conservation, community service, industry and business practices, and sharing nonproprietary information. Leadership as a corporate citizen also entails influencing other organizations, private and public, to partner for these purposes. For example, your organization could lead efforts to help define the obligations of your industry to its communities.

Focus on Results and Creating Value *(Formerly Results Focus)*

A **results focus** and an emphasis on **creating value** helps organizations communicate requirements, monitor actual performance, make adjustments in priorities, and reallocate resources. Without a results focus, organizations can become fixated on internal, self-directed processes and lose sight of the important factors for success, such as customers and their requirements.

Focus on Results and Creating Value

An organization's performance measurements need to focus on key results. Results should be focused on creating and balancing value for all your stakeholders—customers, employees, stockholders, suppliers and partners, the public, and the community. By creating value for all your stakeholders, your organization builds loyalty and contributes to growing the economy. To meet the sometimes conflicting and changing aims that balancing value implies, organizational strategy needs to explicitly include all stakeholder requirements. This will help ensure that actions and plans meet differing stakeholder needs and avoid adverse impacts on any stakeholders. The use of a balanced composite of leading and lagging performance measures offers an effective means to communicate short- and longer-term priorities, to monitor actual performance, and to provide a focus for improving results.

Systems Perspective *(New)*

Taken together, the Baldrige Criteria define the systems required to achieve optimum organizational performance. As with any system, no part can be ignored and still expect the whole to perform at peak levels. What a part of a well-functioning system begins to underperform or work in a manner that is inconsistent with system requirements, the performance of the whole system suffers.

The same is true of a management system. If leaders are ambiguous, plans are not clear, work processes are not consistent, people are not able to do the work they are asked to do, and it is difficult to keep track of progress and make appropriate adjustments, it will be impossible for the organization to achieve maximum levels of performance. For most of the twentieth century, a long list of "management gurus" has suggested a variety of quick and simple remedies to enhance organizational performance. By itself, each quick fix has failed. Hopefully, we have learned that no single solution is sufficient to optimize performance in a complex system. Leaders that approach management from a **systems perspective** are more likely to optimize organizational performance than leaders who continue to take a piecemeal approach to organizational management. There is no magic potion for excellent management or high performance.

Systems Perspective

The Baldrige Criteria provide a systems perspective for managing your organization and achieving Performance Excellence. The core values and the seven Baldrige categories form the building blocks of the system. However, successful management of the overall enterprise requires synthesis and alignment. Synthesis means looking at your organization as a whole and focusing on what is important to the whole enterprise.

Alignment means concentrating on key organizational linkages among requirements given in the Baldrige categories. Alignment means that your senior leaders are focused on strategic directions and on your customers. It means that your senior leaders monitor, respond to, and build on your business results. Alignment means linking your key strategies with your key processes and aligning your resources to improve overall performance and satisfy customers.

Thus, a systems perspective means managing your whole enterprise, as well as its components, to achieve performance improvement.

There are always better ways to do things. Our challenge is to find them, but we are not likely to find them alone. We must create an environment—a work climate where better ways will be sought out, recognized, and put in place by everyone.

Practical Insights

Connections and Linkages

A popular children's activity, connect the dots, helps them understand that, when properly connected, apparently random dots create a meaningful picture. In many ways, the 7 categories, 19 Items, and 27 areas to address in the Baldrige Criteria are like the dots that must be connected to reveal a meaningful picture. With no paths to make the web, or join the dots, human resource development and use are not related to strategic planning; information and analysis are isolated from process management; and overall improvement efforts are disjointed, fragmented, and do not yield robust results. This book describes the linkages for and between each Item. The exciting part about having them identified is you can look for these linkages in your own organization and, if they don't exist, start building them.

Transition Strategies

Putting high-performance management systems in place is a major commitment that will not happen quickly. At the beginning, you will need a transition strategy to get you across the bridge from management by opinion or intuition to more data-driven management. The next part of this section describes one approach that has worked for many organizations in various sectors: creating a performance improvement council.

Performance Improvement Council

Identify a top-level executive leadership group of 6 to 10 members. Each member over that number will seem to double the complexity of issues and make decision making much more cumbersome. The executive leadership group could send a message to the entire organization by naming the group the performance improvement council—reinforcing the importance of continuous performance improvement to the future success of the organization.

The performance improvement council should be the primary policy-making body for the organization. It should spawn other performance improvement councils at lower levels to share practices and policies with every employee in the organization, as well as to involve customers and suppliers. The structure permeates the organization as members of the performance improvement council become area leaders for major improvement efforts and sponsors for several process or continuous improvement task teams throughout the organization. The council structure, networked and cascaded fully, can effectively align the work and optimize performance at all levels and across all functions.

Council Membership

Selecting members for the performance improvement council should be done carefully. Each member should be essential for the success of the operation, and together they must be sufficient for success. The most important member is the senior leader of the organization or work unit. This person must participate actively, demonstrating the kind of leadership that all should emulate. Of particular importance is a commitment to consensus building as the modus operandi for the council. This tool, a core of performance improvement programs, is often overlooked by leadership. Other council members selected should have leadership responsibility for broad areas of the organization such as human resources, operations planning, customers, and data systems.

Performance Improvement Council Learning and Planning

The performance improvement council should be extremely knowledgeable about high performance management systems. If not, as is often the case, performance improvement council members should be among the first in the organization to learn about continuous improvement tools and processes.

To be effective, every member of the council (and every member in the organization) must understand the Baldrige Criteria because the Criteria describe the components of the entire management system. Participation in examiner training has proved to be the very best way to understand the complexities of the system needed to achieve Performance Excellence. Any additional training beyond this should be carried out in the context of planning—that is, learn tools and use them to plan the performance improvement implementation, practices, and policies.

The performance improvement council should:
- Develop an integrated, continuous improvement plan.
- Develop a strategic and business plan.
- Create the web (communication plan and infrastructure) to transmit performance improvement policies throughout the organization.
- Define the roles of employees, including new recognition and reward structures to cause needed behavioral changes.
- Develop a master training and development plan. Involve team representatives in planning so they can learn skills close to when they are needed. Define what is provided to whom, and when and how success will be measured.
- Launch improvement projects that will produce both short- and long-term successes. Improvement projects should be clearly defined by the performance improvement council and driven by the strategic plan. Typical improvement projects include important human resource processes, such as career development, performance measurement, and diversity, as well as improving operational products and services in the line areas.

- Develop a plan to communicate the progress and successes of the organization. Through this approach, the need for performance improvement processes is consistently communicated to all employees. Barriers to optimum performance are weakened and eliminated.
- Create champions to promote Performance Excellence through the categories of the Baldrige Criteria.

Category Champions

This section describes the responsibilities of category champions. The people in the administrative or leadership cabinet should each be the champion of a category.

Organizational Leadership Champion

The Organizational Leadership Champion is a senior executive who, in addition to other executive duties, works to coordinate and enhance leadership effectiveness and alignment throughout the organization. It is both a strategic and an operational activity.

From the strategic side, the champion should focus on ensuring that all senior leaders:
- Understand what is expected of them as leaders of organizational change;
- Agree to achieve consensus, and subsequently, act consistently and speak with one voice as a senior leadership team;
- Serve as role models of Performance Excellence for managers and employees at all levels of the organization;
- Set clear strategy and directions to enhance future opportunities for the organization; and
- Create measurable performance expectations and monitor performance to achieve the key improvements and strategic objectives of the organization. This means that necessary data and analyses must be coordinated to ensure appropriate information is available for the champion and the entire senior leadership team.

From the operational side, the champion should work to identify and eliminate both individual and system deficiencies, territorial conflicts, and knowledge shortfalls that limit a leader's ability to meet expectations and goals consistently.

The champion should be the focal point in the organization to ensure all parts of the organization have systematic processes in place so they fully understand leadership and management requirements.

A process should exist to monitor ongoing initiatives to ensure leaders effectively set and communicate organizational values to employees:

- They must demonstrate that they focus on delivering value to customers and other stakeholders.
- They must aggressively reinforce an environment that promotes empowerment and innovation throughout the workforce. This may involve reviewing policies, systems, work processes, and the use of resources—ensuring sufficient data are available to assist in manager and employee decision making.

The champion should coordinate the activities involving the review of organizational performance and capabilities:

- Key performance measures should be defined.
- Systems to review organizational health, performance, and progress relative to goals should be in place.
- Performance review findings should be communicated widely throughout the organization and, as appropriate, to key suppliers and customers to help ensure organizational alignment.
- Performance review findings should be translated into priorities for improvement and innovation at different levels throughout the organization.
- Performance review findings, together with employee feedback, should be used systematically to assess and improve senior leadership effectiveness and the effectiveness of managers throughout the organization.

Finally, the champion must work as part of the senior leadership team to help coordinate all facets of the management system to drive high performance. This involves teaching the team about the requirements of effective and consistent leadership at all levels and its impact on organizational performance. The senior leader of the organization usually serves as the Organizational Leadership Champion and leads this council.

Strategic Planning Champion

The Strategic Planning Champion is a senior executive who, in addition to other executive duties, works to coordinate and enhance strategic planning and action plan alignment throughout the organization. It is both a strategic and an operational activity.

From the strategic side, the champion should ensure that the focus of strategy development is on sustained competitive leadership, which usually depends on achieving revenue growth, as well as consistently improving operational effectiveness. The Strategic Planning Champion should help the senior leadership team acquire a view of the future and provide clear strategic guidance to the organization through goals, objectives, action plans, and measures.

From the operational side, the champion should work to ensure sufficient data are available about:
- The organization's operational and human resource capabilities;
- Internal and external risks; and
- The competitive environment and other challenges that might affect future direction.

The champion should be the focal point in the organization to ensure all parts of the organization have systematic processes in place so they fully understand the implications of strategy on their daily work.

The champion should ensure that strategy is customer and market focused and is actually used to guide ongoing decision making and resource allocation at all levels of the organization:
- A process should exist to convert strategy into actions at each level of the organization which are aligned to achieve goals necessary for business success.
- Every employee should understand his or her role in carrying out actions to achieve the organization's goals.

The champion should coordinate the activities involving strategy development and deployment to:
- Acquire and use various types of forecasts, projections, scenarios, or other techniques to understand the plausible range of future options;
- Determine how the projected performance of competitors is likely to compare with the projected performance of the organization in the same time frame in order to set goals to ensure competitive advantage;
- Determine what capabilities must be developed within the organization to achieve strategic goals and coordinate with other members of the senior leadership team and category champions to ensure those capabilities are in place;
- Determine what changes in services or products might be needed as a part of strategic positioning and direction;
- Ensure a system is in place to develop action plans that address strategic goals and objectives. Ensure those action plans are understood throughout the organization, as appropriate;
- Ensure a system is in place to identify the human resource requirements necessary to achieve strategic goals and objectives. This may include training, support services for employees, reorganization, and new recruitment, to name a few;

- Ensure a system is in place to allocate resources throughout the organization sufficient to accomplish the action plans;
- Coordinate with the leadership system of performance review to help ensure priorities for improvement and innovation at different levels throughout the organization are aligned with strategy and action plans; and
- Ensure the process for strategic planning, plan deployment, the development of action plans, and the alignment of resources to support actions is systematically evaluated and improved each cycle. Also evaluate and improve the effectiveness of determining the projected performance of competitors for use in goal setting.

Finally, the champion must work as contributing member of the senior leadership team to help coordinate all facets of the management system to drive high performance. This involves teaching the team about the requirements of strategic planning and its impact on organizational performance.

Customer Value Champion

The Customer Value Champion is a senior executive who, in addition to other executive duties, will coordinate and enhance customer satisfaction, relations, and loyalty throughout the organization. It is both a strategic and an operational activity.

From the strategic side, the champion should focus on ensuring that the drivers of customer satisfaction, customer retention, and related market share (which are key factors in competitiveness, profitability, and business success) are considered fully in the strategic planning process. This means that necessary data and analyses must be coordinated to ensure appropriate information is available for the executive planning councils.

From the operational side, the champion should work to identify and eliminate system deficiencies, territorial conflicts, and knowledge shortfalls that limit the organization's ability to meet customer satisfaction, retention, and loyalty goals consistently.

The champion should be the focal point in the organization to ensure all parts of the organization have systematic processes in place so they fully understand key customer, market, and operational requirements as input to customer satisfaction and market goals.

A process should exist to monitor ongoing initiatives to ensure they are aligned with the customer aspects of the strategic direction. This may involve:

- Reviewing policies, systems, work processes, the use of resources, and the availability of employees who are knowledgeable and focus on customer relations and loyalty;
- Ensuring sufficient data are available to assist in decision making about customer issues; and
- Ensuring that strategies and actions relating to customer issues are aligned at all levels of reorganization from the executives to the work unit or individual job level.

The champion should coordinate the activities involving understanding customer requirements, as well as managing the interaction with customers, including how the organization determines customer satisfaction and satisfaction relative to competitors. (Satisfaction relative to competitors and the factors that lead to customer preference are of increasing importance to managing in a competitive environment.) The following elements should be considered when developing the performance requirements for the champion:

- The champion should also examine the means by which customers can seek information, assistance, or comment and complain.
- The champion should coordinate the definition of customer contact requirements and the deployment of those requirements to all points in the organization that have contact with customers.
- The champion should ensure that systems exist to respond quickly and resolve complaints promptly to recover customer confidence that might be otherwise lost.
- The champion should ensure that employees responsible for the design and delivery of products and services receive information about customer complaints so they may eliminate the causes of these complaints.
- The champion should work with appropriate line managers to help set priorities for improvement projects based on the potential impact of the cost of complaints and the impact of customer dissatisfaction and attrition on the organization.
- The champion should be charged with coordinating activities to build loyalty and positive referral, as well as evaluating and improving customer relationship-building processes throughout the organization.

Finally, the champion must work as contributing member of the senior leadership team to help coordinate all facets of the management system to drive high performance. This involves teaching the team about the requirements of customer and market focus and its impact on organizational performance.

Information and Analysis Champion

The Information and Analysis Champion is an executive-level person who, in addition to other executive duties, will coordinate and enhance information and analysis systems throughout the organization to ensure they meet the decision-making needs of managers, employees, customers, and suppliers. It is both a strategic and an operational activity.

From the strategic side, information and data can provide a competitive advantage. The champion should focus on ensuring, to the extent possible, that timely and accurate information and data are available to enhance the delivery of new and existing products and services to meet emerging market needs.

From the operational side, the champion should work to ensure that information and data are available throughout the organization to aid in decision making at all levels. This means coordinating with all other champions to ensure data are available for day-to-day review and decision making at all levels for their areas of responsibility.

The Information and Analysis Champion has responsibility for both information infrastructure, as well as ensuring the appropriate use of data for decision making. The champion should coordinate activities throughout the organization involving data collection, accuracy, analysis, retrieval, and use for decision making. The Champion should ensure:
- Complete data are available and aligned to strategic goals, objectives, and action plans to ensure performance against these goals, objectives, and action plans can be effectively monitored;
- Systems are in place to collect and use comparative data and information to support strategy development, goal setting, and performance improvement;
- Data and information throughout the organization are accurate and reliable to enhance fact-based decision making;
- Data and information are used to support a better understanding of the cost and financial impact of various improvement options;
- Appropriate correlations and performance projections are available to support planning;
- The performance measurement system is evaluated and improved to ensure it meets business needs;
- Data analysis supports the senior executives' organizational performance review and organizational planning;
- Data analysis addresses the overall health of the organization;

- The results of organization-level analysis are available to workgroup and functional-level operations to support decision making at those levels; and
- Data analysis supports daily decisions regarding operations throughout the organization to ensure actions align with plans.

Finally, the champion must work as part of an organizationwide council to help coordinate all facets of the management system to drive high performance.

Human Resource Focus Champion

The Human Resource Focus Champion is an executive-level person who, in addition to other executive duties, will coordinate and enhance systems to enable employees to develop and utilize their full potential, consistent with the organization's strategic objectives. This includes building and maintaining a work environment conducive to full employee participation and growth. It is both a strategic and an operational activity.

From the strategic side, the human resource constraints of the organization must be considered in the development of strategy and, subsequently, eliminated to ensure the workforce is capable of achieving the strategies necessary for business success.

From the operational side, the champion should ensure that the work climate enhances employee satisfaction and well-being and that work is organized and jobs are designed to enable employees to achieve higher levels of performance.

The Human Resource Focus Champion has responsibility for ensuring that employees (including managers and supervisors at all levels; permanent, temporary, and part-time personnel; and contract employees supervised by the organization) receive the same kind of focus and attention as customers so that their needs are met and they can contribute fully to the organization's goals and objectives. The champion should ensure:

- Work and jobs are structured to promote cooperation, collaboration, individual initiative, innovation, and flexibility;
- Managers and supervisors encourage and motivate employees to develop and use their full potential;
- An effective system exists to provide accurate feedback about employee performance and enhance their performance. This includes systems to identify skill gaps and recruit or reassign employees to close those

gaps; as well as ensuring that fair work practices are followed within the organization. This may also include evaluating managers and enhancing their ability to provide accurate feedback and effective coaching to improve employee performance;

- Compensation, recognition, and rewards are aligned to support high-performance objectives of the organization (contained in strategic plans and reported in the balanced scorecard or business results report card);
- Education and training support business objectives and build employee knowledge, skills, and capabilities to enhance employee performance. This includes ensuring employees understand tools and techniques of performance measurement, performance improvement, quality control methods, and benchmarking. This also includes ensuring that managers and supervisors reinforce knowledge and skills on the job;
- The work environment is safe, with measurable performance measures and targets for each key factor affecting employee safety; and
- Factors that affect employee well-being, satisfaction, and motivation are routinely measured and actions are taken promptly to improve conditions that adversely affect morale, motivation, productivity, and other key business results.

Finally, the champion must work as part of an organizationwide council to help coordinate all facets of the management system to drive high performance.

Process Management Champion

The Process Management Champion is an executive-level person who, in addition to other executive duties, will coordinate and enhance all aspects of the organization's systems to manage and improve work processes to meet the organization's strategic objectives. This includes customer-focused design, product and service delivery, internal support services, and supplier and partner systems. It is both a strategic and operational activity.

From the strategic side, rapid and accurate design, development, and delivery of products and services creates a competitive advantage in the marketplace.

From the operational side, the champion should work to ensure all key work processes are examined and optimized to achieve higher levels of performance, reduce cycle time and costs, and subsequently add to organizational profitability.

The Process Management Champion has responsibility for creating a process management orientation within the organization. Since all work is a process, the Process Management Champion must ensure that the process owners (including processes owned by other champions) systematically examine, improve, and execute their processes consistently. The champion should ensure:

- Systematic continuous improvement activities are embedded in all processes, which lead to ongoing refinements;
- Initial and ongoing customer requirements are incorporated into all product and service designs, production and delivery systems, and processes. This includes core production processes, as well as internal support processes, such as finance and accounting, facilities management, research and development, administration, procurement, personnel, and sales and marketing;
- Design, production, and delivery processes are structured and analyzed to reduce cycle time; increase the use of learning from past projects or other parts of the organization; reduce costs; increase the use of new technology and other effectiveness or efficiency factors; and ensure all products and services meet performance requirements; and
- Supplier and partner performance requirements are met and capabilities are improved. This includes minimizing costs associated with inspections, tests, or performance audits; providing timely and actionable feedback to suppliers/partners so they can take quick corrective action as needed; and providing assistance or incentives to help them improve their overall performance and abilities. These actions will, in turn, enhance your organization's performance.

Finally, the champion must work as part of an organizationwide council to help coordinate all facets of the management system to drive high performance.

Business Results Champion

The Business Results Champion is an executive-level person who, in addition to other executive duties, will coordinate the display of the organization's business results. This champion has substantially different work than the champions for Categories 1 through 6. No actions leading to or resulting from the performance outcome data are championed by the Business Results Champion. Those actions are driven by the Category 1 through 6 champions because they have responsibility for taking action to implement and deploy procedures necessary to produce the business results. For example, the Information and Analysis Champion (Category 4), is responsible for collecting data that reflect all areas of strategic importance leading to business results. The Category 4 champion is also responsible for ensuring data accuracy and reliability.

The Business Results Champion is responsible, however, for ensuring that the organization is able to display all business results required by Category 7 to provide evidence of the organization's performance and improvement in key business areas and facilitate monitoring by leaders. These include customer satisfaction, product and service performance, financial and marketplace performance, human resource results, supplier and partner results, and operational performance.

Results must be displayed by appropriate segment and group, such as different customer groups, market segments, employee groups, or supplier groups.

Appropriate comparison data must be included in the business results display to judge the relative "goodness" or "strength" of the results achieved.

Finally, the champion must work as part of an organizationwide council to help coordinate all facets of the management system to drive high performance. For example, if the organization is not collecting data necessary for inclusion in the business results report card, the Business Results Champion coordinates work with the other champions on the council to ensure those data are available.

The Critical Skills

A uniform message, set of skills or core competencies, and constancy of purpose are critical to success. Core training should provide all employees with the knowledge and skills on which to build a learning organization that continually gets better. Such training typically includes team building, leadership skills, consensus building, communications, and effective meeting management. These are necessary for effective teams to become involved in solving critical problems.

Another important core skill involves using a common process to define customer requirements accurately, determining the ability to meet those requirements, measure success, and determine the extent to which customers—internal and external—are satisfied. When a problem arises, employees must be able to define the problem correctly, isolate the **root causes,** generate and select the best solution to eliminate the root causes, and implement the best solution.

It is also important to be able to understand data and make decisions based on facts, not merely intuition or feelings. Therefore, familiarity with tools to analyze work processes and performance data is important. With these tools, work processes can be analyzed and vastly improved. Reducing unnecessary steps in work processes, increasing process consistency, reducing variability, and reducing cycle time are powerful ways to improve quality and reduce cost simultaneously.

Courses in techniques to acquire comparison and benchmarking data, work process improvement and reengineering, supplier partnerships and certification, role modeling for leaders' strategic planning, and customer satisfaction and loyalty will help managers and employees expand their optimization and high-performance thrust across the entire organization.

Lessons Learned

Twenty years ago, the fierce global competition that inspired the quality movement in the United States was felt primarily by major manufacturers. Today, all sectors are under intense pressure to "be the best or be history." The demand for Performance Excellence reaches all corners of the economy, from manufacturing and service industries to professional services, education, health care, public utilities, and government. All of these segments have contributed valuable lessons to the quality movement and have played an important part in our recovery from the economic slump caused by the poor service and products of the 1970s. Relying on the Baldrige model, we will share some of the insights and lessons learned from leaders of high-performing organizations.

A Tale of Two Leaders

It was a time of turbulence; it was a time of peace. It was a time of growth and streamlining. It was the happiest of times; it was also the most painful of times. Most of all it was a time that demanded change—although it was more comfortable to consider it a time for the status quo.

The following tales are of two leaders. One who is consistent and persistent in communicating the direction and message that will bring about excellent results and high performance. Another is uncertain and vague. He does not wish to push his people into anything, let alone the difficult commitment related to using the Baldrige Criteria as the way to run the business. After all, they are still profitable and healthy. Why rock the boat? You may know these people or someone who reminds you of them. If so, you will understand the reason for this section.

There is no lonelier, more challenging, yet critical and rewarding job than that of the leader. I work with many, many leaders who listen to advice carefully. They really want to know the best approaches to use for their organizations. However, what they do with the advice and counsel is always interesting and unpredictable. This section is intended to help those leaders go resolutely down the right path.

Neither leader exists in real life, but both leader profiles are based on actual events and observations of many different people in leadership positions.

The Tale

Background Tale One:

John was the CEO of a Fortune 500 manufacturing company that was slowly but surely losing market share. Shareholders and employees were happy because profits and growth, although slower, were still hearty. However, their business that once enjoyed a near monopoly position was rapidly becoming more and more competitive. Customers that had to beg and plead for limited products and service over the years were happily turning to competitors who were trying in earnest to meet their needs and even delight them. In such an environment, aggressive, customer-focused companies were winning the hearts, minds, and pocketbooks of John's customers. John decided after working with a consulting firm or two and studying the work of Deming, that Performance Excellence was urgently needed to keep the company in business more than five years.

The First Message to the Leadership Team

John called an urgent meeting of his senior team. Many members of this team had been there since the company began its growth spurt and had been good soldiers in times of runaway growth and profit. John was wondering how many of the senior staff would receive the message he was about to send. The meeting was scheduled the next week for five days at the corporate headquarters. Short of an emergency illness, attendance was required.

During the next few days, John received 20 phone calls from secretaries that informed John their bosses could not attend because of other priority commitments. Priorities were quickly realigned when they were informed that all top leaders *would* be in attendance.

The week-long meeting at corporate headquarters began with training. The kind of training where the group was required to participate, listen, and discuss the content. The training was presented by an outside firm with frequent discussions of companywide application and emphasis presented by John. At the end of three days, John took over the meeting and asked for input on how best to apply these principles to the organization at all levels. The leadership group voiced resistance to change, some more than others. They basically voiced concern that "this Performance Excellence stuff with all of its requirements for empowerment and data" would get in the way of their doing business and was not needed.

John clarified the objectives of the group by walking to the white board and writing: "This new program, Performance Excellence, will be in the way of doing business effectively." The senior staff pretty much agreed.

John responded by placing a large *X* through the word *in*. The statement now read, "Performance Excellence, will be the way of doing business effectively." John notified the attendees, "I will negotiate an exit package with anyone who does not understand the implications of this message and who does not want to be part of this new way of doing business."

The Next Steps

John focused on the next two steps: (1) making sure his top team role modeled behavior that would facilitate the needed changes; and (2) planning and implementing a companywide training requirement to communicate the new skills and performance expectations. John started to change his behavior and the behavior of his top staff, feeling that "walking the talk" would signal the importance of new behaviors more than any speech or videotaped presentation. The next top staff meeting was called within a week to plan the design and rollout of training corporatewide, including all foreign and domestic sites. The top staff had very little interest in training, feeling largely that this was a human resource function and should be delegated to that department. Based on the advice of external advisors, John informed the staff that it was now their job to plan, design, and execute this training. A "core design team" was formed with senior leaders and expert content and course design specialists to design the training within 1 month and present it to the senior corporate leaders.

In spite of prior agreements to manage their meetings effectively, to be on time, not interrupt, and follow the agenda, most continued to ignore the rules. Behaviors of the top leadership group at this meeting included the usual set of interruptions, "I told you so's," and everyone talking at the same time. John, whose goal was to create a listening and learning environment, challenged the group to "ante up." He asked that all top leaders bring fifty $20 bills to the meeting. John introduced new meeting ground rules. They were simple. Interruptions, put downs, talking while someone else was, and blocking behaviors were violations of meeting ground rules. On the other hand, building on ideas, clarifying ideas, supporting, and disagreeing respectfully were good meeting behaviors. Every violation was worth a $20 dollar bill. Good meeting behaviors were rewarded, although they did not materialize until several meetings up the road. At first, it seemed that the pot would win big time—no one took John seriously. After about the third meeting, with penalties piling up, their behavior actually changed. Other meeting management skills were slowly introduced, such as time frame limits and action planning. Then John was able to ask his team to role model this behavior to others. He ordered that "This is the way we treat each other at all meetings, including staff meetings, communication forums, and all company business meetings." A core value and new behavior or courtesy and professionalism became deployed companywide through the senior management team.

Training and the Change Process

Each five-day high-performance management course was identical, ensuring a uniform message and set of skills was communicated. Each course was eventually taught by two instructors, a shop supervisor and a manager, so management and the workforce would both be involved. John personally taught the top leadership team the entire five-day course, assisted by a member of the design team, and this tale spread across the organization like wildfire. It was the thing to be invited to take part in this instruction because their leader had done it. The core skills became part of the fabric of the organization—the way to conduct business. They included fact-based decisions, a focus on customers, and using and improving processes. Also included was a way to solve problems continually with a well-defined process at the level the problem was occurring.

The focus had shifted from status quo to a thirst for improvement. Improvement began to bring rewards, whereas the status quo was disdained. A comprehensive business evaluation was conducted, and improvement targets were identified. Clear assignments with reasonable goals were cascaded to all levels of the organization. Performance planning, goals, compensation, and recognition were aligned to support the overall business strategy. Managers who did not work to meet these new goals, who did not role model the behaviors necessary to achieve high performance, were reassigned to jobs that did not require their management skills. New role models emerged to lead the organization at all levels. Within three years, the company regained market share, improved profitability, expanded its employee base, and became, once again, one of the world's most admired companies.

Background Tale Two

Jerry was the CEO of a West Coast manufacturing company that also was a proud member of the Fortune 500. Company performance had been uneven over the past few years. Profits were low this year relative to previous years, but the company still met financial targets. Product demands were high and the outlook was fairly good for the next quarter. The industry as a whole was fairly evenly matched as far as management problems. Trends for return on investment were also uneven. Other indicators, such as sales volume and net profit, were up and down. Investors were not happy, especially when other companies consistently outperformed them. Jerry thought that it was time to do something different. Jerry consulted several valuable and trusted advisors and then decided that Performance Excellence might be worth considering.

The First Message to the Leadership Team

Jerry scheduled a series of weekly dinner meetings over the next month (January) and engaged several different top consultants to talk to the group about the business case for using high-performance management. He invited 50 top-level managers from across the country to attend. Most top leaders attended the meetings, enjoyed the dinners, and Jerry attended most but not all of them. The sessions were interesting—the top leaders found the meetings were a great forum for politicking, posturing, wining and dining, and trying to sharpshoot the consultant. Jerry asked his top leaders to come together for a half day in the spring to discuss the content and direction of the high performance initiative, being convinced intellectually by the dinner discussions that this was the right direction for the company. At the half-day meeting, it was obvious that about half of the group agreed with the CEO and about half were uncertain or downright resistant, particularly one very senior vice president. Jerry left the team with this message, "Let me take your comments under advisement and think about them as we go forward." Later, at the consultant's suggestion, he conducted an organizational assessment to identify problems that might be contributory to the uneven, up-and-down performance. The assessment uncovered several serious problems that required change, yet the senior leaders continued to resist.

The Next Steps

Jerry finally hired one of the external advisors who withstood the test of several dinner meetings and the challenges of his threatened senior management team. The advisor was asked to speak to the top leaders of Jerry's entire U.S.-based company about what a great group they were and how important the Performance Excellence initiative was going to be for the company. The advisor closed by telling them that only the best go after high performance; if they did not, their competitors would. During the following discussion sessions, Jerry's chief operating officer (COO) announced to the group that he was far from convinced and stated he was not going to change the way he did business. That comment went unchallenged by Jerry or anyone else in the company. Frustration continued to build.

In an effort to regain momentum, Jerry wanted to create a change team. He asked each division to send a person to "facilitate" the initiative and be trained by the external team. The people selected were far from the best each division could offer, since no selection criteria were provided. They supplied people that were expendable. The people who formed the facilitator group, for their part, were very enthusiastic but not particularly respected or credible. They were given absolutely no relief from any regular duties, so they were stretched very thin. Also, the division heads were not supportive in any way of their participation, so they were almost punished for participating on this team. As the facilitators worked to please the demands of the CEO, there was no clear charter or mission as to what they were actually supposed to accomplish—no way to assess their performance or their accomplishment of their mission.

The power struggle intensified between the COO (who thought this was not the way to go and would have none of it), and the CEO. The CEO and the top management team arranged to travel to a leadership conference where they could hear presentations from high-performance organizations that had used the Performance Excellence techniques successfully. The CEO made it a priority to plan to attend only morning presentations so everyone could play tennis together each afternoon. Tennis, not high performance, was the main topic of discussion at the evening dinners. A good time was had by all, but no consensus around change developed or was even discussed.

Training and the Change Process

Still, Jerry wanted the facilitators to continue their work to assist change. The internal facilitators were placed in charge of conducting training for the entire organization. After the initial training was designed, a date was set to present a half-day version to the senior staff. Although the entire training was a four-day course, the senior staff did not feel they needed the same skills as the workforce. However, Jerry made it a high priority for his direct reports to attend. At the last minute, Jerry had to attend a function related to the board of directors and did not attend.

The training was, to put it mildly, a disaster. The executives, prompted by the snide comments of the COO, never gave it a chance. They concluded that the training was not effective and should not be rolled out to the employees. In the face of compelling opposition, Jerry quietly diverted his attention elsewhere.

Summary

It is probably obvious what the current state is of John's high-performance "way to run the business" versus the high-performance "initiative" at Jerry's company. Perhaps you could spot some of the problems each type of leader addressed and solutions they supported.

Using symbols and language to manage the change to high performance is tricky and usually demands that some external person is involved who can provide sound advice, based on experience and expertise, to the CEO. Using power constructively is absolutely critical, since failure of the top leader to use all forms of power and influence available will intensify conflict and power struggles that act as a de facto barrier to change.

Motivating people to act constructively and not feel threatened is another challenge. Providing a clear focus on the future state while rewarding behavior that facilitates the transition will work to ensure the change actually happens. Jerry's vision was unclear. He did not act as a leader. He ensured his facilitators would never succeed by never championing their work in any way. The next time Jerry gets a new idea, these people (if they are still employees) will take a nosedive rather than be at the forefront of the initiative.

John never lost his vision, control, or influence as CEO. He ensured his management team would also retain control by first insisting they climb on board and then giving them the skills and support to spread the approaches throughout the company. He used many points of contact for the seeds to take root.

Leadership

Based on the CEO research cited earlier, coupled with the relentless pace of change in all sectors and increasingly global competition, there are several strong messages leaders need to understand. ***Then they must be willing to take the necessary steps to change.*** This will require an assessment of current management systems ***and*** a willingness to drive the necessary adjustment. Once the assessment is complete and priorities are agreed upon, line up plans and resources and support the change wholeheartedly. ***Focus on the marketplace for your cues to change.*** Ask for example:

- Is your competition growing weaker?
- Is the economy more stable and secure?
- Are the demands of all of your customers declining?
- Do you have all of the resources you need to meet your future goals?
- Do you believe your employees will be willing or able to continue working at the pace you have set for them? Will they do more?

If answer is NO to any of these questions, read on.

Assess management systems and launch improvements. This will require your organization to assess their management against the Baldrige Criteria. After the assessment is complete, identify the vital few next steps, assign responsibility, make improvements, and reevaluate.

Great Leaders Are Great Communicators Who Lead by Example

One characteristic of a high-performance organization is outstanding performance results. How does an organization achieve such results? How does it become world-class? We have found unanimous agreement on the critical and fundamental role of leadership. There is not one example of an organization or unit within an organization that achieves superior levels of performance without the personal and active involvement of its top leadership. Top leaders in these organizations create a powerful vision that focuses and energizes the workforce. Everyone is pulling together toward the same goals. Frequently, an inspired vision, combined with appropriately aligned recognition and reward, is the catalyst that builds trust and launches initiatives to overcome the organizational status quo.

Great leaders are great communicators. They identify clear objectives and a game plan so the organization succeeds in its mission. They assign accountability, ensure that employees have the tools and skills required, and create a work climate where individual initiative and the transfer of learning thrives. They reward teamwork and data-driven improvement. While practicing what they preach, they serve as role models for continuous improvement, consensus building, and fact-based decision making; they push authority and accountability to the lowest possible levels.

One lesson from great leaders is to refrain from the use of the word "quality." Too often, when skilled, hard-working, dedicated employees are told by leaders, "We are going to start a quality effort," they conclude that their leaders believe they have not been working hard enough. The workforce hears an unintended message, "We have to do this because we are not good." They frequently retort with, "We already do quality work!" Registered professionals (engineers, chemists, psychologists, physicians, teachers) often exacerbate the communication problem by arguing that they, not customers, are the best ones in a position to know and define "quality." These messages confuse the workforce. Unfortunately, the use of the word *quality* can create an unintended barrier of mistrust and negativism that leaders must overcome before even starting on the road to Performance Excellence.

As an alternative, we advise leaders to create a work climate that enables employees to develop and use their full potential, to improve continually the way they work—to seek higher performance levels and reduce activities that do not add value or optimize performance. Most employees readily agree that there is always room for improvement—all are exposed to work that does not add value.

The use of the word *quality* can also open leadership to challenges as to what definition of quality the organization should use. This leads to our second lesson learned.

Leaders will have to overcome two organizational tendencies—to reject any management model or approach "not invented here" and to think that there are many equally valid models. Quality differs from a decision tree or problem-solving model where there are many acceptable alternatives. The Baldrige model—and the many national, state, and organization assessment systems based on it—is accepted as the standard for defining Performance Excellence in organizations worldwide. Its criteria provide validated, leading-edge practices for managing an organization to achieve peak performance. A decade of extraordinary business results shown by Baldrige Award winners and numerous state-level, Baldrige Award-based winners have helped convince those willing to listen and learn.

To be effective, leaders must understand the Baldrige model and communicate to the workforce and leadership system their intention to use that model for assessment and improvement. Without clear leadership commitment to achieving the requirements of the comprehensive Baldrige model, resources may be spent chasing facts, narrow focuses, and isolated strategies, such as activity-based costing, management by objective, reengineering, project management, quality circles, and ISO 9000 certification, to name a few. Without clear leadership there will be many "hikers" walking around but no marked trails for them to follow. Once leaders understand the system and realize that it is their responsibility to share the knowledge and mark the trails clearly, performance optimization is attainable. This brings us to our third leadership lesson learned.

A significant portion of senior leaders' time—as much as 60 percent to 80 percent—should be spent in visible Baldrige-related leadership activities, such as goal setting, planning, reviewing performance, recognizing and rewarding high performance, and spending time understanding and communicating with customers and suppliers, *not* micromanaging subordinates' work. The senior leaders' perspective in goal setting, planning, and reviewing performance must look at the inside from the outside. Looking at the organization through the critical eyes of external customers, suppliers, and other stakeholders is a vital perspective.

The primary role of the effective senior leader is to focus the organization on satisfying customers through an effective leadership system. Leaders must role model the tools of consensus building and decision making as the organization focuses on its vision, mission, and strategic direction to keep customers loyal.

Falling back on command-and-control behavior will be self-defeating. The leadership system will suffer from crossed wires and mixed messages. Such commandments as "I want this mission rolled out by the end of the second quarter" fall into the self-defeating, major mistake category. However, leaders must be clear and resolute.

Using the consensus approach to focus the organization on its mission and vision will take longer, of course. This is similar to taking more time during the product design phase to ensure that problems are prevented later. The additional time is necessary for organizational learning, support, and buy-in, particularly around two areas—integrating global marketplace realities and better understanding the competitive environment. The resulting vision will have more depth and focus. The leadership system will be stronger. Finally, the deployment of the vision and focus will take a shorter time because of the buy-in and support created during the process.

L Is for Listen

Successful leaders know the power of listening to their people—those they rely on to achieve their goals. One vital link to the pulse of the organization is employee feedback. To determine whether what you have said has been understood, ask for feedback and then listen carefully. To know whether what you have outlined as a plan makes sense or has gaping faults, ask for feedback and then listen. Your leadership system cannot improve without your listening and acting on employee feedback, and your goals and action plans cannot be improved without it. In fact, the 2000 Baldrige Criteria [Item 1.1b(4)] specifically examines the extent to which leaders use employee feedback in assessing and improving their leadership effectiveness and the effectiveness of managers at all levels.

Manage and Drive Change

Business leaders can count on relentless, rapid change being part of the business world. The rate of change confronting business today is far faster than that driven by the Industrial Revolution. Skills driven by the Industrial Revolution carried our parents through a 40-year work life. Human knowledge now doubles every 5 to 7 years, instead of the 40 years it took in the 1930s. Today, our children are told to expect five career (not job) changes during their work life.

There are several lessons for leaders today. Change may not occur on the schedule they set for it. It is often faster or too uneven to predict at all. Also, change driven by leaders is often resisted by those most successful—they have difficulty seeing the need to change. Take, for example, a school district that scheduled a quality improvement workshop for its middle school faculty. The day before the training, the district leadership received a letter protesting the workshop on the grounds it was not needed. The letter was signed by the 20 best teachers in the school. To the credit of the school district leadership, they held the workshop anyway, and the truly outstanding teachers saw the value in continuous improvement once they began to listen.

Leaders who hold the values of high performance will need to drive change to make the necessary improvements. Change will not happen naturally. It is rarely driven by those at the bottom (except for revolutionaries). Embracing the concepts of organizational learning (not just individual) will facilitate change in the organization. Leaders will need organizational learning as an ally as they manage change and drive it through the organization.

Strategic Planning

Deploy Through People Not Paper

Strategic planning is performance improvement planning, deployment, and implementation. The organization's strategic plan is also its quality—business, human resources—performance improvement plan. Easily enough said, but trying to get agreement on exactly what strategic planning is will result in an interesting variety of ideas. Therefore, the planning process should begin by ensuring that all contributors agree on terminology. Otherwise, the strategic plan, in fact, may be incomplete—a marketing plan, a budget plan, or a financial business plan, depending on who is leading the team.

Developing separate plans for each aspect of business success is counterproductive. It guarantees a nonintegrated and short-lived systematic performance improvement effort. Therefore, leaders should concentrate on the few critical improvement goals in the strategic plan necessary for organizational success, such as improving customer loyalty and reducing errors or cycle time. The well-developed strategic plan also:

- Documents the financial impact of achieving these few goals;
- Details actions to support the goals; and
- Discusses the competitive environment that drives the goals.

One highly successful organization simplified this document to a single electronic page, to which senior leaders referred each month by computer during performance results reviews. Everyone at all levels used their own one-page document to deploy the plan and define actions needed.

The most critical lesson learned when it comes to strategic plans is that there can be no rest until it is certain every person in the organization understands his or her role in the plan and how their contribution will be measured.

Customer and Market Focus

Customers Expect Solutions to Problems They Don't Know They Have

The high-performing organization systematically determines its customers' short-term and long-term service and product requirements. It does this based on information from former, as well as current and potential, customers. It builds relationships with customers and continuously obtains information, using it to improve its service and products and understand better customer preferences. The smart organization prioritizes the drivers of satisfaction and loyalty of its customers, compares itself to its competitors, and continuously strives to improve its satisfaction and loyalty levels.

As the organization becomes more and more systematic and effective in determining customer needs, it learns that there is high variation in customer needs. The more sophisticated the measurement system, the more variation will become apparent. It is particularly important that organizations focus on this vital process and make it a top priority that their customers have access to people to make known their requirements and their preferences. How else can modern organizations ensure they are building relationships with their customers? After all, few of us have storefronts on Main Street where our customers come and chat regularly.

One specific lesson learned comes from voice mail—a big step forward in convenience and efficiency can be a big step backward in customer relationship building if used poorly. For example, a major international financial institution put their highest priority customers on a new voice mail system. Customers were never informed about the system and one day called their special line to find rock music and a three-tiered voice mail system instead of their personal financial account manager. This is a good example of a step in the wrong direction. Customers were never asked about their requirements and preferences, and the organization heard about it quickly in the form of lost accounts and angry, frustrated customers.

Another important first lesson is to segment customers according to their needs and preferences and do what is necessary to build strong, positive relationships with them. More and more customers are looking for service providers to define their unique needs for them and respond to those unique needs. In short, customers are expecting solutions to problems that they, the customers, have not yet realized.

Organizations that make it easy for customers to complain are in a good position to hear about problems early so that they can fix them and plan ahead to prevent them. If organizations handle customer complaints effectively at the first point of contact, customer loyalty and satisfaction will increase. If organizations do not make it easy for customers to complain, when finally given the chance to provide feedback, they will not bother to complain; they simply will no longer do business with these organizations.

As the customer-focused organization matures, it will likely evolve around customer types. This evolution leads to restructuring that is guided by shared organizational values. The speed with which this restructuring occurs varies according to marketplace conditions and the organization's ability to change. Today, we see more restructuring that eliminates parochial, regional centers in favor of creating customer service groups that meet customer requirements around the world using up-to-date technologies.

The next lesson has to do with educating the organization's leadership in the fundamentals of customer loyalty and customer satisfaction research models before beginning to collect customer satisfaction data. Failure to do this may affect the usefulness of the data as a strategic tool. At the very least, it will make the development of data collection instruments a long, misunderstood effort, creating rework and unnecessary cost.

Do not expect everyone to welcome customer feedback—many fear accountability. Time and time again, the organizations most resistant to surveying customers, conducting focus groups, and making it easy for customers to complain are the same organizations that do not have everyday contact handling systems, response-time standards, or trained and empowered frontline employees to serve customers and deal with their concerns promptly. Frontline employees who are not ready to acknowledge customer concerns are not capable of assuming responsibility to solve customer problems.

No single feedback tool is intended to stand alone. A mail-based survey does not take the place of personal interviews. Focus groups do not replace surveys. The high-performance organization uses multiple listening posts and trains frontline employees to collect customer feedback and improve those listening posts. In the high-performance organization, for example, even an accounts receivable system is viewed as a listening post.

Do not lose sight of the fact that the best customer feedback method, whether it be a survey, focus group, or one-on-one interview, is only a tool:
- Make sure the data gathered are actionable.
- Aggregate the data from all sources to permit complete analyses.
- Use the data to improve strategic planning and operating processes.

Finally, be aware that customers are not interested in your problems. They merely want products or services delivered as promised. They become loyal when consistent value is provided that sets you above all others. Merely meeting their basic expectations brands you as marginal. To be valued, you must consistently delight and exceed the customers' expectations.

Information and Analysis

Data-Driven Management and Avoiding Contephobia

The high-performance organization collects, manages, and analyzes data and information to drive excellence and improve its overall performance. Said another way, information is used to drive actions. Using data and information as strategic weapons, effective leaders compare their organization constantly to competitors, similar service providers, and world-class organizations.

While people tend to think of data and measurement as objective and hard, there is often a softer by-product of measurement. That by-product is the basic human emotion of fear. This perspective on data and measurement leads to the first lesson learned about information and analysis. Human fear must be recognized and managed in order to practice data-driven management.

This fear can be found in two types of people. The first are those who have a simple fear of numbers—those who hated mathematics in school and probably stretch their quantitative capabilities to balance their checkbook. These individuals are lost in numerical data discussions. When asked to measure or when presented with data, they can become fearful, angry, and resistant. Their reactions can actually undermine improvement efforts.

The second type of individual understands numbers and realizes that numbers can impose higher levels of accountability. The fear of accountability, *contephobia* (from fourteenth-century Latin "to count," modified by the French "to account"), is based on the fear of real performance failure that numbers might reveal or, more often, an overall fear of the unknown that will drive important decisions. Power structures can and do shift when decisions are data driven.

Fearful individuals can undermine effective data-driven management systems. In managing this fear, leaders must believe and communicate through their behavior that a number is not inherently right or wrong. It is important for leaders at all levels to demonstrate that system and process improvement, not individuals, are the focus of performance improvement.

A mature, high-performance organization will collect data on competitors and similar providers and benchmark itself against world-class leaders. Some individuals may not be capable of seeing the benefit of using this process performance information. This type of data is known as **benchmarking** data. The focus is on identifying, learning from, and adopting best practices or methods from similar processes, regardless of industry or product similarity. Adopting the best practices of other organizations has driven quantum leap improvements and provided great opportunities for breakthrough improvements.

Lesson number two, therefore, is that an organization that has difficulty comparing itself with dissimilar organizations is not ready to benchmark and is not likely to be able to optimize its own performance as a result.

The third lesson in this area relates to not being a DRIP. This refers to a tendency to collect so much data (which contributes to contephobia) that the organization becomes <u>d</u>ata <u>r</u>ich and <u>i</u>nformation <u>p</u>oor. This is wrong. Avoid wasting capital resources and stretch the resources available for managing improvement by asking this question: "Will these data help make improvements for our customers, key financials, employees, or top result areas?" If the answer is no, do not waste time collecting, analyzing, and trying to use the data.

Human Resource Focus

Human Resource (Not the Department)

Personnel departments have been renamed in many organizations, often to "human resources." This name change is intended to draw attention to the fact that people are valuable resources of the organization, not just commodities to be hired and fired and filed. Now, however, the leap made by successful organizations is that human resources need to be part of every strategic and operational decision of the organization. This focus goes far beyond the department of human resources. In high-performing organizations, employees are treated like any valuable asset of the organization—investment and development are critical to optimize the asset. People should be perceived as internal customers and a vital part of the chain that eventually serves an external customer.

One of the valuable lessons learned in this regard is not to let an out-of-date or territorial "personnel or human resources department" use archaic rules to stop your performance improvement program. Although many human resources professionals are among the brave pioneers in high-performance organizations, others have tried to keep compensation and promotions tied to "seat time" and tenure rather than performance. This outdated approach will definitely stop progress in its tracks or slow it significantly.

The Big Challenge Is Trust

The high-performing organization values its employees and demonstrates this by enabling people to develop and realize their full potential while providing them incentives to do so. The organization that is focused on human resource excellence maintains a climate that builds trust. Trust is essential for employee participation, engagement, personal and professional growth, and high organizational performance.

The first human resource lesson is perhaps the most critical one. That is, revise—overhaul, if necessary—recognition, compensation, promotion, and feedback systems to support high-performance work systems. If leaders personally demonstrate all the correct leadership behaviors yet continue to recognize and reward "fire fighting" performance, offer pay and bonuses tied only to traditional bottom-line results, and promote individuals who do not represent high-performance role models—those leaders will find their improvement effort is short-lived. The leadership system with all its webs and intricate circuits will short out due to mixed signals.

Promotion, compensation, recognition, and reward must be tied to the achievement of key business results, including customer satisfaction, innovation, and performance improvement. The promotion/compensation/recognition tool is a powerful tool in aligning, or misaligning, the work of the organization.

A second human resource lesson learned relates to training and development. Training is not a panacea or a goal in itself. The organization's direction and goals must support training, and training must support organization priorities.

Its human resources are the competitive edge of a high-performing organization. Training must be part of an overall business strategy. If not, money and resources are probably better spent on a memorable holiday party.

Timing is critical. Broad-based workforce skill training should not come first. Many organizations rush out and train their entire workforce only to find themselves having to retrain months or years later. Key participants should be involved in planning skill training so that important skills are delivered just in time for them to use in their assignments.

Continuous skill development requires management support to reinforce and strengthen skills on the job. Leadership development at all levels of the organization needs to be built into employee development. New technology has increased training flexibility so that all knowledge does not have to be transferred in a classroom setting. Consider many options when planning how best to update skills. After initial skill building occurs, high-performing organizations emphasize organizational learning where employees take charge of their own learning, using training courses as only one avenue for skill upgrading. Transferring learning to other parts of the organization or projects is a valuable organizational learning strategy and reinforcement technique. Training must be offered when an application exists to use and reinforce the skill. Otherwise, most of what is learned will be forgotten. The effectiveness of training must be assessed based on the impact on the job, not merely the likability of the instructor or the clarity of course materials.

Employee surveys are often used to measure employee satisfaction and improve employee satisfaction. Surveys are especially useful to identify key issues that should be discussed in open employee forums. Such forums are truly useful if they clarify perceptions, provide more in-depth understanding of employee concerns, and open the communication channels with leaders. Organizations have success in improving employee satisfaction by conducting routine employee satisfaction surveys, meeting with employees to plan improvements, and tying improvements in satisfaction ratings to managers' compensation.

Two final human resource excellence lessons have to do with engaging and involving employees in decisions about their work. Involving employees in decision making without the right skills or a sense of direction produces chaos, not high performance. Consider the following:
- First, leaders who empower employees before communicating and testing that a sense of direction has been fully understood will find that they are managing chaos.

- Second, not everyone wants to be empowered, and to do so represents a barrier to high performance. While there may be individuals who truly seek to avoid responsibility for making improvements, claiming "that's management's job," these individuals do not last long in a high-performing organization. They begin to stick out like a lone bird in the winter. Team members who want the organization to thrive and survive do not permit such people to influence (or even remain on) their team.

The bigger reason for individuals failing to "take the empowerment and run with it" is management's mixed messages. In short, management must convince employees that they (managers) really believe that employees know their own processes best and can improve them. Consistent leadership is required to help employees overcome legitimate, long-standing fear of traditional management practices used so often in the past to control and punish.

Remember, aligning compensation and reward systems to reinforce performance plans and core values is one of the most critical factors in enhancing organizational performance; however, getting employees to believe their leaders really trust them to improve their own processes is difficult.

Process Management

Listen to Process Owners and Keep Them Involved

Process management involves the **continuous improvement** of processes required to meet customer requirements and deliver quality products and services. Virtually every high-performance organization identifies key processes and manages them to ensure that customer requirements are met consistently and performance is continuously improved.

The first lesson learned has to do with the visibility of processes. Many processes are highly visible, such as serving a meal or purchasing. However, when a process is hard to observe, such as course design or customer response, as so many are in the service sector, it cannot be assumed that everyone will see the organization as a collection of processes. The simple exercise of drawing a process flow diagram with people involved in an invisible process can be a struggle, but it also can be a valuable revelation. With no vantage point from which to see work as a process, many people never think of themselves as engaged in a process. Some even deny it. The fact that all work—visible and invisible—is part of a process must be understood throughout the organization before employees can begin to manage and improve key processes.

Once this is understood, a second process management lesson comes to light. Process owners are the best ones, but not the only ones, to improve their processes. They must be part of process improvement teams. These teams are often made up of carefully selected cross-discipline, cross-functional, multi-level people who bring fresh insight to the examination of a process. Do not lose sight of the process owner—the person with expert knowledge of the process who should be accountable for long-term improvement to it. To try to ensure that all of its process improvement teams were cross-functional and multilevel, one organization enlisted volunteers to join process improvement teams. Using this democratic but misguided process, a marketing process improvement team ended up with no marketing expertise among its members. Instead, a group of frustrated support and technical staff members, who knew nothing about marketing, wasted time and money mapping and redesigning a process doomed to fail.

The third process management lesson learned involves an issue mentioned earlier. When focusing too closely on internal process data, there is a tendency to lose sight of external requirements. Organizations often succeed at making their processes better, faster, and (maybe) cheaper for them but not necessarily to the benefit of their customers. When analyzing internal process data, someone must stubbornly play the role of advocate for the external customers' perspective. Ensure that the data will help make improvements for customers, key financials, employees, or top result areas. Avoid wasting resources on process improvements that do not benefit customers, employees, or the key performance of your organization.

A fourth lesson involves design processes, an important but often neglected part of process management. The best organizations have learned that improvements made early in the process, beginning with design, save more time and money than those made farther "downstream." To identify how design processes can be improved, it is necessary to include ongoing evaluation and improvement cycles.

Business Results

Encourage Activities That Lead to Desired Business Results

Results fall into five broad categories:
- Customer focused, such as customer satisfaction and product and service quality:
- Financial and market:
- Human resource:
- Supplier and partner:
- Organizational effectiveness, such as key design, production, delivery and support performance and regulatory/legal compliance.

Being customer focused is a critical and ongoing result that every successful organization or work unit within an organization must achieve. Systems must exist to make sure that the data from customer satisfaction and dissatisfaction are used at all levels to plan and make improvements. Remember that when customers are asked their opinion, an expectation is created in their minds that the information will be used to make improvements that benefit them.

Some organizations have found it beneficial to have their customers analyze some of their business results with the idea of learning from them, as well as building and strengthening relationships. This may or may not be appropriate for your organization, but many successful organizations have shared results with key customer groups at a level appropriate for their specific organization.

Product and service quality results provide useful information on key measures of the product or service itself. This information allows an organization to predict whether customers are likely to be satisfied—usually without asking them. For example, one of the nation's most successful and fastest-growing coffee shops knows from its customers that a good cup of coffee is hot, has a good taste, is not too bitter, and has a rich aroma. The measures for these product characteristics are temperature, pH (acidity), and the time lapse between brewing and serving. With these measures, they can predict whether their customers are likely to be satisfied with the coffee before they serve it. One important lesson in this area is to select measures that correlate with, and predict, customer preference, satisfaction, and loyalty.

Financial and market performance is a key to survival. Organizations that make improvements that do not ultimately improve financial performance are wasting resources and growing weaker financially. This is true for both private sector (for-profit) and public sector (not-for-profit, education, government) organizations. It is important to avoid overreliance on financial results. Financial results are the lagging indicators of organization performance. Leaders who focus primarily on financials often overlook or cannot respond quickly to changing business needs. Focusing on finances to run the business—to the exclusion of leading indicators, such as operational performance and employee satisfaction—is like driving your car by looking only in the rearview mirror. You cannot avoid potholes and turns in the road.

Human resource performance results provide an early alert to problems that may threaten success. Absenteeism, turnover, accidents, low morale, grievances, and poor skills or ineffective training suboptimize organizational effectiveness. By monitoring performance in these areas, leaders can adjust quickly and prevent little problems from overwhelming the organization.

Supplier quality performance can significantly affect organizational operating effectiveness and customer satisfaction. To the extent an organization depends on suppliers, it must ensure that supplier performance improves— otherwise, it must absorb (or pass on to customers) supplier waste, errors, inefficiency, and rework. An organization that tolerates poor supplier performance places its own business at risk.

Organizational effectiveness operational and service results pertain to measures of internal effectiveness that may not be of immediate interest to customers, such as **cycle time** (how long it takes to brew a pot of coffee), **waste** (how many pots you have to pour out because the coffee sat too long), and payroll accuracy (which may upset the affected workers). Ultimately, improving internal work process efficiency can result in reduced cost, rework, waste, scrap, and other factors that affect the bottom line, whether profit driven or budget driven. As a result, customers are indirectly affected. To stay in business, to remain competitive, or to meet increased performance demands with fewer resources, the organization will be required to improve processes that enhance operational and support service results. The results also need to address the organization performance regarding regulatory, legal compliance and citizenship. Results relating to accomplishment of organizational strategy are also to be addressed.

Award Criteria Framework

The Baldrige Performance Excellence Criteria contain three basic elements:
- **Strategy and action plans.** The context for aligning work and achieving Performance Excellence
- **System.** Consisting of the driver triad and work core, producing business results
- **Information and analysis.** The brain center of high-performing organizations

Figure 1 depicts the entire system. Figures 2, 3, and 4 break out the major components of the system.

Strategy and Action Plans

Strategy and action plans are the set of organization-level requirements, derived from short- and long-term strategic planning, that must be done well for the organization's strategy to succeed. Strategy and action plans set the context for action in high-performing organizations and provide the vehicle through which leaders drive the organization to achieve success. Strategy and action plans guide overall resource decisions and drive the alignment of measures for all work units to ensure customer satisfaction and market success.

Strategy and action plans are represented in the framework as an umbrella that covers the organization's entire work system.

Criteria for Performance Excellence—Systems Framework

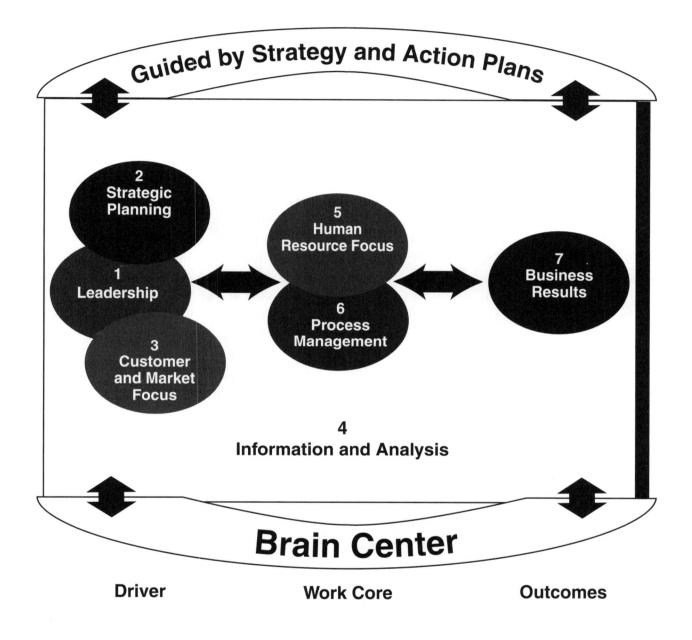

Figure 1

System   The **system** is comprised of the six Baldrige Categories in the center of the figure that define the organization, its operations, and its results. The system is further shown to be comprised of two core activities that produce key business results.

- The driver triad
- The work core

The business outcomes are a composite of customer, financial, and nonfinancial performance results, including human resource development and public responsibility.

The Driver Triad   As Figure 2 indicates, the **driver triad** consists of three categories.
- Leadership
- Strategic Planning
- Customer and Market Focus

The processes that make up these categories require leaders to set direction and expectations for the organization to meet customer and market requirements (Category 1). Customer and market focus (Category 3) processes produce the information that leaders use to determine what current and potential customers want. Strategic planning (Category 2) and goal setting provide the vehicle for determining the short- and long-term strategies for success, as well as communicating and aligning the work of the organization. Leaders use this information to set direction and goals, monitor progress, make resource decisions, and take corrective action when progress does not proceed according to plan.

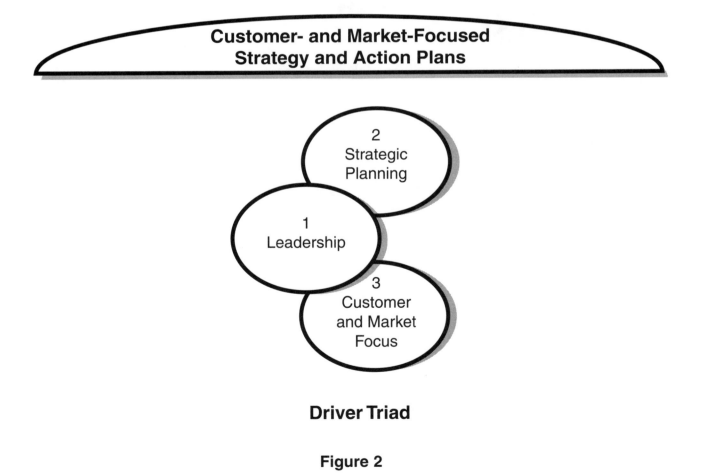

Driver Triad

Figure 2

The Work Core   The work core, as the name suggests, describes the processes through which the core work of the organization takes place. As Figure 3 indicates, the work core consists of human resource focus (Category 5) and process management (Category 6), which produce the business results (Category 7).

These categories recognize that the people of an organization are responsible for doing the work. To achieve Performance Excellence, these people must possess the right skills and must be allowed to work in an environment that promotes initiative and self-direction. The work processes provide the structure for continuous learning and improvement to optimize performance.

Business results reflect the organization's actual performance in terms critical for success. These include customer satisfaction, financial and market performance, human resource performance, supplier performance, and internal operating effectiveness.

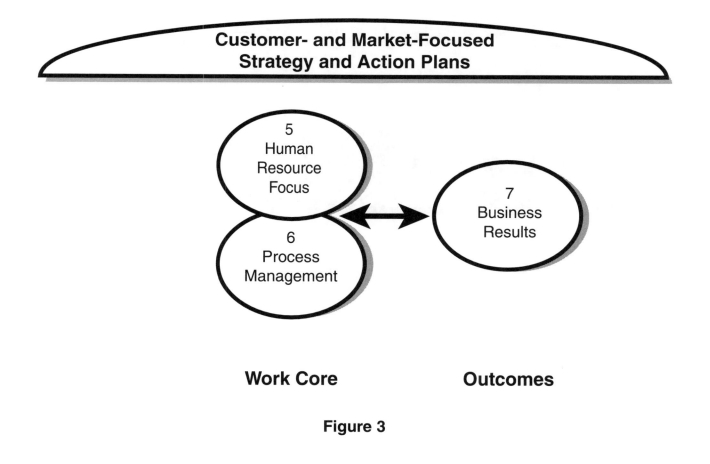

Figure 3

Information and Analysis

Figure 4 depicts how information and analysis (Category 4) is the foundation for the entire management system. Information and analysis is the "brain center" of the management system. It is the platform on which the entire system operates. Information and analysis processes are critical to the effective management of the organization and to a fact-based system for improving organizational performance and competitiveness.

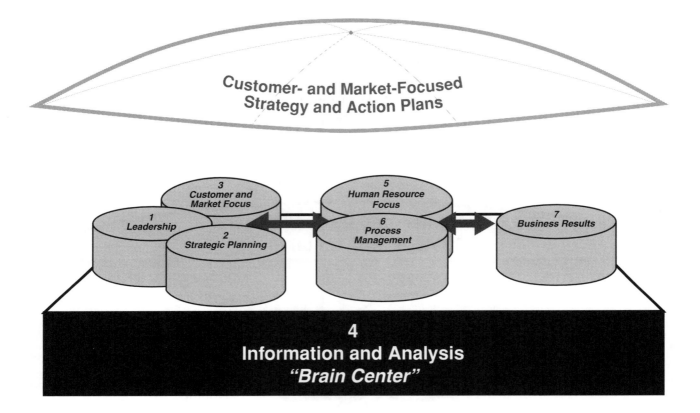

Figure 4

Award Criteria Organization

The seven Criteria categories are subdivided into Items and areas to address. Figure 5 demonstrates the organization of Category 1.

Items

There are 19 Items, each focusing on a major requirement. Item titles and point values are on page 72.

Areas to Address

Items consist of one or more areas to address (areas). Information is submitted by applicants in response to the specific requirements of these areas. There are 27 areas to address.

Subparts

There are 85 subparts in the 2000 Criteria, the same as the 1999 Criteria. Areas consist of one or more subparts, where numbers are shown in parentheses. A response should be made to each subpart.

Notes

In 2000, the notes have been increased to 49 from the 1999 total of 46. **Notes do not add requirements.** Examiners may not use the explanations in the notes as if they were Criteria requirements.

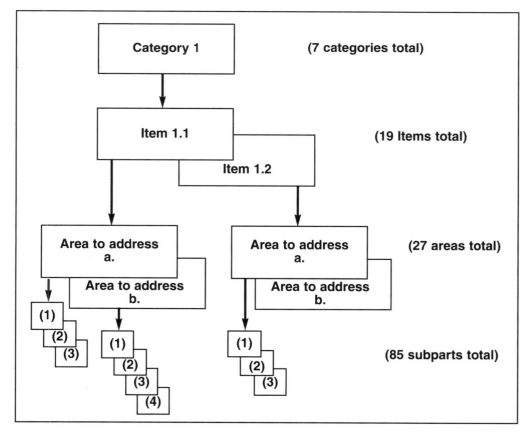

Figure 5

Baldrige Award Categories and Point Values

Examination Categories/Items		Maximum Points
1 **Leadership**	**(125 points)**	
1.1 Organizational Leadership		85
1.2 Public Responsibility and Citizenship		40
2 **Strategic Planning**	**(85 points)**	
2.1 Strategy Development		40
2.2 Strategy Deployment		45
3 **Customer and Market Focus**	**(85 points)**	
3.1 Customer and Market Knowledge		40
3.2 Customer Satisfaction and Relationships		45
4 **Information and Analysis**	**(85 points)**	
4.1 Measurement of Organizational Performance		40
4.2 Analysis of Organizational Performance		45
5 **Human Resource Focus**	**(85 points)**	
5.1 Work Systems		35
5.2 Employee Education, Training, and Development		25
5.3 Employee Well-Being and Satisfaction		25
6 **Process Management**	**(85 points)**	
6.1 Product and Service Processes		55
6.2 Support Processes		15
6.3 Supplier and Partnering Processes		15
7 **Business Results**	**(450 points)**	
7.1 Customer Focused Results		115
7.2 Financial and Market Results		115
7.3 Human Resource Results		80
7.4 Supplier and Partner Results		25
7.5 Organizational Effectiveness Results		115
Total Points		**1000**

Key Characteristics—2000 Performance Excellence Criteria

The Criteria focus on business results and the processes required to achieve them. Business results are a composite of the following:
- Customer satisfaction and retention;
- Financial and marketplace performance;
- Product and service performance;
- Productivity, operational effectiveness, and responsiveness;
- Human resource performance and development;
- Supplier performance and development; and
- Public responsibility and good citizenship.

These results areas cover overall organization performance, including financial performance. The results areas also recognize the importance of suppliers and of community and national well-being. The use of a composite of indicators helps to ensure that strategies are balanced—that they do not inappropriately trade off among important stakeholders or objectives or between short- and long-term goals.

The Criteria allow wide latitude in how requirements are met. Accordingly, the Criteria do not prescribe:
- Specific tools, techniques, technologies, systems, measures, or starting points; that organizations should or should not have departments for quality, planning, or other functions; and
- How the organization or business units within the organization should be organized.

Processes to achieve Performance Excellence are very likely to change as needs and strategies evolve. Hence, the Criteria themselves are regularly evaluated as part of annual performance reviews to ensure that they continue to distinguish high-performing organizations from all others.

The Criteria do not prescribe specific approaches or methods, because:
- The focus is on results, not on procedures, tools, or organizational structure. Organizations are encouraged to develop and demonstrate creative, adaptive, and flexible approaches for meeting basic requirements. Nonprescriptive requirements are intended to foster incremental and major (breakthrough) improvement, as well as basic change;
- Selection of tools, techniques, systems, and organizations usually depends on many factors, such as business size, business type, the

organization's stage of development, and employee capabilities and responsibilities; and

- Focusing on common requirements within an organization, rather than on common procedures, fosters better understanding, communication, sharing, and alignment, while supporting creativity and diversity in approaches.

The Criteria support a systems approach to organizationwide goal alignment. The systems approach to goal alignment is embedded in the integrated structure of the Criteria and the results-oriented, cause-effect linkages among the Criteria parts.

The measures in the Criteria tie directly to customer value and to overall performance that relate to key internal and external requirements of the organization. Measures serve both as a communications tool and a basis for deploying consistent overall performance requirements. Such alignment ensures consistency of purpose while at the same time supporting speed, innovation, and decentralized decision making.

Learning Cycles and Continuous Improvement

In high-performing organizations, action-oriented learning takes place through feedback between processes and results facilitated by learning or continuous improvement cycles. The learning cycles have four clearly defined and well-established stages:

1. **Plan.** Planning, including design of processes, selection of measures, and deployment of requirements
2. **Do.** Execute plans
3. **Study/check.** Assess progress, taking into account internal and external results
4. **Act.** Revise plans based on assessment findings, learning, new inputs, and new requirements

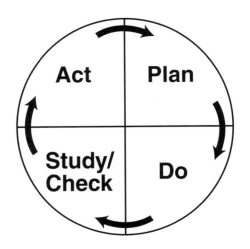

Goal-Based Diagnosis

The Criteria and the scoring guidelines make up the diagnostic assessment system. The Criteria, as discussed previously, are a set of 19 Items. The scoring guidelines spell out the assessment dimensions—approach, deployment, and results—and the key factors used to assess against each dimension. An assessment provides a profile of strengths and areas for improvement to help organizations identify areas that, if addressed, will move the organization ahead. As a result, this diagnostic assessment is a useful management tool that goes beyond traditional performance reviews.

Changes from the 1999 Award Criteria

The Criteria for Performance Excellence have evolved significantly over the last several years toward comprehensive coverage of strategy-driven performance, addressing the needs of all stakeholders—customers, employees, stockholders, suppliers and partners, and the public. During this period of time, other sections of the Criteria booklet have not fully kept pace with the evolving Criteria. For 2000, there are no changes to the Criteria.

Item requirements; revisions have been made in other important sections of the Criteria booklet. The most significant changes are summarized as follows:
- Several core values and concepts have been revised.
- The Glossary of Key Terms has been revised and expanded.
- The Scoring Guidelines have been revised slightly for Approach/Deployment Items.
- The Guidelines for Responding to Approach/ Deployment Items have been modified to explain the desired responses for questions that begin with *how* and for questions that begin with *what*.

A more detailed explanation of the most significant changes follow.

Core Values and Concepts

Many of the core values and concepts have been changed to better align with the foundation for the current Criteria. The number of core values and concepts remains constant at 11.

Seven core values and concepts replacements have been made:
- Visionary Leadership replaces Leadership
- Customer Driven replaces Customer-Driven Quality
- Organizational and Personal Learning replaces Continuous Improvement and Learning
- Valuing Employees and Partners replaces Valuing Employees
- Agility replaces Fast Response
- Focus on the Future replaces Long-Range View of the Future
- Focus on Results and Creating Value replaces Results Focus.

The seven new Core Values and Concepts are intended to provide a more holistic and current view of organizational Performance Excellence.

Two of the 1999 core values and concepts have been incorporated into the 2000 core values and concepts:
- Design Quality and Prevention
- Partnership Development

Two new core values and concepts have been added to underpin the current Criteria:
- Managing for Innovation
- Systems Perspective

Two 1999 core values and concepts remain:
- Management by Fact
- Public Responsibility and Citizenship

Glossary of Key Terms

- The following key terms have been added to the Glossary: analysis, approach, deployment, empowerment, results, strategic objectives, and systematic. All of these terms have very specific meanings in the Baldrige context.

Scoring Guidelines

- The word *effective* replaces the word *sound* for Approach/Deployment Items in the Scoring Guidelines. Effective relates to producing the desired result and to appropriateness for intended use. Effective is a better term in the context of a Baldrige assessment.

1 Leadership—125 Points

The Leadership Category examines how your organization's senior leaders address values and performance expectations, as well as a focus on customers and other stakeholders, empowerment, innovation, learning, and organizational directions. Also examined is how your organization addresses its responsibilities to the public and supports its key communities.

The leadership system must promote core values, set high performance expectations, and promote an organizationwide focus on customers, employee empowerment, learning, and innovation. The Leadership category looks at how senior leaders guide the organization in setting directions and seeking future opportunities. Senior leaders must communicate clear values and high performance expectations that address the needs of all stakeholders. The category also looks at the how the organization meets its responsibilities to the public and how it practices good citizenship.

The category is broken into two Items:

Organizational Leadership
- Communicating and reinforcing clear values, performance expectations, and a focus on creating value for customers and other stakeholders.
- Reinforce environment for empowerment and innovation and employee and organizational learning.
- Reviewing organizational performance and capabilities, competitiveness, and progress relative to goals, and setting priorities for improvement.
- Evaluating and improving the effectiveness of senior leadership and management throughout the organization, including employee input in the process.

Public Responsibility and Citizenship
- For regulatory and other legal requirements in such areas as safety, environmental protection, and waste management; anticipating public concerns and addressing risks to the public; and ensuring ethical business practices.
- For strengthening and supporting key communities.

1.1 Organizational Leadership (85 Points)
Approach/Deployment Scoring

Describe how senior leaders guide your organization and review organizational performance.

Within your response, include answers to the following questions:

a. Senior Leadership Direction

(1) How do senior leaders set, communicate, and deploy organizational values, performance expectations, and a focus on creating and balancing value for customers and other stakeholders? Include communication and deployment through your leadership structure and to all employees.

(2) How do senior leaders establish and reinforce an environment for empowerment and innovation, and encourage and support organizational and employee learning?

(3) How do senior leaders set directions and seek future opportunities for your organization?

b. Organizational Performance Review

(1) How do senior leaders review organizational performance and capabilities to assess organizational health, competitive performance, and progress relative to performance goals and changing organizational needs? Include the key performance measures regularly reviewed by your senior leaders.

(2) How do you translate organizational performance review findings into priorities for improvement and opportunities for innovation?

(3) What are your key recent performance review findings, priorities for improvement, and opportunities for innovation? How are they deployed throughout your organization and, as appropriate, to your suppliers/partners and key customers to ensure organizational alignment?

(4) How do senior leaders use organizational performance review findings and employee feedback to improve their leadership effectiveness and the effectiveness of management throughout the organization?

Note:

Your organizational performance results should be reported in Items 7.1, 7.2, 7.3, 7.4, and 7.5.

The first part of this Item [1.1a] looks at how senior leaders create and sustain values that promote high performance throughout the organization. In promoting high performance, leaders should develop and implement systems to ensure values are understood and consistently followed. An organization's failure to achieve high levels of performance can usually be traced to a failure in leadership:

- To consistently promote high performance, leaders must clearly set direction and make sure everyone in the organization understands his or her responsibilities. Success requires a strong future orientation and a commitment to improvement and the disciplined change that is needed to carry it out. This requires creating an environment for learning and innovation, as well as the means for rapid and effective application of knowledge.

- Leaders must also ensure that organizational values actually guide the behavior of managers and employees throughout the organization or the values are meaningless. To enhance Performance Excellence, the "right" values must be adopted. These values must include a focus on customers and other stakeholders. The failure to ensure a customer focus usually causes the organization and its employees to focus internally. The lack of a customer focus forces workers to default to their own ideas of what customers really "need." This increases the risk of becoming arrogant and not caring about the requirements of customers. It also increases the potential for creating and delivering products and services that no customer wants or values. That, in turn, increases rework, scrap, waste, and added cost/lower value.

- In addition, it is the responsibility of top leadership to create an environment that engages employees and promotes employee innovation, learning, and knowledge sharing.

The second part of this Item [1.1b] looks at how senior leaders review organizational performance in a disciplined, fact-based manner. This organizational review should cover all areas of performance and provide a complete and accurate picture of the "state of health" of the organization. This includes not only how well the organization is currently performing, but also how well it is moving to secure future success:

- Key performance measures should focus on and reflect the key drivers of success leaders regularly review. These measures should relate to the strategic objectives necessary for success.

- Leaders should use these reviews to drive improvement and change. These reviews should provide a reliable means to guide the improvement and change needed to achieve the organization's key objectives.

- Leaders must create a consistent process to translate the review findings into an action agenda sufficiently specific for deployment throughout the organization and to suppliers/partners and key customers as appropriate.
- In addition, leaders and managers at all levels must evaluate their personal effectiveness. To ensure the evaluation is accurate, employees must provide feedback to the leaders and managers.
- Finally, leaders and managers at all levels should take action, based on the feedback, to improve their effectiveness.

1.1 Organizational Leadership

How senior leaders guide the organization in setting direction and developing and sustaining an effective leadership system throughout the organization

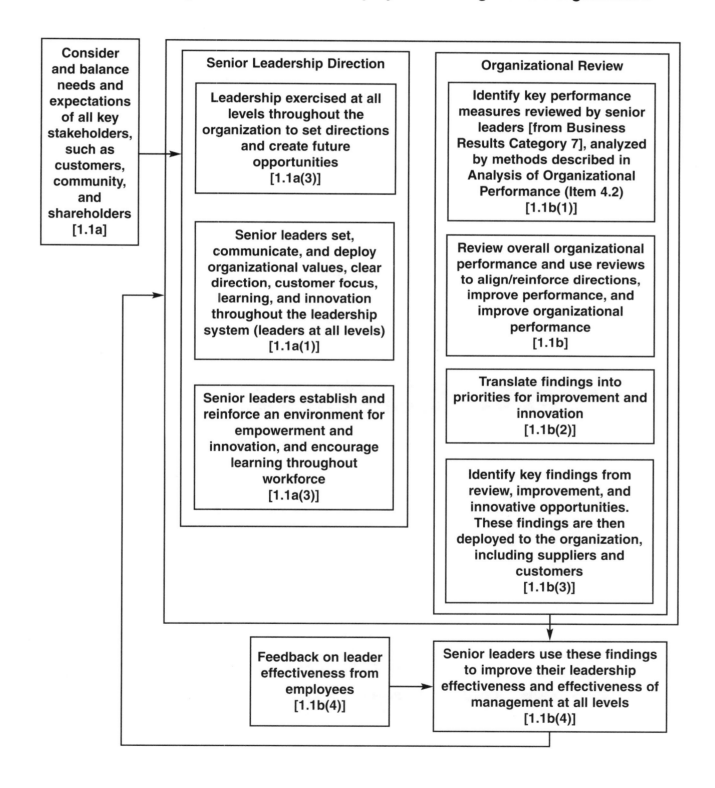

1.1 Organizational Leadership Item Linkages

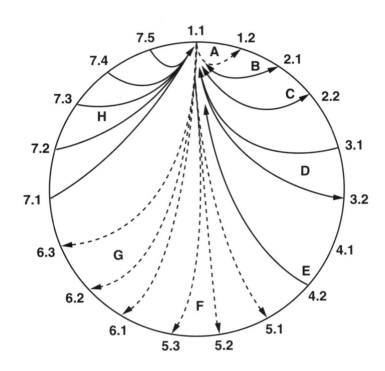

Note: See page 2 for a key to the meaning of the arrows.

	Nature of Relationship
A	Leaders at all levels [1.1] must role model and support corporate responsibility and practice good citizenship [1.2].
B	Leaders [1.1] participate in the strategic planning process [2.1]. Leaders also use the time lines for achieving strategic objectives [2.1b] as a basis for defining and monitoring expected progress closely [1.1b].
C	Leaders ensure that plans are deployed at all levels throughout the organization and used to align work [2.2a]. Leaders [1.1] also approve the goals and measurements set forth in the plan [2.2b]. They are responsible for using comparative data to set stretch goals.
D	Leaders [1.1] use information from customers [3.1 and 3.2] to set direction and create opportunity for the organization. Leaders [1.1] also have a responsibility for personally building relationships with key customers [3.2a] (creating a bidirectional relationship).
	Continued on next page

	Nature of Relationship (continued)
E	Leaders [1.1] use analyses of data [4.2] to monitor organizational performance and understand relationships among performance, employee satisfaction, customers, markets, and financial success. These analyses are also used for decision making at all levels to set priorities for action and allocate resources for maximum advantage.
F	Leaders [1.1] at all levels work to improve the organization's work and job design and ensure that the compensation and recognition system [5.1] encourages employees at all levels to achieve Performance Excellence. Leaders [1.1] are also responsible for supporting appropriate skill development of all employees through training and development systems and the use of learning on the job [5.2], as well as creating effective systems to enhance employee satisfaction, well-being, and motivation [5.3]. Leaders are also responsible for evaluating and refining all of these processes.
G	Leaders [1.1] at all levels are responsible for creating an environment that supports high performance, including monitoring processes for design and delivery [6.1], support services [6.2], and better supplier and partner performance [6.3]. Leaders must ensure that design, production/delivery, support, and supplier performance processes are aligned and consistently evaluated and refined.
H	Senior leaders [1.1b] use performance results data [Category 7] for many activities, including strategic planning [2.1], setting goals and priorities, allocating resources [2.2], reinforcing or rewarding employee performance [5.1], and improving their effectiveness and the effectiveness of leaders at all levels [1.1b(4)].

1.1 Organizational Leadership—Sample Effective Practices

A. Senior Leadership Direction

- All senior leaders are personally involved in performance improvement.
- Senior leaders spend a significant portion of their time on performance improvement activities.
- Senior leaders carry out many visible activities (for example, goal setting, planning, and recognition and reward of performance and process improvement).
- Senior leaders regularly communicate Performance Excellence values to managers and ensure that managers demonstrate those values in their work.
- Senior leaders participate on performance improvement teams and use quality tools and practices.
- Senior leaders spend time with suppliers, partners, and customers.
- Senior leaders mentor managers and ensure that promotion criteria reflect organizational values.
- Senior leaders study and learn about the improvement practices of other organizations.
- Senior leaders clearly and consistently articulate values (customer focus, customer satisfaction, role model leadership, continuous improvement, workforce involvement, and performance optimization) throughout the organization.
- Senior leaders ensure that organizational values are used to provide direction to all employees in the organization to help achieve the mission, vision, and performance goals.
- Senior leaders use effective and innovative approaches to reach out to all employees to spread the organization's values and align its work to support organizational goals.
- Senior leaders effectively surface problems and encourage employee risk taking.
- Roles and responsibilities of managers are clearly defined, understood by them, and used to judge their performance.
- Managers walk the talk (serve as role models) in leading quality and systematic performance improvement.
- Job definitions with quality indices are clearly delineated for each level of the organization, objectively measured, and presented in a logical and organized structure.
- Many different communication strategies are used to reinforce quality values.
- Leader behavior (not merely words) clearly communicates what is expected of the organization and its employees.

- Systems and procedures are deployed that encourage cooperation and a cross-functional approach to management, team activities, and problem solving.
- Leaders monitor employee acceptance and adoption of vision and values, using annual surveys, employee focus groups, and e-mail questions.
- A systematic process is in place for evaluating and improving the integration or alignment of quality values throughout the organization.

B. Organizational Performance Review

- Reviews against measurable performance standards are held frequently.
- Actions are taken to assist units that are not meeting goals or performing to plan.
- Senior leaders systematically and routinely check the effectiveness of their leadership activities (for example, seeking annual feedback from employees and peers (upward evaluation) and take steps to improve.
- Leaders at all levels determine how well they carried out their activities (what went right or wrong and how they could be done better).
- There is evidence of adopting changes to improve leader effectiveness.
- Priorities for organizational improvement and innovation are driven by customer, performance, and financial data.
- Senior leaders base their business decisions on reliable data and facts pertaining to customers, operational processes, and employee performance and satisfaction.
- Senior leaders hold regular meetings to review performance data and communicate problems, successes, and effective approaches to improve work.
- Senior leaders conduct monthly reviews of organizational and key supplier performance. This requires that subordinates conduct biweekly reviews and that workers and work teams provide daily performance updates. Corrective actions are developed to improve performance that deviates from planned performance.

1.2 Public Responsibility and Citizenship (40 Points)
Approach/Deployment Scoring

Describe how your organization addresses its responsibilities to the public and how your organization practices good citizenship.

Within your response, include answers to the following questions:

a. Responsibilities to the Public
(1) How do you address the impacts on society of your products, services, and operations? Include your key practices, measures, and targets for regulatory and legal requirements and for risks associated with your products, services, and operations.
(2) How do you anticipate public concerns with current and future products, services, and operations? How do you prepare for these concerns in a proactive manner?
(3) How do you ensure ethical business practices in all stakeholder transactions and interactions?

b. Support of Key Communities
How do your organization, your senior leaders, and your employees actively support and strengthen your key communities? Include how you identify key communities and determine areas of emphasis for organizational involvement and support.

Notes:

N1 Public responsibilities in areas critical to your business also should be addressed in Strategy Development (Item 2.1) and in Process Management (Category 6). Key results, such as results of regulatory/legal compliance or environmental improvements through use of "green" technology or other means, should be reported as Organizational Effectiveness Results (Item 7.5).

N2 Areas of community support appropriate for inclusion in 1.2b might include your efforts to strengthen local community services, education, the environment, and practices of trade, business, or professional associations.

N3 Health and safety of employees are not addressed in Item 1.2; you should address these factors in Item 5.3.

This Item looks at how the organization fulfills its public responsibilities and encourages, supports, and practices good citizenship.

The first part of this Item [1.2a] looks at how the organization addresses current and future impacts on society in a proactive manner and how it ensures ethical business practices in all stakeholder interactions. The practices are expected to cover all relevant and important areas—products, services, and operations:

- An integral part of performance management and improvement is proactively addressing legal and regulatory requirements and risk factors. Addressing these areas requires establishing appropriate measures and/or indicators that senior leaders track in their overall performance review. The organization should be sensitive to issues of public concern, whether or not these issues are currently embodied in law. The failure to address these areas can expose the organization to future problems when it least expects them. Problems can range from a sudden decline in consumer confidence to extensive and costly litigation. In this regard, it is important to anticipate potential problems the public may have with both current and future products. Sometimes, a well intended product or service could create adverse public consequences.

- For example, consider the use of automatic teller machines (ATMs), or cash machines as they are called today. When these machines were first introduced, many in the industry believed that the public would never accept the machines as a surrogate for a human being. For the most part, these machines were considered an eyesore and were installed in out-of-the-way places, usually at the back of the bank building. However, the extraordinary success of these devices resulted in hundreds of millions of people conducting cash transactions outside the relative safety of the bank building. This gave rise to more robberies, abductions, and even murder. By failing to consider the potential adverse consequence of these cash machines located in out-of-the-way places, banks were exposed to increased litigation and costs associated with relocating or providing appropriate security enclosures in an effort to reduce public risk.

- Good public responsibility implies going beyond minimum compliance with laws and regulations. Top-performing organizations frequently serve as role models of responsibility and provide leadership in areas key to business success. For example, a manufacturing company might go beyond the requirements of the environmental protection regulations and develop innovative and award-winning systems to protect the environment and reduce pollution.

- Ensuring ethical business practices are followed by all employees lessens the organizations risk of adverse public reaction, as well as criminal prosecution. Programs to ensure ethical business practices typically seek to prevent activities that might be perceived as criminal or near criminal. Examples of unethical business practices might include falsifying expense reports or quality-control data, accepting lavish gifts from a contractor, or seeking kickbacks.

The second part of this Item [1.2b] looks at how the organization, its senior leaders, and its employees identify, support, and strengthen key communities as part of good citizenship practices:

- Good citizenship practices typically vary according to the size, complexity, and location of the organization. Larger organizations are generally expected to have a more comprehensive approach to citizenship than small organizations.
- Examples of organizational community involvement include influencing the adoption of higher standards in education by communicating employability requirements to schools and school boards; partnering with other businesses and health-care providers to improve health in the local community by providing education and volunteer services to address public health issues; and partnering to influence trade and business associations to engage in beneficial, cooperative activities, such as sharing best practices to improve overall U.S. global competitiveness and the environment.
- In addition to activities directly carried out by the organization, opportunities to practice good citizenship include employee community service that is encouraged and supported by the organization. Frequently, the organization's leaders actively participate on community boards and actively support their work.

1.2 Public Responsibility and Citizenship

How the organization addresses public responsibilities and practices good citizenship

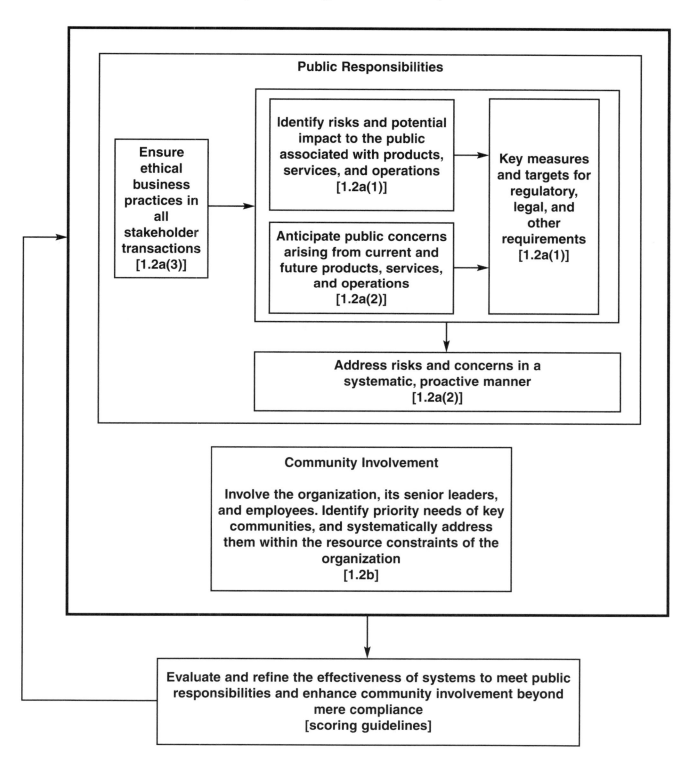

1.2 Public Responsibility and Citizenship Item Linkages

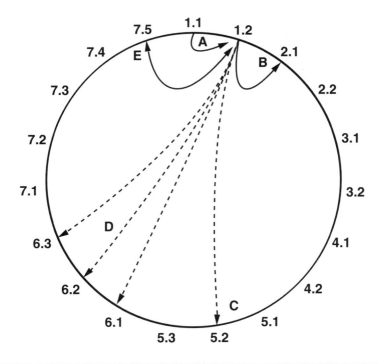

	Nature of Relationship
A	Senior leaders [1.1] have a responsibility for setting policies and ensuring that practices and products of the organization and its employees do not adversely affect society or violate ethical standards, regulations, or law [1.2a]. They are also responsible to be personally involved and to ensure that the organization and its employees strengthen key communities in areas, such as local community services, education, the environment, business and professional associations, and health and welfare [1.2b].
B	Public health and safety concerns, environmental protection, and waste management issues [1.2] are important factors to consider in strategy development [2.1].
C	Training [5.2] is provided to ensure all employees understand organization ethical and business practices, as well as the importance of strengthening key communities [1.2].
D	Managers at all levels have responsibility for ensuring that work practices of the organization [6.1 and 6.2] and its suppliers [6.3] are consistent with the organization's standards of ethics and public responsibility [1.2].
E	Key results, such as results of regulatory compliance, environmental improvements, and support to key communities, are reported in Organization-Effectiveness Results [7.5]. In addition, these results are monitored to determine if process changes are needed. (Compliance results in areas of employee safety are reported in 7.3, based on processes described in Item 5.3, Employee Well-Being and Satisfaction, and are not a part of the requirements in 1.2.)

1.2   Public Responsibility and Citizenship—Sample Effective Practices

A. Responsibilities to the Public

- The organization's principal business activities include systems to analyze, anticipate, and minimize public hazards or risk.
- Indicators for risk areas are identified and monitored.
- Continuous improvement strategies are used consistently, and progress is reviewed regularly.
- The organization considers the impact its operations, products, and services might have on society and considers those impacts in planning.
- The effectiveness of systems to meet or exceed regulatory or legal requirements is systematically evaluated and improved.

B. Support of Key Communities

- Senior leaders and employees at various levels in the organization are involved in professional organizations, committees, task forces, or other community activities.
- Organizational resources are allocated to support involvement in community activities outside the organization.
- Employees participate in local, state, or national quality award programs and receive recognition from the organization.
- Employees participate in a variety of professional quality and business improvement associations.
- The effectiveness of processes to support and strengthen key communities is systematically evaluated and improved.

2 Strategic Planning—85 Points

The **Strategic Planning** Category examines your organization's strategy development process, including how your organization develops strategic objectives, action plans, and related human resource plans. Also examined are how plans are deployed and how performance is tracked.

The Strategic Planning Category looks at the organization's process for strategic and action planning, and deployment of plans to make sure everyone is working to achieve those plans. Customer-driven quality and operational Performance Excellence are key strategic issues that need to be integral parts of the organization's overall planning:

- Customer-driven quality is a strategic view of quality. The focus is on the drivers of customer satisfaction, customer retention, new markets, and market share—key factors in competitiveness, profitability, and business success; and
- Operational performance improvement contributes to short-term and longer-term productivity growth and cost/price competitiveness. Building operational capability—including speed, responsiveness, and flexibility—represents an investment in strengthening your competitive position now and into the future.

Over the years, much debate and discussion has taken place around planning. Professors in our colleges and universities spend a great deal of time trying to differentiate strategic planning, long-term planning, short-term planning, tactical planning, operational planning, quality planning, business planning, and human resource planning to name a few. However, a much simpler view might serve us better. For our purposes, the following captures the essence of planning:

- *Strategic planning is simply an effort to identify the things we must do to be successful in the future.*
- Once we have determined what we must do to be successful (the plan), we must take steps to execute that plan (the actions).

Accordingly, the key role of strategic planning is to provide a basis for aligning the organization's work processes with its strategic directions, thereby ensuring people and processes in different parts of the organization are not working at cross purposes. To the extent that alignment does not occur, the organization's effectiveness and competitiveness is reduced.

The Strategic Planning category looks at how the organization:
- Understands the key customer, market, and operational requirements as input to setting strategic directions. This helps to ensure that ongoing process improvements are aligned with the organization's strategic directions.
- Optimizes the use of resources and ensures bridging between short-term and longer-term requirements that may entail capital expenditures, supplier development, new human resource recruitment strategies, reengineering key processes, and other factors affecting business success.
- Ensures that deployment will be effective—that there are mechanisms to transmit requirements and achieve alignment on three basic levels: (1) the organization/executive level; (2) the key process level; and (3) the work-unit/individual-job level.

The requirements for the Strategic Planning category are intended to encourage strategic thinking and acting—to develop a basis for achieving and maintaining a competitive position. These requirements do not demand formalized plans, planning systems, departments, or specific planning cycles. They do, however, require plans and the alignment of actions to those plans at all levels of the organization. An effective system to improve performance and competitive advantage requires fact-based strategic guidance, particularly when improvement alternatives compete for limited resources. In most cases, priority setting depends heavily upon a cost rationale. However, an organization might also have to deal with critical requirements, such as public responsibilities that are not driven by cost considerations alone.

Strategic planning consists of the planning process, the identification of goals and actions necessary to achieve success, and the deployment of those actions to align the work of the organization.

Strategy Development
- Customers: market requirements and evolving expectations
- Competitive environment: industry, market, and technology
- Financial and societal risks
- Human resource capabilities and needs
- Operational capabilities and needs, including resource availability
- Supplier capabilities and needs
- Develop clear strategic objectives with timetables

Strategy Deployment (cont.)

- Translate strategy into action plans and related human resource plans
- Align and deploy action plan requirements, performance measures, and resources throughout the organization
- Project expected performance results, including assumptions of competitor performance increases

2.1 Strategy Development (40 points)
Approach/Deployment Scoring

Describe your organization's strategy development process to strengthen organizational performance and competitive position. Summarize your key strategic objectives.

Within your response, include answers to the following questions:

a. **Strategy Development Process**
   (1) What is your strategic planning process? Include key steps and key participants in the process.
   (2) How do you consider the following key factors in your process? Include how relevant data and information are gathered and analyzed.

   The factors are:
   - Customer and market needs/expectations, including new product/service opportunities
   - Your competitive environment and capabilities, including use of new technology
   - Financial, societal, and other potential risks
   - Your human resource capabilities and needs
   - Your operational capabilities and needs, including resource availability
   - Your supplier and/or partner capabilities and needs

b. **Strategic Objectives**
   What are your key strategic objectives and your timetable for accomplishing them? In setting objectives, how do you evaluate options to assess how well they respond to the factors in 2.1a(2) most important to your performance?

Notes:
N1. Strategy development refers to your organization's approach (formal or informal) to a future-oriented basis for business decisions, resource allocations, and management. Such development might utilize various types of forecasts, projections, options, scenarios, and/or other approaches to addressing the future.

Continued on next page

N2. The word *strategy* should be interpreted broadly. It might be built around or lead to any or all of the following: new products, services, and markets; revenue growth; cost reduction; business acquisitions; and new partnerships and alliances. Strategy might be directed toward becoming a preferred supplier, a low-cost producer, a market innovator, and/or a high-end or customized service provider.

Strategy might depend upon or require you to develop different kinds of capabilities, such as rapid response, customization, market understanding, lean or virtual manufacturing, relationships, rapid innovation, technology management, leveraging assets, business process excellence, and information management. Responses to Item 2.1 should address the key factors from your point of view.

N3. Item 2.1 addresses your overall organizational directions and strategy, that might include changes in services, products, and/or product lines. However, the Item does not address product and service design; you should address these factors in Item 6.1.

This Item looks at how the organization sets strategic directions and develops your strategic objectives, with the aim of strengthening your overall performance and competitiveness.

The first part of this Item [2.1a(1)] asks the organization to describe its strategic planning process and identify the key participants. This helps examiners understand the steps and data used in the planning process. It is usually a good idea to provide a flowchart of the planning process. This helps examiners understand how the planning process works without wasting valuable space in the application.

An organization must consider the key factors that affect its future success. These factors cover external and internal influences on the organization. Although the organization is not limited to the number of factors it considers important in planning, the six factors identified in Item 2.1a(2) must be addressed unless a valid rationale can be offered as to why the factor is not appropriate. Together, these six factors will cover the most important variables for any organization's future success:
  • The planning process should examine all the key influences, risks, challenges, and other requirements that might affect the organization's future opportunities and directions—taking as long term a view as possible. This approach is intended to provide a thorough and realistic context for the development of a customer- and market-focused strategy to guide ongoing decision making, resource allocation, and overall management.

- This planning process should cover all types of businesses, competitive situations, and strategic issues. The Item does not require formalized planning, planning departments, planning cycles, or a specified way of visualizing the future.
- This Item focuses on identifying the factors and actions the organization must take to achieve a leadership position in a competitive market. This usually requires ongoing revenue growth and improvements in operational effectiveness. Achieving and sustaining a leadership position in a competitive market requires a view of the future that includes not only the markets or segments in which the organization competes, but also how it competes. How it competes presents many options and requires that you understand the organization's and your competitors' strengths and weaknesses. No specific time horizon for planning is required by the Criteria.
- In order to maintain competitive leadership, an increasingly important part of strategic planning requires processes to project the competitive environment accurately. Such projections help detect and reduce competitive threats, shorten reaction time, and identify opportunities. Depending on the size and type of business, maturity of markets, pace of change, and competitive parameters (such as price or innovation rate), organizations might use a variety of modeling, scenario, or other techniques and judgments to project the competitive environment.

The second part of this Item [2.1b] asks for a summary of the organization's key strategic objectives and the timetable for accomplishing them.

- The purpose of the timetable is to provide a basis for projecting the path that improvement is likely to take. This allows the organizations' leaders to monitor progress more accurately. Consider Figure 2.1. The performance goal four years into the future is to achieve a level of performance of 100. Currently, the organization is at 20. At the end of year 1, the organization achieved a performance level of 40, represented by the circle symbol. It appears that that level of performance is on track toward the goal of 100. However, unless the expected trajectory is known, it is not possible to evaluate the progress accurately.

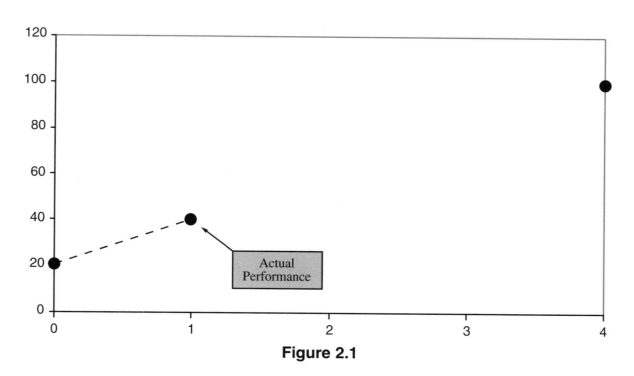

Figure 2.1

In Figure 2.2, the planned trajectory is represented by the triangle symbols. When compared with the current level of performance (the circle symbol), it is clear that there is a performance shortfall of approximately 30.

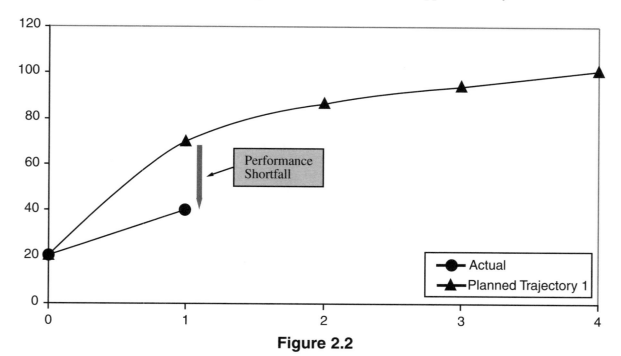

Figure 2.2

In Figure 2.3, the planned trajectory is represented by the square symbols. When compared with the current level of performance (the circle symbol), it is clear that the performance is ahead of schedule. There are several possible decisions that leaders could make based on this information. It might mean that the original estimates/goals were low and should be reset. It might also mean that the process did not need all of the resources it had available. These resources may be better used in areas where performance is not ahead of schedule.

In any case, without knowing the expected path toward a goal, it requires leaders to guess whether the level of progress is appropriate or not.

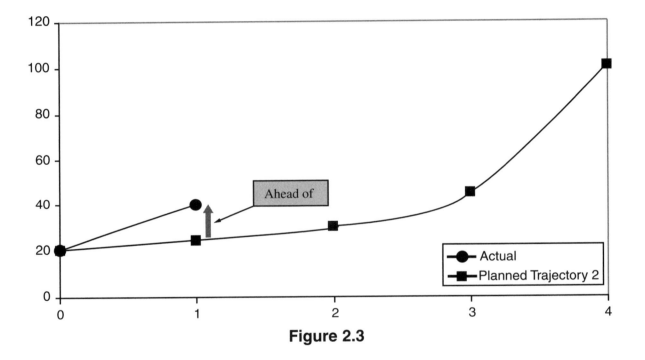

Figure 2.3

- Finally, the last part of this Item requires the organization to evaluate the options it considered in the strategic planning process to ensure it responded fully to the six factors identified in Item 2.1a(2) that were most important to business success. This last step helps the organization "close the loop" to make sure that the factors influencing organization success were adequately analyzed and support key strategic objectives.

2.1 Strategy Development

How the organization sets strategic direction to define and strengthen competitive position

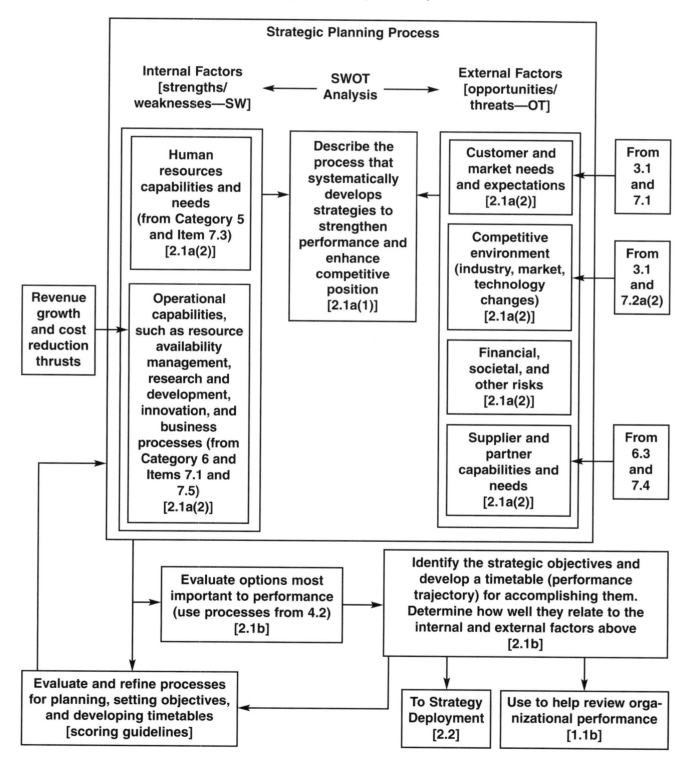

2.1 Strategy Development Item Linkages

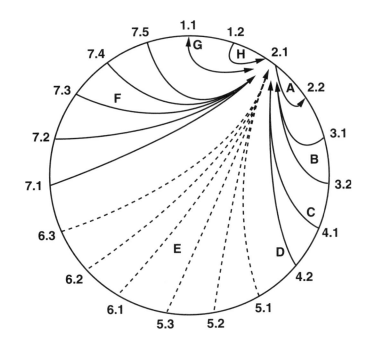

	Nature of Relationship
A	The planning process [2.1] produces a set of actionable plans that are deployed to the work-force [2.2].
B	The business planning process [2.1] includes information on current and potential customer requirements and the projected competitive environment [3.1], as well as intelligence obtained from customer-contact people (complaints and comments) [3.2a].
C	Key organizational [4.1] and competitive comparison data [4.2] are used for planning [2.1].
D	Analytical data [4.2], including data on work process improvement strategies, realigning work processes, improving operational performance, and reducing waste are used in the planning process [2.1].
E	Information on human resource capabilities [Category 5] and work process capabilities [Category 6] is considered in the strategic planning process as part of the determination of internal strengths and weaknesses. To avoid cluttering diagrams 5.1–6.3, these arrows will not be repeated there.
	Continued on next page

	Nature of Relationship (continued)
F	Customer-focused and financial and market results [7.1 and 7.2] and human resource, supplier and partner, and organization effectiveness results [7.3, 7.4, and 7.5] are used in the planning process [2.1] to set priorities and goals (which are reported in 2.2).
G	The planning process [2.1] includes senior leader participation and guidance, as well as participation by leaders at all levels [1.1]. In addition, the timelines or performance trajectory [2.1b] provide a basis for leaders monitoring progress [1.1b]. Without timelines, it is difficult to determine if the organization is on track.
H	Public health, environmental, waste management, and related concerns [1.2a] are considered, as appropriate, in the strategy development process [2.1].

Note: The many inputs to strategy development will not all be repeated on other linkage diagrams to avoid clutter.

2.1 Strategy Development—Sample Effective Practices

A. Strategy Development Process

- Business goals, strategies, and issues are addressed and reported in measurable terms. Goals consider future requirements needed to achieve organizational leadership after considering the quality levels other organizations are likely to achieve.
- The planning and goal-setting process encourages input (but not necessarily decision making) from a variety of people at all levels throughout the organization.
- Data on customer requirements, key markets, benchmarks, supplier and partner, human resource, and organizational capabilities (internal and external factors) are used to develop business plans.
- Plans are evaluated each cycle for accuracy and completeness—more often if needed to keep pace with changing business requirements.
- Areas for improvement in the planning process are identified systematically and carried out each planning cycle.
- Refinements in the process of planning, plan deployment, and receiving input from work units have been made. Improvements in plan cycle time, plan resources, and planning accuracy are documented.

B. Strategic Objectives

- Strategic objectives are identified and a timetable for accomplishing the objectives are set.
- Options to obtain best performance for the strategic objectives are systematically evaluated against the internal and external factors used in the strategy development process.

2.2 Strategy Deployment (45 points)
Approach/Deployment Scoring

Describe your organization's strategy deployment process. Summarize your organization's action plans and related performance measures. Project the performance of these key measures into the future.

Within your response, include answers to the following questions:

a. **Action Plan Development and Deployment**
   (1) How do you develop action plans that address your key strategic objectives? What are your key short- and longer-term action plans? Include key changes, if any, in your products/services and/or your customers/markets.
   (2) What are your key human resource requirements and plans, based on your strategic objectives and action plans?
   (3) How do you allocate resources to ensure accomplishment of your overall action plan?
   (4) What are your key performance measures and/or indicators for tracking progress relative to your action plans?
   (5) How do you communicate and deploy your strategic objectives, action plans, and performance measures/indicators to achieve overall organizational alignment?

b. **Performance Projection**
   (1) What are your two- to five-year projections for key performance measures and/or indicators? Include key performance targets and/or goals, as appropriate.
   (2) How does your projected performance compare with competitors, key benchmarks, and past performance, as appropriate? What is the basis for these comparisons?

Notes:
N1. Action plan development and deployment are closely linked to other Items in the Criteria and to the Performance Excellence framework on page 6. Examples of key linkages are:
   • Item 1.1 for how your senior leaders set and communicate directions;
   • Category 3 for gathering customer and market knowledge as input to your strategy and action plans, and for deploying action plans;
   • Category 4 for information and analysis to support your development of strategy, to provide an effective performance basis for your performance measurements, and to track progress relative to your strategic objectives and action plans;

Continued on next page

- Category 5 for your work system needs, employee education, training, and development needs, and related human resource factors resulting from action plans;
- Category 6 for process requirements resulting from your action plans; and
- Item 7.5 for accomplishments relative to your organizational strategy.

N2. Measures and/or indicators of projected performance (2.2b) might include changes resulting from new business ventures, business acquisitions, new value creation, market entry and/or shifts, and/or significant anticipated innovations in products, services, and/or technology.

The first part of this Item looks at how the organization translates its strategic objectives into action plans to accomplish the objectives and to enable assessment of progress relative to your action plans. The aim is to ensure that your strategies are deployed for goal achievement.

The first part of this Item [2.2a] calls for information on how action plans are developed and deployed. This includes spelling out key performance requirements and measures, as well as aligning work throughout the organization. Leaders must develop action plans that address the key strategic objectives (which were developed using the processes and Item 2.1). Organizations must summarize key short- and longer-term action plans. Particular attention is given to products/services, customers/markets, human resource requirements, and resource allocations.

Of central importance in this area is how alignment and consistency are achieved—for example, via key processes and key measurements. Alignment and consistency are intended also to provide a basis for setting and communicating priorities for ongoing improvement activities—part of the daily work of all work units. You also are asked to specify key measures and/or indicators used in tracking progress relative to the action plans and how you communicate and align strategic objectives, action plans, and performance.

Without effective alignment, routine work and acts of improvement can be random and serve to suboptimize organizational performance. In Figure 2.4 the arrows represent the well-intended work carried out by employees of organizations who lack a clear set of expectations and direction. Each person, each manager, and each work unit works diligently to achieve goals they believe are important. Each is pulling hard—but not necessarily in ways that ensure Performance Excellence. This encourages the creation of "feifdoms" within organizations.

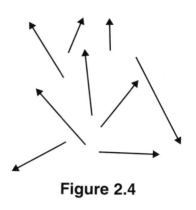

Figure 2.4

With a clear, well-communicated strategic plan, it is easier to know when daily work is out of alignment. The large arrow in Figure 2.5 represents the strategic plan pointing the direction the organization must take to be successful and achieve its mission and vision. The strategic plan and accompanying measures make it possible to know when work is not aligned and help employees, including leaders, to know when adjustments are required.

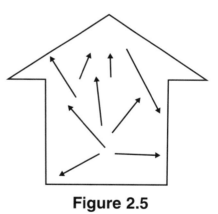

Figure 2.5

A well-deployed and understood strategic plan helps everyone in the organization distinguish between random acts of improvement and aligned improvement. Random acts of improvement give a false sense of accomplishment and rarely benefit the organization. For example, a decision to improve a business process that is not aligned with the strategic plan (as the small bold arrow in Figure 2.6 represents) usually results in a wasteful expenditure of time, money, and human resources—improvement without benefiting customers or enhancing operating effectiveness.

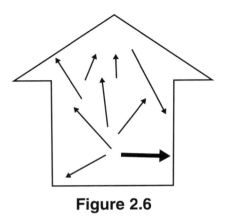

Figure 2.6

On the other hand, by working systematically to strengthen processes that are aligned with the strategic plan, the organization moves closer to achieving success, as Figure 2.7 indicates. Ultimately, all processes and procedures of an organization should be aligned to maximize the achievement of strategic plans, as Figure 2.8 demonstrates.

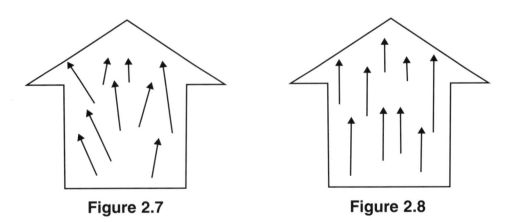

Figure 2.7   **Figure 2.8**

Critical action plan resource requirements include human resource plans that support your overall strategy. Examples of possible human resource plan elements are:
- Redesign of your work organization and/or jobs to increase employee empowerment and decision making;
- Initiatives to promote greater labor-management cooperation, such as union partnerships;
- Initiatives to foster knowledge sharing and organizational learning;
- Modification of your compensation and recognition systems to recognize team, organizational, stock market, customer, or other performance attributes; and

- Education and training initiatives, such as developmental programs for future leaders, partnerships with universities to help ensure the availability of future employees, and/or establishment of technology-based training capabilities.

Finally, the second part of this Item [2.2b] asks the organization to provide a two-to-five year projection of key performance measures and/or indicators, including key performance targets and/or goals. This projected performance is the basis for comparing past performance and performance relative to competitors and benchmarks, as appropriate:

- Projections and comparisons in this area are intended to help the organization's leaders improve their ability to understand and track dynamic, competitive performance factors. Through this tracking process, they should be better prepared to take into account its rate of improvement and change relative to competitors and relative to their own targets or stretch goals. Such tracking serves as a key diagnostic management tool.

- In addition to improvement relative to past performance and to competitors, projected performance also might include changes resulting from new business ventures, entry into new markets, product/service innovations, or other strategic thrusts. Without this comparison information, it is possible to set goals that, even if attained, may not result in competitive advantage. More than one high-performing company has been surprised by a competitor that set and achieved more aggressive goals. Consider the following example represented by Figure 2.9. Imagine that you are ahead of your competition and committed to a 10 percent increase in profit over your base year. After eight years you are twice as profitable. To your surprise, you find that your competitor has increased 20 percent each year. You have achieved your goal, but your competitor has beaten you, making slightly more. After 10 years, the competitor has a significant lead. It is not enough to make your goals unless your goals place you in a competitive position.

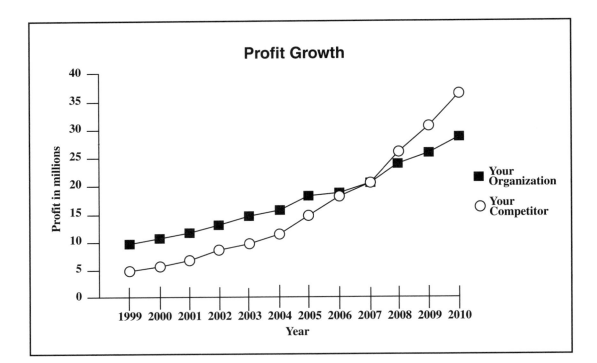

Figure 2.9

2.2 Strategy Deployment

Summary of strategy, action plans, and performance projections; how they are developed, communicated, and deployed.

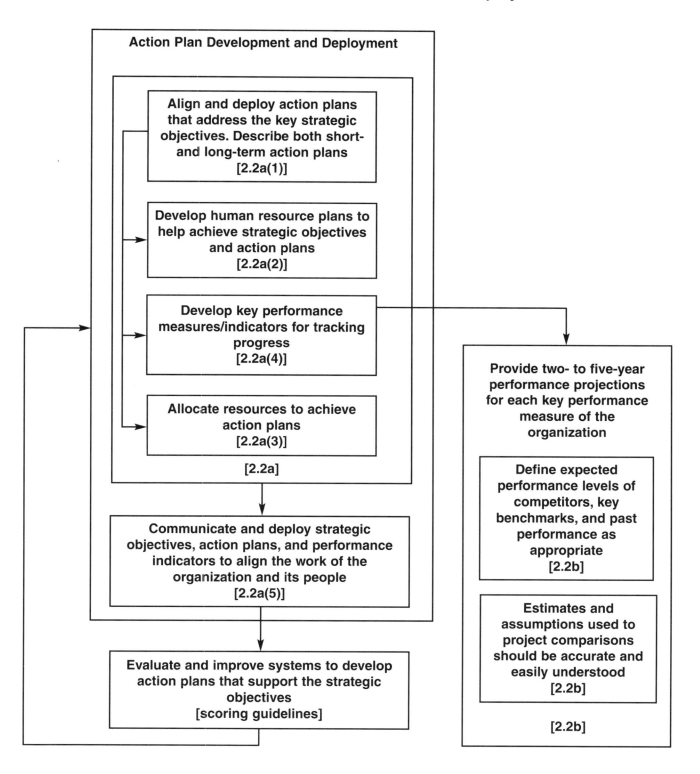

2.2 Strategy Deployment Item Linkages

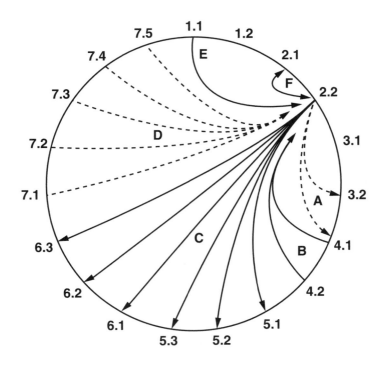

Nature of Relationship	
A	The goals and strategy [2.2] will influence the data and measures that need to be collected to monitor alignment [4.1], customer relations management, and customer satisfaction determination [3.2].
B	Benchmarking comparison data [4.1] and analytical processes [4.2] are used to set organizational measures and objectives [2.2].
C	Measures, objectives, and plans, deployed to the workforce [2.2] are used to drive and align actions to achieve improved performance [Category 6] and develop human resources [Category 5].
D	Results data [Category 7] are used to help set goals [2.2]. (To avoid clutter, these relationships will not be repeated on the Category 7 linkage diagrams.)
E	The leadership team [1.1] sets the organization's goals and objectives [2.2].
F	The planning process [2.1] develops the strategic objectives that produce action plans to support these objectives [2.2].

2.2   Strategy Deployment—Sample Effective Practices

A. Action Plan Development and Deployment

- Plans are in place to optimize operational performance and improve customer focus using tools, such as reengineering, streamlining work processes, and reducing cycle time.
- Strategies to retain or establish leadership positions exist for major products and services for key customers or markets.
- Strategies to achieve key organizational results (operational performance requirements) are defined.
- Planned quality and productivity levels are defined in measurable terms for key features of products and services.
- Planned actions are challenging, realistic, achievable, and understood by employees throughout the organization. Each employee understands his or her role in achieving strategic and operational goals and objectives.
- Resources are available and committed to achieve the plans (no unfunded mandates).
- Plans are realistic and used to guide operational performance improvements.
- Incremental (short-term) strategies to achieve long-term plans are defined in measurable terms.
- Business plans, short- and long-term goals, and performance measures are understood and used to drive actions throughout the organization.
- Each individual in the organization, at all levels, understands how his or her work contributes to achieving organizational goals and plans.
- Plans are followed to ensure that resources are deployed and redeployed as needed to support goals.
- Capital projects are funded according to business improvement plans.
- Human resource plans support strategic plans and goals. Plans show how the workforce will be developed to enable the organization to achieve its strategic goals.
- Key issues of training and development, hiring, retention, employee participation, involvement, empowerment, and recognition and reward are addressed as a part of the human resource plan.
- Innovative strategies may involve one or more of the following:
  - Redesign of work to increase employee responsibility
  - Improved labor-management relations (That is, prior to contract negotiations, train both sides in effective negotiation skills so that people focus on the merits of issues, not on positions. The goal is to improve relations and shorten negotiation time by 50 percent.)

- Forming partnerships with education institutions to develop employees and ensure a supply of well-prepared future employees
- Developing gain-sharing or equity-building compensation systems for all employees to increase motivation and productivity
- Broadening employee responsibilities; creating self-directed or high-performance workteams
- Key performance measures (for example, employee satisfaction or work climate surveys) have been identified to gather data to manage progress. (Note: Improvement results associated with these measures should be reported in 7.3.)
- The effectiveness of human resource planning and alignment with strategic plans is evaluated systematically.
- Data are used to evaluate and improve performance and participation for all types of employees (for example, absenteeism, turnover, grievances, accidents, recognition and reward, and training participation).
- Routine, two-way communication about performance of employees occurs.
- The process to develop action plans to support strategic objectives is systematically evaluated.

B. Performance Projection

- Projections of two- to five-year changes in performance levels are developed and used to track progress.
- Data from competitors, key benchmarks, and/or past performance form a valid basis for comparison. The organization has strategies and goals in place to meet or exceed the planned levels of performance for these competitors and benchmarks.
- Plans include expected future levels of competitor or comparison performance and are used to set and validate the organization's own plans and goals.

3 Customer and Market Focus— 85 Points

Customer and Market Focus addresses how the organization seeks to understand the voices of customers and of the marketplace. The category stresses relationships as an important part of an overall listening, learning, and Performance Excellence strategy. Your customer satisfaction and dissatisfaction results provide vital information for understanding your customers and the marketplace. In many cases, such results and trends provide the most meaningful information, not only on your customers' views but also on their marketplace behaviors—repeat business and positive referrals.

This category identifies the systems for gathering intelligence about customer requirements and levels of satisfaction that leaders use to plan, set direction, and set goals. In addition, information about customer satisfaction and dissatisfaction, including complaints, are used to identify systems and processes needing improvement. Information from complaints helps production and design identify and prevent future problems.

Customer and market focus contains two Items that focus on understanding customer and market requirements, and determining satisfaction.

Customer and Market Knowledge
- Determining market or customer segments
- Determining customer information validity
- Determining important product or service features
- Using complaint information and data from potential and former customers

Customer Satisfaction and Relationships
- Making customer contact and feedback easy and useful
- Handle complaints effectively and responsively
- Ensure complaint data are used to eliminate causes of complaints
- Build customer relationships and loyalty
- Systematically determine customer satisfaction and the satisfaction of competitor's customers

3.1 Customer and Market Knowledge (40 points)
Approach/Deployment Scoring

Describe how your organization determines short- and longer-term requirements, expectations, and preferences of customers and markets to ensure the relevance of current products/services and to develop new opportunities.

Within your response, include answers to the following questions:

a. Customer and Market Knowledge

(1) How do you determine or target customers, customer groups, and/or market segments? How do you consider customers of competitors and other potential customers and/or markets in this determination?

(2) How do you listen and learn to determine key requirements and drivers of purchase decisions for current, former, and potential customers? If determination methods differ for different customers and/or customer groups, include the key differences.

(3) How do you determine and/or project key product/service features and their relative importance/value to customers for purposes of current and future marketing, product planning, and other business developments, as appropriate? How do you use relevant information from current and former customers, including marketing/sales information, customer retention, won/lost analysis, and complaints in this determination?

(4) How do you keep your listening and learning methods current with business needs and directions?

Notes:

N1. If your products and services are sold to end users via other businesses, such as retail stores or dealers, customer groups [3.1a(1)] should include both the end users and these intermediate businesses.

N2. Product and service features [3.1a(3)] refer to all important characteristics and to the performance of your products and services throughout their full life cycle and the full "consumption chain." The focus should be on features that bear upon customer preference and repurchase loyalty—for example, those features that differentiate your products and services from competing offerings. Those features might include factors, such as price, value, delivery, customer or technical support, and the sales relationship.

This Item looks at the organization's key processes for gaining knowledge about its current and future customers and markets, in order to offer relevant products and services, understand emerging customer requirements and expectations, and keep pace with changing markets and marketplaces. This information is intended to support marketing, business development, and planning. In a rapidly changing competitive environment, many factors may affect customer preference and loyalty, making it necessary to listen and learn on a continuous basis. To be effective, such listening and learning strategies need to have a close connection with the organization's overall business strategy. For example, if the organization customizes its products and services, the listening and learning strategy needs to be backed by a capable information system—one that rapidly accumulates information about customers and makes this information available where needed throughout the organization or elsewhere within the overall value chain.

The organization must have a process for determining or segmenting key customer groups and markets. To ensure a complete and accurate picture of customer requirements and concerns is obtained, organizations should consider the requirements of potential customers, including competitors' customers. (Note: A potential customer is a customer the organization wants but who is currently being served by a competitor.) In addition, the organization should tailor its listening and learning techniques to different customer groups and market segments. A relationship or listening strategy might work with some customers, but not with others.

- Information sought should be sensitive to specific product and service requirements and their relative importance or value to the different customer groups. This determination should be supported by use of information and data, such as complaints and gains and losses of customers.
- In addition to defining customer requirements, organizations must determine key requirements and drivers of purchase decisions and key product/service features. In other words, the organization must be able to prioritize key customer requirements and drivers of purchase decisions. These priorities are likely to be different for different customer groups and market segments. Knowledge of customer groups and market segments allows the organization to tailor listening and learning strategies and marketplace offerings, to support marketing strategies, and to develop new business.
- In a rapidly changing competitive environment, many factors may affect customer preference and loyalty. This makes it necessary to listen and learn on a continuous basis. To be effective as an organization, listening and learning need to be closely linked with the overall business strategy and strategy planning process.

- Electronic commerce is changing the competitive arena rapidly. This may significantly affect relationships with customers and the effectiveness of listening and learning strategies. It may also force the organization to redefine customer groups and market segments.
- A variety of listening and learning strategies are commonly used. The selection of a particular strategy depends upon the type and size of the organization and other factors. Some examples of listening and learning strategies include:
- Close integration with key customers;
- Rapid innovation and field trials of products and services to better link research and development (R&D) and design to the market;
- Close tracking of technological, competitive, and other factors that may bear upon customer requirements, expectations, preferences, or alternatives;
- Defining the customers' value chains and how they are likely to change;
- Focus groups with leading-edge customers;
- Use of critical incidents, such as complaints, to understand key service attributes from the point of view of customers and customer-contact employees;
- Interviewing lost customers to determine the factors they use in their purchase decisions; and
- Won/lost analysis relative to competitors.

Finally, the organization must have a system in place to improve its customer listening and learning strategies to keep current with changing business needs and directions. If the organization competes in a rapidly changing environment, it may need to evaluate and improve its customer listening and learning strategies more frequently. The organization should be able to demonstrate that it has made appropriate improvements to ensure its techniques for understanding customer requirements and priorities keeps pace with changing business needs.

3.1 Customer and Market Knowledge

How the organization determines longer-term requirements, expectations, and preferences of target or potential customers and markets to anticipate their needs and to develop business opportunities

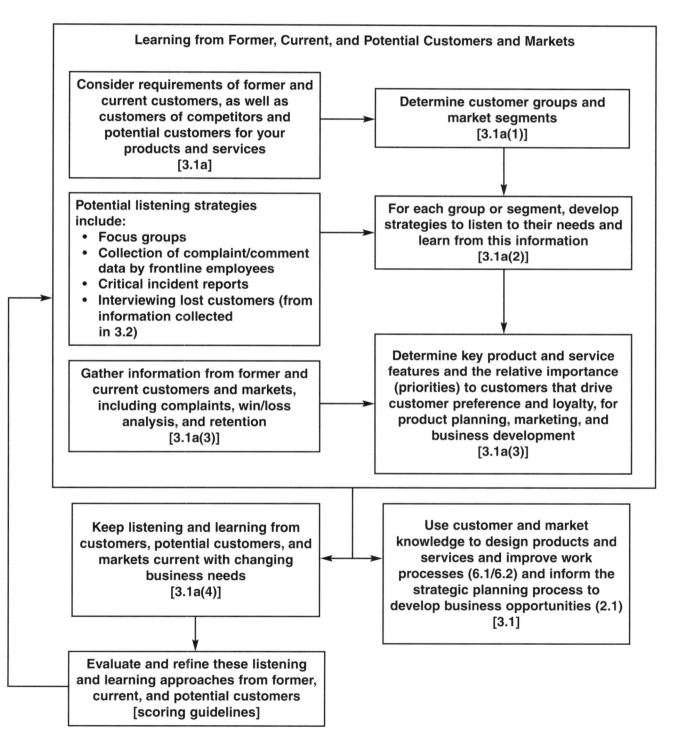

3.1 Customer and Market Knowledge Item Linkages

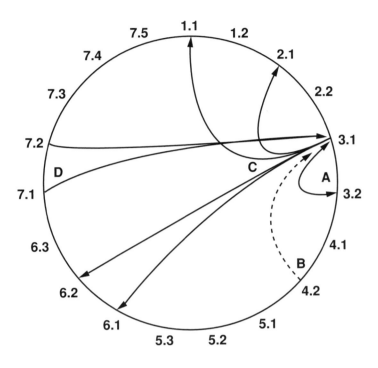

	Nature of Relationship
A	Customer complaints [3.2a] are used to help assess current customer expectations and refine requirements [3.1]. Information about customer requirements [3.1] is used to build instruments to assess customer satisfaction [3.2b].
B	Information from customer satisfaction data are analyzed [4.2] and used to help determine ways to assess current and potential customer requirements [3.1].
C	Information about current and future customer and market requirements [3.1] is used for strategic planning [2.1], to design products and services, revise work processes [6.1 and 6.2], and to help leaders set directions for the organization [1.1].
D	Customer satisfaction data and complaints [7.1] and market growth data [7.2] are used to assess customer expectations and refine requirements [3.1]. In addition, processes to gather intelligence about customer requirements [3.1] are used to define and produce customer satisfaction results [7.1].

3.1   Customer and Market Knowledge—Sample Effective Practices

A. Customer and Market Knowledge

- Various systematic methods are used to gather data and identify current requirements and expectations of customers (for example, surveys, focus groups).
- Key product and service features are defined. Product and service features refer to all important characteristics and to the performance of products and services that customers experience or perceive throughout their use. The focus is primarily on factors that bear on customer preference and loyalty—for example, those features that enhance or differentiate products and services from competing offerings.
- Customer requirements are identified or grouped by customer segments.
- Customer data, such as complaints and gains or losses of customers, are used to support the identification of key customer requirements.
- Various systematic methods are used to identify the future requirements and expectations of customers.
- Customers of competitors are considered and processes are in place to gather expectation data from potential customers.
- Effective listening and learning strategies include:
  - Close monitoring of technological, competitive, societal, environmental, economic, and demographic factors that may bear on customer requirements, expectations, preferences, or alternatives;
  - Focus groups with demanding or leading-edge customers;
  - Training of frontline employees in customer listening;
  - Use of critical incidents in product or service performance or quality to understand key service attributes from the point of view of customers and frontline employees;
  - Interviewing lost customers;
  - Won/lost analysis relative to competitors; and
  - Analysis of major factors affecting key customers.
- Analytical tools, such as forced choice or paired choice (where customers select between options A and B, A and C, B and C, and so forth). Using this technique, organizations quickly prioritize requirements and focus on delivering those that make the greatest impact on satisfaction, repeat business, and loyalty.

  Methods to listen and learn from customers are evaluated and improved through several cycles. Examples of factors that are evaluated include:
  - The adequacy and timeliness of customer-related information;
  - Improvement of survey design;

- Approaches for getting reliable and timely information—surveys, focus groups, customer-contact personnel; and
- Improved aggregation and analysis of information.

• Best practices for gathering customer requirements and forecasting are gathered and used to make improvements.

3.2 Customer Satisfaction and Relationships (45 points)
Approach/Deployment Scoring

Describe how your organization determines the satisfaction of customers and builds relationships to retain current business and to develop new opportunities.

Within your response, include answers to the following questions:

a. Customer Relationships
(1) How do you determine key access mechanisms to facilitate the ability of customers to conduct business, seek assistance and information, and make complaints? Include a summary of your key mechanisms.
(2) How do you determine key customer contact requirements and deploy these requirements to all employees involved in the response chain?
(3) What is your complaint management process? Include how you ensure that complaints are resolved effectively and promptly, and that all complaints received are aggregated and analyzed for use in overall organizational improvement.
(4) How do you build relationships with customers for repeat business and/or positive referral?
(5) How do you keep your approaches to customer access and relationships current with business needs and directions?

b. Customer Satisfaction Determination
(1) What processes, measurement methods, and data do you use to determine customer satisfaction and dissatisfaction? Include how your measurements capture actionable information that reflects customers' future business and/or potential for positive referral. Also include any significant differences in processes or methods for different customer groups and/or market segments.
(2) How do you follow up with customers on products/services and recent transactions to receive prompt and actionable feedback?
(3) How do you obtain and use information on customer satisfaction relative to competitors and/or benchmarks, as appropriate?
(4) How do you keep your approaches to satisfaction determination current with business needs and directions?

Notes:
N1. Customer relationships (3.2a) might include the development of partnerships or alliances.

Continued on next page

N2. Customer satisfaction and dissatisfaction determination (3.2b) might include any or all of the following: surveys, formal and informal feedback from customers, use of customer account data, and complaints.

N3. Customer satisfaction measurements might include both a numerical rating scale and descriptors for each unit in the scale. Actionable customer satisfaction measurements provide reliable information about customer ratings of your specific product, service, and relationship features; the linkage between these ratings; and your customer's likely future actions—repurchase and/or positive referral. Product and service features might include overall value and price.

N4. Your customer satisfaction and dissatisfaction results and information on product/ service measures that contribute to customer satisfaction or dissatisfaction should be reported in Item 7.1. These latter measures might include trends and levels in performance of customer-desired product features or customer complaint handling effectiveness (such as complaint response time, effective resolution, and percent of complaints resolved on first contact).

This Item [3.2] looks at the organization's processes for determining customer satisfaction and building customer relationships, with the aim of acquiring new customers, retaining existing customers, and developing new opportunities. Relationships provide an important means for organizations to understand and manage customer expectations and to develop new business. Also, customer-contact employees may provide vital information to build partnerships and other longer-term relationships with customers.

Overall, Item 3.2 emphasizes the importance of obtaining actionable information, such as feedback and complaints from customers. To be actionable, the information gathered should meet two conditions:
- Responses should be tied directly to key business processes, so opportunities for improvement are clear; and
- Responses should be translated into cost/revenue implications to support the setting of improvement priorities.

This Item also addresses how the organization determines customer satisfaction and satisfaction relative to competitors. Satisfaction relative to competitors and the factors that lead to preference are of critical importance to managing in a competitive environment.

The first part of this Item [3.2a(1)] looks at the organization's processes for providing easy access for customers and potential customers to seek information or assistance and/or to comment and complain.

- This access makes it easy to get timely information from customers about issues that are of real concern to them. Timely information, in turn, is transmitted to the appropriate place in the organization to drive improvements or new levels of product and service.
- Information from customers should be actionable. To be actionable, organizations should be able to tie the information to key business processes and be able to determine cost/revenue implications for improvement priority setting.

Organizations must also determine key customer contact requirements and make sure all employees who are involved in responding to customers understand these requirements:

- Customer contact requirements essentially refer to customer expectations for service after contact with the organization has been made. Typically, the organization translates customer contact requirements into customer service standards. Customer contact requirements should be set in measurable terms to permit effective monitoring and performance review.
- A good example of a measurable customer contact requirement might be the customer expectation that a malfunctioning computer would be back on-line within 24 hours of the request for service. Another example might be the customer requirement that a knowledgeable and polite human being is available within 5 minutes to resolve a problem with software. In both cases, a clear requirement and a measurable standard were identified.
- A bad example of customer service standard might be "we get back to the customer as soon as we can." With this example, no standard of performance is defined. Some customer contact representatives might get back to the customer within a matter of minutes. Others might take hours or days. The failure to define precisely the contact requirement makes it difficult to allocate appropriate resources to meet that requirement consistently.
- These customer service standards must be deployed to all employees who are in contact with customers. Such deployment needs to take into account all key points in the response chain—all units or individuals in the organization that make effective interactions possible. These standards then become one source of information to evaluate the organization's performance in meeting customer contact requirements.

Organizations should capture, aggregate, analyze, and learn from the complaint information and comments it receives. A prompt and effective response and solutions to customer needs and desires are a source of satisfaction and loyalty.

- The principal issue in complaint management is prompt and effective resolution of complaints, including recovery of customer confidence. This is enhanced by resolution made by the first person the customer contacts. This helps ensure higher levels of loyalty than if the customer never had a problem in first place. Even if the organization ultimately resolves a problem, the likelihood of maintaining a loyal customer is nearly cut in half each time that customer is referred to another place in the organization.
- The organization must also have a mechanism for learning from complaints and ensuring that design/production/delivery process employees receive information needed to eliminate the causes of complaints. Effective elimination of the causes of complaints involves aggregation of complaint information from all sources for evaluation and use in overall organizational improvement—both design and delivery stages (see Items 6.1 and 6.2).
- Complaint aggregation, analysis, and root cause determination should lead to effective elimination of the causes of complaints and to priority setting for process, product, and service improvements. Successful outcomes require effective deployment of information throughout the organization.

For long-term success, organizations should build strong relationships with its customers, since business development and product/service innovation increasingly depend on maintaining close relationships with your customers:

- Organizations should keep approaches to all aspects of customer relationships current with changing business needs and directions, since approaches to and bases for relationships may change quickly.
- Organizations should also develop an effective process to determine the levels of satisfaction and dissatisfaction for the different customer groups. Satisfied customers are a requirement for loyalty, repeat business, and positive referrals.

Finally, organizations should systematically follow up with customers regarding products, services, and recent transactions, and as well as determine the customers' satisfaction relative to competitors so that you may improve future performance:

- A key aspect of customer satisfaction determination is satisfaction relative to competitors and competing or alternative offerings. Such information might be derived from your own comparative studies or from independent studies. The factors that lead to customer preference are of critical importance in understanding factors that drive markets and potentially affect longer-term competitiveness.

The second part of this Item [3.2b] looks at how the organization determines customer satisfaction and dissatisfaction. Four types of requirements are considered:

- The organization must gather information on customer satisfaction and dissatisfaction, including any important differences in approaches for different customer groups or market segments. This highlights the importance of the measurement scale in determining those factors that best reflect customers' market behaviors—repurchase, new business, and positive referral.
- The organization should follow up with customers regarding products, services, and recent transactions to determine satisfaction and to resolve problems quickly.
- The organization should determine the levels of customer satisfaction relative to competitors. Such information might be derived from organization-based comparative studies or independent studies. The purpose of this comparison is to develop information that can be used for improving performance relative to competitors and to better understand the factors that drive markets.
- The organization keeps their approaches to determining customer satisfaction current with changing business needs and directions.

The customer satisfaction data gathered from the complaint management process in Item 3.2a ensure timely resolution of problems and can help recover or build customer loyalty. Data collected by survey or similar means, as required by Item 3.2b, produce information at the convenience of the organization. However, data from the complain processes in Item 3.2a are collected at the customer's convenience. Customers complain when they have a problem. They do not tend to hold their complaint until the organization finds it convenient to ask them. Although the complaint-type customer feedback (from Item 3.2a) is timely, it is often difficult to develop reliable trend data. The processes in Item 3.2b make it easier to track satisfaction over time. Both techniques are valuable in helping to understand the dynamics that build loyalty. To be effective, both should be used to drive improvement actions.

3.2 Customer Satisfaction and Relationships

How customer satisfaction is determined, relationships strengthened, and current products and services enhanced to support customer- and market-related planning

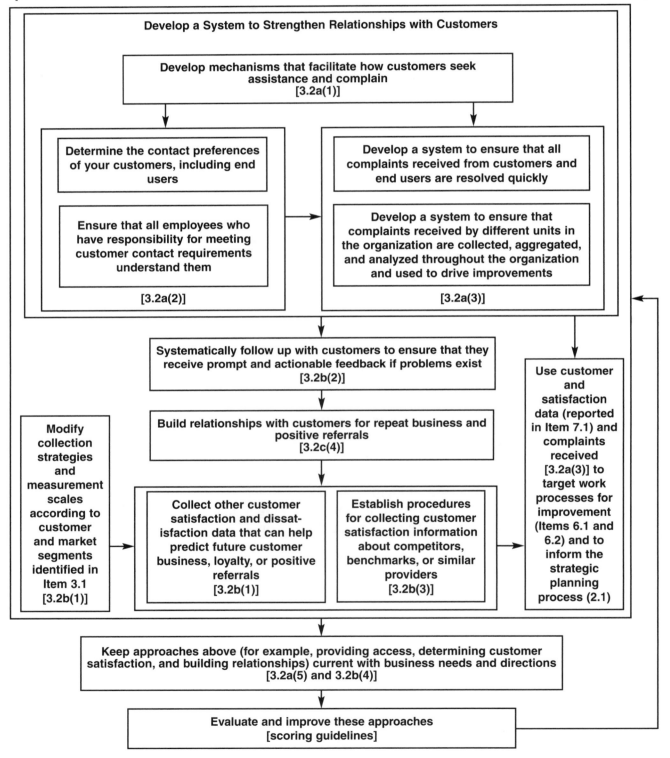

Develop a System to Strengthen Relationships with Customers

Develop mechanisms that facilitate how customers seek assistance and complain
[3.2a(1)]

Determine the contact preferences of your customers, including end users

Ensure that all employees who have responsibility for meeting customer contact requirements understand them

[3.2a(2)]

Develop a system to ensure that all complaints received from customers and end users are resolved quickly

Develop a system to ensure that complaints received by different units in the organization are collected, aggregated, and analyzed throughout the organization and used to drive improvements

[3.2a(3)]

Systematically follow up with customers to ensure that they receive prompt and actionable feedback if problems exist
[3.2b(2)]

Build relationships with customers for repeat business and positive referrals
[3.2c(4)]

Modify collection strategies and measurement scales according to customer and market segments identified in Item 3.1
[3.2b(1)]

Collect other customer satisfaction and dissatisfaction data that can help predict future customer business, loyalty, or positive referrals
[3.2b(1)]

Establish procedures for collecting customer satisfaction information about competitors, benchmarks, or similar providers
[3.2b(3)]

Use customer and satisfaction data (reported in Item 7.1) and complaints received [3.2a(3)] to target work processes for improvement (Items 6.1 and 6.2) and to inform the strategic planning process (2.1)

Keep approaches above (for example, providing access, determining customer satisfaction, and building relationships) current with business needs and directions
[3.2a(5) and 3.2b(4)]

Evaluate and improve these approaches
[scoring guidelines]

3.2 Customer Satisfaction and Relationships Item Linkages

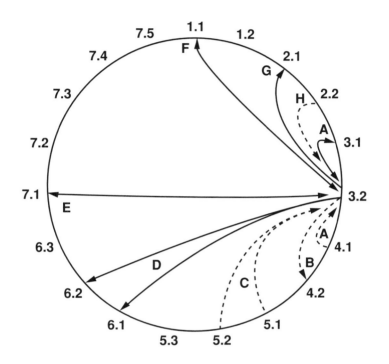

	Nature of Relationship
A	Information concerning customer requirements and expectations [3.1] and benchmark data [4.1] are used to set and deploy customer contact requirements (service standards) [3.2a]. Customer complaint data [3.2a] are used to help assess customer requirements and expectations [3.1].
B	Customer relations and satisfaction data [3.2] are analyzed and used to set priorities for action [4.2].
C	Training [5.2] and improved flexibility and self-direction [5.1] can enhance the development and effectiveness of customer-contact employees [3.2a].
D	Information collected through customer relations employees [3.2a] is used to enhance design of products and services and to improve operational and support processes [6.1 and 6.2].
	Continued on next page

	Nature of Relationship (continued)
E	Information from customer relations processes [3.2a] can help in the design of customer satisfaction measures [3.2b] and even produce data on customer satisfaction [7.1]. In addition, customer satisfaction results data [7.1] are used to set customer contact requirements (service standards) [3.2a]. Efforts of improved accessibility and responsiveness in complaint management [3.2a] should result in improved complaint response time, effective complaint resolution, and a higher percentage of complaints resolved on first contact. These results should be reported in 7.1.
F	Priorities and customer-contact requirements (service standards) for customer service personnel [3.2a] are driven by top leadership [1.1]. Leaders at all levels [1.1] personally interact with and build better relationships with customers. They receive useful information from those customers to improve management of decision making.
G	Information about customer complaints and satisfaction collected by customer-contact employees [3.2a] is used in the planning process [2.1].
H	Goals and strategy [2.2] influence customer relations management [3.2a] and customer satisfaction determination processes [3.2b].

3.2 Customer Satisfaction and Relationships—Sample Effective Practices

A. Customer Relationships

- Several methods are used to ensure ease of customer contact, 24 hours a day if necessary (for example, toll-free numbers, pagers for contact personnel, web sites, e-mail, surveys, interviews, focus groups, electronic bulletin boards).
- Customer-contact employees are empowered to make decisions to address customer concerns.
- Adequate staff are available to maintain effective customer contact.
- Performance expectations are set for employees whose job brings them in regular contact with customers.
- The performance of employees against these expectations is measured and tracked.
- A system exists to ensure that customer complaints are resolved promptly and effectively.
- Complaints and customer concerns are resolved at first contact. This often means training customer-contact employees and giving them authority for resolving a broad range of problems.
- Complaint data are tracked and used to initiate prompt corrective action to prevent the problem from recurring.
- Procedures are in place and evaluated to ensure that customer contact is initiated to follow up on recent transactions to build relationships.
- Training and development plans and replacement procedures exist for customer-contact employees.
- Objective customer-contact requirements (service standards) have been derived from customer expectations (for example, timeliness, courtesy, efficiency, thoroughness, and completeness).
- Requirements for building relationships are identified and may include factors, such as product knowledge, employee responsiveness, and various customer contact methods.
- A systematic approach exists to evaluate and improve service and customer relationships.

B. Customer Satisfaction Determination

- Several customer satisfaction indicators are used (for example, repeat business measures, praise letters, and direct measures using survey questions and interviews).

- Comprehensive satisfaction and dissatisfaction data are collected and segmented or grouped to enable the organization to predict customer behavior (likelihood of remaining a customer).
- Customer satisfaction and dissatisfaction measurements include both a numerical rating scale and descriptors assigned to each unit in the scale. An effective (actionable) customer satisfaction and dissatisfaction measurement system provides the organization with reliable information about customer ratings of specific product and service features and the relationship between these ratings and the customer's likely market behavior.
- Customer dissatisfaction indicators include complaints, claims, refunds, recalls, returns, repeat services, litigation, replacements, performance rating downgrades, repairs, warranty work, warranty costs, misshipments, and incomplete orders.
- Satisfaction data are collected from former customers.
- Competitors' customer satisfaction is determined using various means, such as external or internal studies.
- Methods are in place to ensure objectivity of these data.
- Organization-based or independent organization comparative studies take into account one or more indicators of customer dissatisfaction, as well as satisfaction. The extent and types of such studies depend on industry and organization size.
- The process of collecting complete, timely, and accurate customer satisfaction and dissatisfaction data is regularly evaluated and improved. Several improvement cycles are evident.

4 Information and Analysis—85 Points

> The **Information and Analysis** Category examines your organization's performance measurement system and how your organization analyzes performance data and information.

Information and Analysis is the main point within the Criteria for all key information to effectively measure performance and manage the organization, and to drive improvement of performance and competitiveness. In the simplest terms, Category 4 is the brain center for the alignment of the organization's operations and its strategic directions. However, since information and analysis might themselves be primary sources of competitive advantage and productivity growth, the category also includes such strategic considerations.

Information and analysis evaluates the selection, management, and effectiveness of use of information and data to support processes, action plans, and the performance management system. The analysis and review of data are evaluated.

Measurement of Organizational Performance
- This Item looks at the mechanical processes associated with data collection, information, and measures (including comparative data) for planning, decision making, improving performance, and supporting action plans and operations.

Analysis of Organizational Performance
- This Item looks at the analytical processes used to make sense out of the data. It also looks at how these analyses are deployed throughout the organization and used to support organization-level review, decision making, and planning.

4.1 Measurement of Organizational Performance (40 points)
Approach/Deployment Scoring

Describe how your organization provides effective performance measurement systems for understanding, aligning, and improving performance at all levels and in all parts of your organization.

Within your response, include answers to the following questions:

a. *Measurement of Organizational Performance*
  (1) How do you address the major components of an effective performance measurement system, including the following key factors?
  - Selection of measures/indicators, and extent and effectiveness of their use in daily operations
  - Selection and integration of measures/indicators and completeness of data to track your overall organizational performance
  - Selection, and extent and effectiveness of use of key comparative data and information
  - Data and information reliability
  - A cost/financial understanding of improvement options
  - Correlations/projections of data to support planning
  (2) How do you keep your performance measurement system current with business needs and directions?

Notes:

N1. The term *information and analysis* refers to the key metrics used by your organization to measure and analyze performance. Performance measurement is used in fact-based decision making for setting and aligning organizational directions and resources use at your work unit, key process, departmental, and whole-organization levels.

N2. Deployment of data and information might be via electronic or other means. Reliability [4.1a(1)] includes reliability of software and delivery systems.

N3. Comparative data and information include benchmarking and competitive comparisons. Benchmarking refers to processes and results that represent best practices and performance for similar activities, inside or outside your organization's industry. Competitive comparisons refer to performance relative to competitors in your organization's markets.

This Item [4.1] looks at to the mechanical aspects of the selection, management, and use of data and information for performance measurement, in support of organizational planning and performance improvement. The aim is to serve as a key foundation for consistently good decision making.

The organization should select and use measures for tracking daily operations. It should select and integrate measures for monitoring overall organizational performance:

- Alignment and integration are key concepts for successful implementation of your performance measurement system. They are viewed in terms of extent and effectiveness of use to meet your performance assessment needs. Alignment and integration include how measures are aligned throughout the organization, how they are integrated to yield organizationwide measures, and how performance measurement requirements are deployed by your senior leaders to track workgroup and process-level performance on key measures targeted for organizationwide significance and/or improvement.
- Performance data and information are especially important in business networks, alliances, and supply chains. Your responses to this Item should take into account this strategic use of data and information and should recognize the need for rapid data validation and reliability assurance given the increasing use of electronic data transfer.
- Organizations must ensure data and information reliability since reliability is critical to good decision making, successful monitoring of operations, and successful data integration for assessing overall performance.

You are asked how you select and use competitive comparisons and benchmarking information to help drive performance improvement:

- The use of competitive and comparative information is important to all organizations. The major premises for using competitive and comparative information are (1) the organization needs to know where it stands relative to competitors and to best practices; (2) comparative and benchmarking information often provides the impetus for significant ("breakthrough") improvement or change; and (3) preparation for comparing performance information frequently leads to a better understanding of your processes and their performance. Benchmarking information also may support business analysis and decisions relating to core competencies, alliances, and outsourcing.
- Your effective selection and use of competitive comparisons and benchmarking information require (1) determination of needs and priorities; (2) criteria for seeking appropriate sources for comparisons—from within and outside the organization's industry and markets; and (3) use of data and information to set stretch targets and to promote major, nonincremental improvements in areas most critical to the organization's competitive strategy.

Finally, you are asked how you keep the organization's performance measurement system current with changing business needs. This involves ongoing evaluation and demonstrated refinement.

4.1 Measurement of Organizational Performance

How the organization selects, manages, and uses information and data to support decision making for key processes and to improve performance

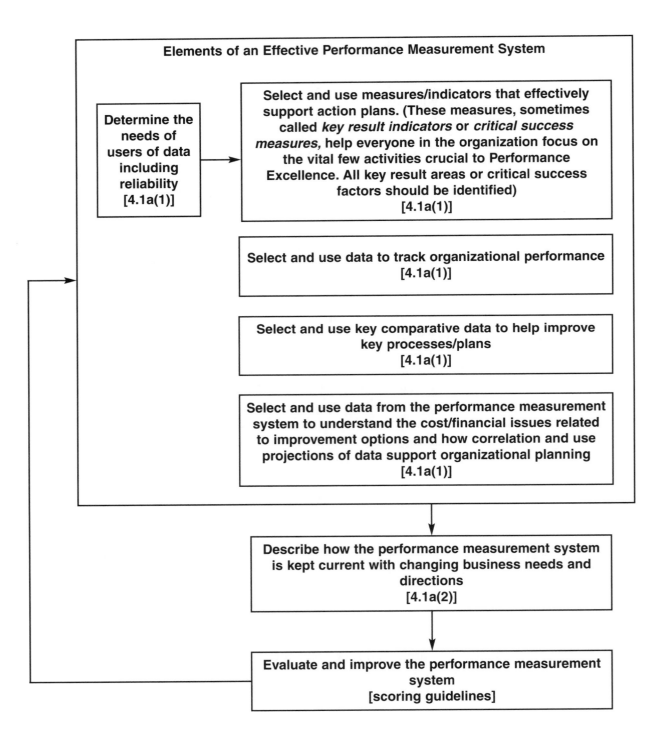

Elements of an Effective Performance Measurement System

Determine the needs of users of data including reliability [4.1a(1)]

Select and use measures/indicators that effectively support action plans. (These measures, sometimes called *key result indicators* or *critical success measures,* help everyone in the organization focus on the vital few activities crucial to Performance Excellence. All key result areas or critical success factors should be identified) [4.1a(1)]

Select and use data to track organizational performance [4.1a(1)]

Select and use key comparative data to help improve key processes/plans [4.1a(1)]

Select and use data from the performance measurement system to understand the cost/financial issues related to improvement options and how correlation and use projections of data support organizational planning [4.1a(1)]

Describe how the performance measurement system is kept current with changing business needs and directions [4.1a(2)]

Evaluate and improve the performance measurement system [scoring guidelines]

4.1 *Measurement of Organizational Performance Item Linkages*

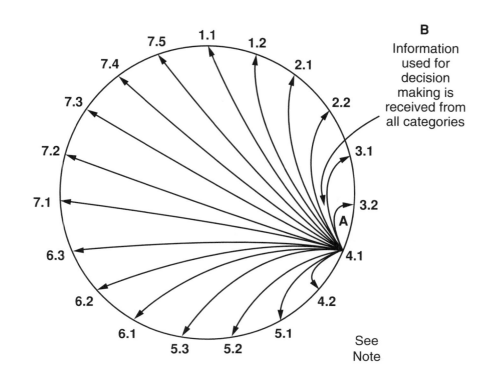

Nature of Relationship	
A	Information collected [4.1] is used for planning [2.1], goal setting [2.2], analysis [4.2], benchmarking priority setting [4.1], day-to-day leadership [1.1], setting public responsibility standards (regulatory, legal, ethical) for community involvement [1.2], monitoring of quality and operational performance results [7.2, 7.3, 7.4, 7.5], improving work processes [6.1, 6.2, 6.3] and human resource systems [5.1, 5.2, 5.3], determining customer requirements [3.1], managing customer complaints and building customer relations [3.2a], and determining customer satisfaction [3.2b] and reporting customer satisfaction [7.1].
B	Information used for decision making and continuous improvement [4.1] is collected from all categories.

Note: Because the information collected and used for decision-making links with all other Items, the linkage arrows will not all be repeated on the other Item maps. The more relevant connections will be identified.

4.1 Measurement of Organizational Performance—Sample Effective Practices

A. Measurement of Organizational Performance

- Data collected at the individual worker level are consistent across the organization to permit consolidation and organizationwide performance monitoring.
- Every person has access to the data they need to make decisions about their work, from top leaders to individual workers or teams of workers.
- Quality and operational data are collected and routinely used for management decisions.
- Internal and external data are used to describe customer satisfaction and product and service performance.
- The cost of quality and other financial concerns are measured for internal operations and processes.
- Data are maintained on employee-related issues of satisfaction, morale, safety, education and training, use of teams, and recognition and reward.
- Supplier performance data are maintained.
- The performance measurement system is systematically evaluated and refined.
- Improvements have been made to reduce cycle time for data collection and to increase data access, reliability, and use.
- Employees, customers, and suppliers are involved in validating data.
- A systematic process exists for data review and improvement, standardization, and easy employee access to data. Training on the use of data systems is provided as needed.
- Data used for management decisions' focus on critical success factors are integrated with work processes for the planning, design, and delivery of products and services.
- Users of data help determine what data systems are developed and how data are accessed.
- A systematic process is in place for identifying and prioritizing comparative information and benchmark targets.
- Research has been conducted to identify best-in-class organizations, which may be competitors or noncompetitors.
- Key processes or functions are the subject of benchmarking. Activities, such as those that support the organization's goals and objectives, action plans, and opportunities for improvement and innovation are the subject of benchmarking.

- Benchmarking covers key products, services, customer satisfiers, suppliers, employees, and support operations.
- The organization reaches beyond its own business to conduct comparative studies.
- Benchmark or comparison data are used to improve the understanding of work processes and to discover the best levels of performance that have been achieved. Based on this knowledge, the organization sets goals or targets to stretch performance, as well as drive innovations.
- A complete understanding of the cost and benefit of improvement options exists.
- Correlations and projections of data are used to support business planning at all levels.
- Any systematic process is in place to improve the use of benchmark or comparison data in the understanding of all work processes.

4.2 Analysis of Organizational Performance (45 points)
Approach/Deployment Scoring

Describe how your organization analyzes performance data and information to assess and understand overall organizational performance.

Within your response, include answers to the following questions:

a. Analysis of Organizational Performance

(1) How do you perform analyses to support your senior executives' organizational performance review and your organizational planning? How do you ensure that the analyses address the overall health of your organization, including your key business results and strategic objectives?

(2) How do you ensure that the results of organizational-level analysis are linked to workgroup and/or functional-level operations to enable effective support for decision making?

(3) How does analysis support daily operations throughout your organization? Include how this analysis ensures that measures align with action plans.

Note:

N1. Analysis includes trends, projections, comparisons, and cause-effect correlations intended to support your performance reviews and the setting of priorities for resource use. Accordingly, analysis draws upon all types of data: customer-related, financial and market, operational, and competitive.

N2. Your performance results should be reported in Items 7.1, 7.2, 7.3, 7.4, and 7.5.

This Item looks at the techniques the organization uses to analyze business data and gain valuable insight about its performance, as a basis for assessing overall organizational health. The Item serves as a central analysis point in an integrated performance measurement and management system that relies on financial and nonfinancial data and information. The aim of analysis is to guide decision making at all levels of the organization and improve the consistency of process management to help achieve key business results and strategic objectives.

Data and information from all parts of in the organization should be used to support senior leaders' assessment of overall organizational health, organizational planning, and daily operations.

Individual facts and data do not usually provide an effective basis for organizational priority setting. This Item emphasizes that close alignment is needed between your analysis and the organizational performance review and between your analysis and organizational planning. This ensures that analysis is relevant to decision making and that decision making is based on relevant facts.

Action depends upon understanding cause-effect connections among processes and between processes and business/performance results. Process actions and their results may have many resource implications. Organizations have a critical need to provide an effective analytical basis for decisions because resources for improvement are limited and cause-effect connections are often unclear.

Analyses that the organization conducts to gain an understanding of performance and needed actions may vary widely, depending upon your type of organization, size, competitive environment, and other factors. Examples of possible analyses include:

- How product and service quality improvement correlates with key customer indicators, such as customer satisfaction, customer retention, and market share;
- Cost/revenue implications of customer-related problems and problem resolution effectiveness;
- Interpretation of market share changes in terms of customer gains and losses and changes in customer satisfaction;
- Improvement trends in key operational performance indicators, such as productivity, cycle time, waste reduction, new product introduction, and defect levels;
- Relationships between employee/organizational learning and value added per employee;
- Financial benefits derived from improvements in employee safety, absenteeism, and turnover;
- Benefits and costs associated with education and training, improved organizational knowledge management, and sharing;
- The ability to identify and meet employee requirements correlates with employee retention, motivation, and productivity;
- Individual or aggregate measures of productivity and quality relative to competitors;
- Cost trends relative to competitors;

- Relationships between product/service quality, operational performance indicators, and overall financial performance trends as reflected in such indicators as operating costs, revenues, asset utilization, and value added per employee;
- Allocation of resources among alternative improvement projects based on cost/revenue implications and improvement potential;
- Net earnings derived from quality/operational/human resource performance improvements;
- Comparisons among business units showing how quality and operational performance improvement affect financial performance;
- Contributions of improvement activities to cash flow, working capital use, and shareholder value;
- Profit impacts of customer retention;
- Cost/revenue implications of new market entry, including global market entry or expansion;
- Cost/revenue, customer, and productivity implications of engaging in and/or expanding electronic commerce;
- Market share versus profits; and
- Trends in economic, market, and shareholder indicators of value.

4.2 Analysis of Organizational Performance

How the organization analyzes performance to assess the overall health of the organization

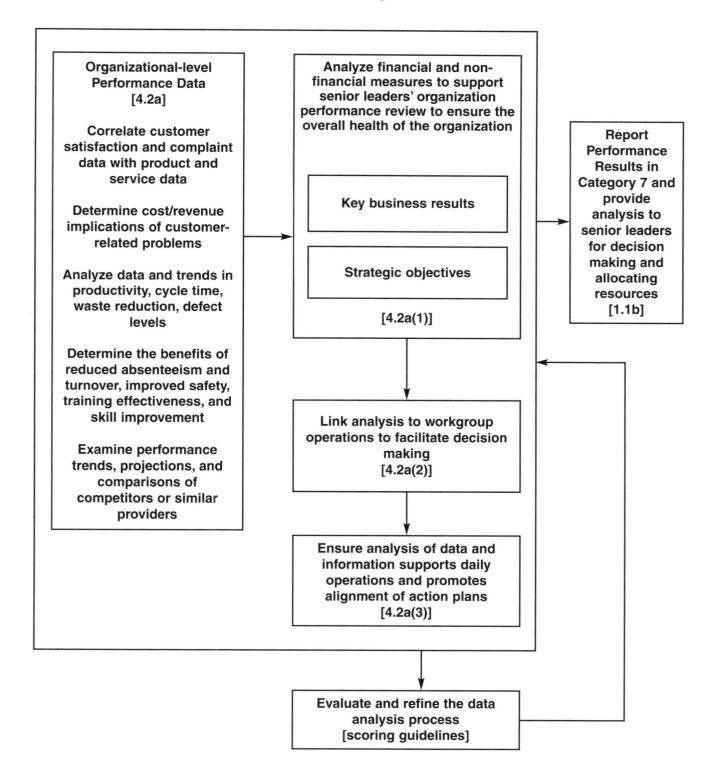

4.2 Analysis of Organizational Performance Item Linkages

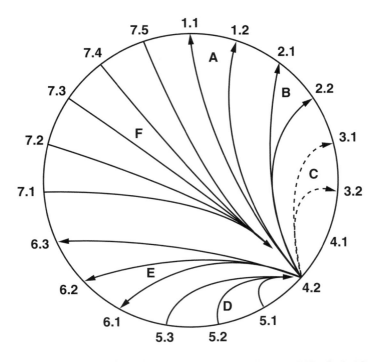

Nature of Relationship	
A	Leaders at all levels [1.1] use data and information [4.2] to review overall performance, assess progress relative to plans, ensure regulatory, legal, and public responsibilities are met or exceeded [1.2], and identify key areas for improvement.
B	Aggregated information is analyzed [4.2] and used in the strategic planning process [2.1] and to help set goals [2.2].
C	Information from customer satisfaction data [7.1] are analyzed [4.2] and used to help determine ways to assess customer requirements [3.1], to determine standards or required levels of customer service and relationship development [3.2a], and to design instruments to assess customer satisfaction [3.2b].
D	Information regarding human resources capabilities, including work system efficiency, initiative, and self-direction [5.1], training and development [5.2], and well-being and satisfaction [5.3] is analyzed [4.2] to improve safety, retention, absenteeism, and organizational effectiveness.
E	Data are aggregated and analyzed [4.2] to improve work processes [6.1, 6.2, 6.3] that will reduce cycle time, waste, and defect levels.
F	Performance data from all parts of the organization are integrated and analyzed [4.2] to assess performance in key areas, such as customer-related performance [7.1], operational performance [7.5], financial and market performance [7.2], human resource performance [7.3], and supplier and partner performance [7.4], relative to competitive performance in all areas.

4.2 Analysis of Organizational Performance—Sample Effective Practices

A. Analysis of Organizational Performance

- Systematic processes are in place for analyzing all types of data and to determine overall organizational health, including key business results, action plans, and strategic objectives. Part of the process is a method to evaluate the effectiveness of the analysis process and improve.
- Facts, rather than intuition, are used to support most decision making at all levels based on the analyses conducted to make sense out of the data collected.
- The analysis process itself is analyzed to make the results more timely and useful for decision making for quality improvement at all levels.
- Analysis processes and tools, and the value of analyses to decision making, are systematically evaluated and improved.
- Analysis is linked to workgroups to facilitate decision making (sometimes daily) throughout the organization.
- Analysis techniques enable meaningful interpretation of the cost and performance impact of organization processes. This analysis helps people at all levels of the organization make necessary trade-offs, set priorities, and reallocate resources to maximize overall organization performance.

5   *Human Resource Focus—85 Points*

The **Human Resource Focus** Category examines how your organization enables employees to develop and utilize their full potential, aligned with the organization's objectives. Also examined are your organization's efforts to build and maintain a work environment and an employee support climate conducive to Performance Excellence, full participation, and personal and organizational growth.

Human Resource Focus addresses key human resource practices—those directed toward creating a high-performance workplace and toward developing employees to enable them and the organization to adapt to change. The category covers human resource development and management requirements in an integrated way, that is, aligned with the organization's strategic directions. Included in the focus on human resources is a focus on the work environment and the employee support climate.

To ensure the basic alignment of human resource management with overall strategy, the Criteria also include human resource planning as part of organizational planning in the Strategic Planning category. Human resource focus evaluates how the organization enables employees to develop and use their full potential.

Work Systems
- Design, organize, and manage work and jobs to optimize employee performance and potential
- Recognition and reward practices support objectives for customer satisfaction, performance improvement, and employee and organization learning goals
- Identify skills needed by potential employees, recruit, and hire

Employee Education, Training, and Development
- Deliver, evaluate, and reinforce appropriate training to achieve action plans and address organization needs, including building knowledge, skills, and abilities to improve employee development and performance

Employee Well-Being and Satisfaction

- Improve employee safety, well-being, development, and satisfaction and maintain a work environment free from distractions to high performance
- Leaders at all levels encourage and motivate employees to reach full potential
- Systematically evaluate employee well-being, satisfaction, and motivation and identify improvement priorities that promote key business results

5.1 Work Systems (35 Points)
Approach/Deployment Scoring

Describe how your organization's work and job design, compensation, career progression, and related workforce practices enable employees to achieve high performance in your operations.

Within your response, include answers to the following questions:

a. **Work Systems**

(1) How do you design, organize, and manage work and jobs to promote cooperation and collaboration, individual initiative, innovation, flexibility, and to keep current with business needs?

(2) How do your managers and supervisors encourage and motivate employees to develop and utilize their full potential? Include formal and/or informal mechanisms you use to encourage and support employees in job- and career-related development/learning objectives.

(3) How does your employee performance management system, including feedback to employees, support high performance?

(4) How do your compensation, recognition, and related reward/incentive practices reinforce high performance?

(5) How do you ensure effective communication, cooperation, and knowledge/skill sharing across work units, functions, and locations, as appropriate?

(6) How do you identify characteristics and skills needed by potential employees; how do you recruit and hire new employees? How do you take into account key performance requirements, diversity of your community, and fair workforce practices?

Notes:

N1. The term *employees* refers to your organization's permanent, temporary, and part-time personnel, as well as any contract employees supervised by your organization. Employees include managers and supervisors at all levels. You should address contract employees supervised by a contractor in Item 6.3.

N2. The term *work design* refers to how your employees are organized and/or organize themselves in formal and informal, temporary, or longer-term units. This might include work teams, process teams, customer action teams, problem-solving teams, centers of excellence, functional units, cross-functional teams, and departments—self-managed or managed by supervisors. The term *job* design refers to responsibilities, authorities, and tasks of individuals. In some work systems, jobs might be shared by a team, based upon cross-training.

N3. Compensation and recognition include promotions and bonuses that might be based upon performance, skills acquired, and other factors. Recognition includes monetary and nonmonetary, formal and informal, and individual and group recognition.

This Item looks at the organization's systems for work and job design, compensation, employee performance management, motivation, recognition, communication, and hiring, with the aim of enabling and encouraging all employees to contribute effectively and to the best of their ability. These systems are intended to foster high performance, to result in individual and organizational learning, and to enable adaptation to change.

Work and jobs should be designed in such a way as to allow employees to exercise discretion and decision making, resulting in high performance:

- High-performance work is enhanced by systems that promote employee flexibility, innovation, knowledge and skill sharing. Work should support organizational objectives, customer focus, and rapid response to changing business needs and requirements of the marketplace. To achieve high levels of organizational performance, it is essential to develop fully the capabilities of the workforce. In addition to the enabled employees and proper work system design, high-performance work requires ongoing education and training, and information systems that ensure proper information flow. To help employees realize their full potential, many organizations use individual development plans prepared with the input of each employee and designed to address his or her career and learning objectives.
- The ability to respond quickly to changing customer and workplace requirements demands a workforce characterized by initiative and self-direction. Hierarchical, command-and-control management styles work directly against fast response and high-performance capability. After all, the opposite of individual initiative is an environment where managers demand review and approval of decisions that are typically better made by employees doing the work.
- Factors to consider in work and job design include simplification of job classifications, cross-training, job rotation, use of teams (including self-directed teams), and changes in work layout and location. Effective communication across functions and work units is also important to ensure a focus on customer requirements and to ensure an environment of trust, knowledge sharing, and mutual respect.

Leaders and managers throughout the organization should consistently encourage and motivate employees to achieve Performance Excellence objectives. Employee compensation, recognition, and reward should be lined up to support business objectives. In addition, to make sure all employees understand their responsibilities, systems should exist to promote effective communication and cooperation at all levels of the organization.

- Once the organization determines its key strategic objectives, it should review compensation, reward, and recognition systems to ensure they support those objectives. The failure to do this creates an environment where employees are focused on one set of activities (based on their compensation plan), but the organization has determined that another set of activities (the action plans to achieve the strategic objectives) is necessary for success.
- Compensation and recognition might be tied to demonstrated skills and/or to peer evaluations. Compensation and recognition approaches also might include profit sharing, team or unit performance, and linkage to customer satisfaction and loyalty measures, which are typical business objectives.

Finally, organizations must profile, recruit, and hire employees who will meet skill requirements. Obviously, the right workforce is a key driver of high performance:

- As the pool of skilled talent continues to shrink, it becomes more important than ever for organizations to specifically define the skills needed by potential employees and create a work environment to attract them. Accordingly, it is critical to take into account characteristics of diverse populations to make sure appropriate support systems exist that make it possible to attract skilled workers.

5.1 Work Systems

How the organization's work and job design, compensation and recognition approaches, career progression, recruitment, and diversity practices enable and encourage all employees to contribute effectively to achieving high performance

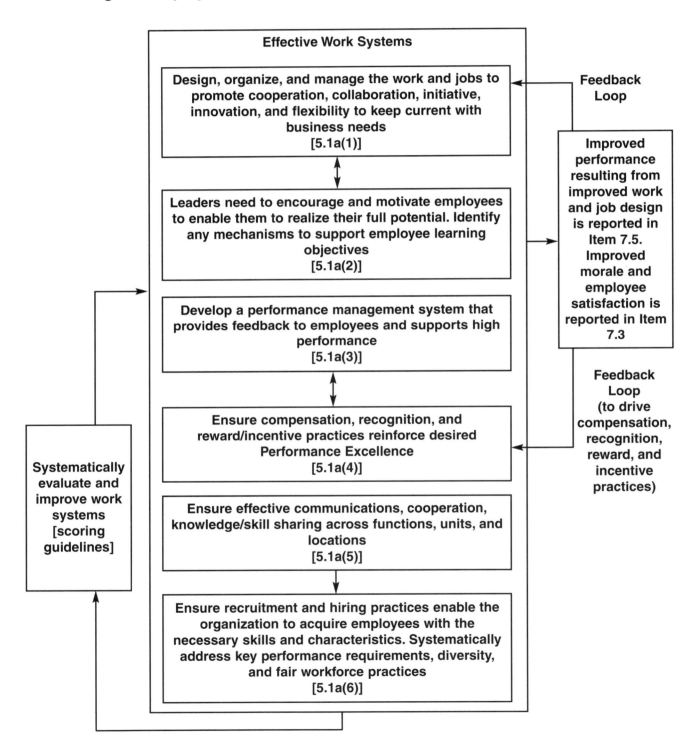

5.1 Work Systems Item Linkages

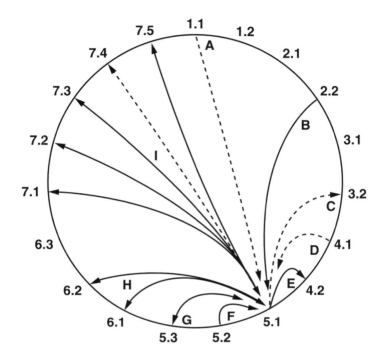

Nature of Relationship	
A	Leaders at all levels [1.1] set the policies and role model actions essential to improving work and job design to enhance employee performance, initiative, self-direction, and involvement in quality improvement [5.1].
B	Human resource development plans and goals [2.2] address ways to improve employee performance and involvement [5.1], training [5.2], and satisfaction and well-being [5.3].
C	Improved flexibility and self-direction [5.1] can enhance the effectiveness of customer-contact employees [3.2a].
D	Key comparison data [4.1] are often used to improve work systems, and reward and recognition [5.1].
E	Information regarding work systems effectiveness, design effectiveness, and employee involvement and recognition [5.1] is used to gain a better understanding of operational performance and organizational capabilities [4.2].
Continued on next page	

	Nature of Relationship (continued)
F	Effective training [5.2] is critical to enable employees or managers at all levels to improve skills and improve their ability to manage, organize, and design better work processes [5.1].
G	An improved work climate [5.3b] enhances employee participation, self-direction, and initiative [5.1] and vice versa.
H	High-performance, streamlined work systems, and effective compensation and recognition [5.1] are essential to improving operational and support processes [6.1 and 6.2]. In addition, the analysis of work processes (identifying inefficiencies) is used to inform or drive the improvements in flexibility and job design [5.1].
I	Recognition or rewards [5.1] are based in part on performance results [Category 7], particularly in areas of operating effectiveness [7.5], financial and market performance [7.2], and customer satisfaction [7.1]. Improvements in work and job design [5.1] result in improved employee motivation and satisfaction [7.3] and improved operating effectiveness [7.5]. Processes to improve initiative and flexibility [5.1] can enhance all performance results [Category 7].

5.1 Work Systems—Sample Effective Practices

A. Work Systems

- Fully using the talents of all employees is a basic organizational value.
- Managers use cross-functional workteams to break down barriers, improve effectiveness, and meet goals.
- Teams have access to data and are authorized to make decisions about their work.
- Employee opinion is sought regarding work design and work processes.
- Prompt and regular feedback is provided to teams regarding their performance. Feedback covers both results and team process.
- Although lower-performing organizations use teams for special improvement projects (while the "regular work" is performed using traditional approaches), higher-performing organizations use teams and self-directed employees as the way regular work is done.
- Self-directed or self-managed workteams are used throughout the organization. They have authority over matters, such as budget, hiring, and team membership and roles.
- A systematic process is used to evaluate and improve the effectiveness and extent of employee involvement.
- Many indicators of employee involvement effectiveness exist, such as the improvements in time or cost reduction produced by teams.
- The performance management system provides feedback to employees that supports their ability to contribute to a high-performing organization.
- Compensation, recognition, and rewards/incentives are provided for generating improvement ideas. Also, a system exists to encourage and provide rapid reinforcement for submitting improvement ideas.
- Compensation, recognition, and rewards/incentives are provided for results, such as for reductions in cycle time and exceeding target schedules with error-free products or services at less-than-projected cost.
- Employees, as well as managers, participate in creating the compensation, recognition, and rewards/incentives practices and help monitor its implementation and systematic improvement.
- The organization evaluates its approaches to employee performance and compensation, recognition, and rewards to determine the extent to which employees are satisfied with them, the extent of employee participation, and the impact of the system on improved performance (reported in Item 7.3).
- Evaluations are used to make improvements. The best organizations have several improvement cycles. (Many improvement cycles can occur in one year.)

- Performance measures exist for employee involvement, self-direction, and initiative. Goals for these measures are expressed in measurable terms. These measurable goals form at least a good part of the basis for performance recognition.
- Recognition, reward/incentives, and compensation are influenced by customer satisfaction ratings, as well as other performance measures.

5.2 Employee Education, Training, and Development (25 points)
Approach/Deployment Scoring

Describe how your organization's education and training support the achievement of your business objectives, build employee knowledge, skills, and capabilities, and contribute to improved employee performance.

Within your response, include answers to the following questions:

a. Employee Education, Training, and Development
  (1) How does your education and training approach balance short- and longer-term organizational and employee needs, including development, learning, and career progression?
  (2) How do you design education and training to keep current with business and individual needs? Include how job and organizational performance are used in education and training design and evaluation.
  (3) How do you seek and use input from employees and their supervisors/managers on education and training needs, expectations, and design?
  (4) How do you deliver and evaluate education and training? Include formal and informal education, training, and learning, as appropriate.
  (5) How do you address key developmental and training needs, including diversity training, management/leadership development, new-employee orientation, and safety, as appropriate?
  (6) How do you address Performance Excellence in your education and training? Include how employees learn to use performance measurements, performance standards, skill standards, performance improvement, quality control methods, and benchmarking, as appropriate.
  (7) How do you reinforce knowledge and skills on the job?

Notes:
  Education and training delivery [5.2a(4)] might occur inside or outside your organization and involve on-the-job, classroom, computer-based, distance learning, and/or other types of delivery (formal or informal).

This Item looks at the organization's system for workforce education, training, and on-the-job reinforcement of knowledge and skills, with the aim of meeting ongoing needs of employees and a high-performance workplace.

To help the organization achieve its high-performance objectives, education and training must be effectively designed, delivered, reinforced on the job, and evaluated. To optimize organization effectiveness, the education and training system should place special emphasis on meeting individual career progression and organizational business needs:

- Education and training needs might vary greatly depending on the nature of the organization's work, employee responsibility, and stage of organizational and personal development. These needs might include knowledge-sharing skills, communications, teamwork, problem solving, interpreting and using data, meeting customer requirements, process analysis and simplification, waste and cycle time reduction, and priority setting based on strategic alignment or cost/benefit analysis. Education needs also might include basic skills, such as reading, writing, language, and arithmetic.

Organizations should consider job and organizational performance in education and training design and evaluation in support of a fact-based management system. Employees and their supervisors should help determine training needs and contribute to the design and evaluation of education and training, because these individuals frequently are best able to identify critical needs and evaluate success:

- Education and training delivery might occur inside or outside the organization and could involve on-the-job, classroom, computer-based, distance learning, or other types of delivery. Training also might occur through developmental assignments within or outside the organization.
- When you evaluate education and training, you should seek effectiveness measures as a critical component of evaluation. Such measures might address impact on individual, unit, and organizational performance; impact on customer-related performance; and cost/benefit analysis of the training.
- Although this Item does not require specific training for customer-contact employees, the Item does require that education and training "keep current with business and individual needs" and "address Performance Excellence." If an objective of the organization is to enhance customer satisfaction and loyalty, it may be critical to identify job requirements for customer-contact employees and then provide appropriate training to these employees. Such training is increasingly important and common among high-performing organizations. It frequently includes acquiring critical knowledge and skills with respect to products, services, and customers; skills on how to listen to customers; recovery from problems or failures; and learning how to manage customer expectations effectively.

The organization must address Performance Excellence in its education and training programs:

- Employees and supervisors should use performance measures and standards to ensure excellence in education and training.
- Performance excellence education and training may be similar to the "quality" training organizations provided in the past. This may include the use of performance measures, skill standards, quality control methods, benchmarking, problem-solving processes, and performance improvement techniques.
- Finally, the organization should address key developmental and training needs, including high priority needs, such as management/leadership development, diversity training, and safety. Succession planning and leadership development at all levels is becoming more critical as organizations find it more difficult to recruit and retained skilled workers and leaders.

5.2 Employee Education, Training, and Development

How the organization's education and training addresses business objectives, building employee knowledge, skills, and capabilities, and contributes to improving employee performance

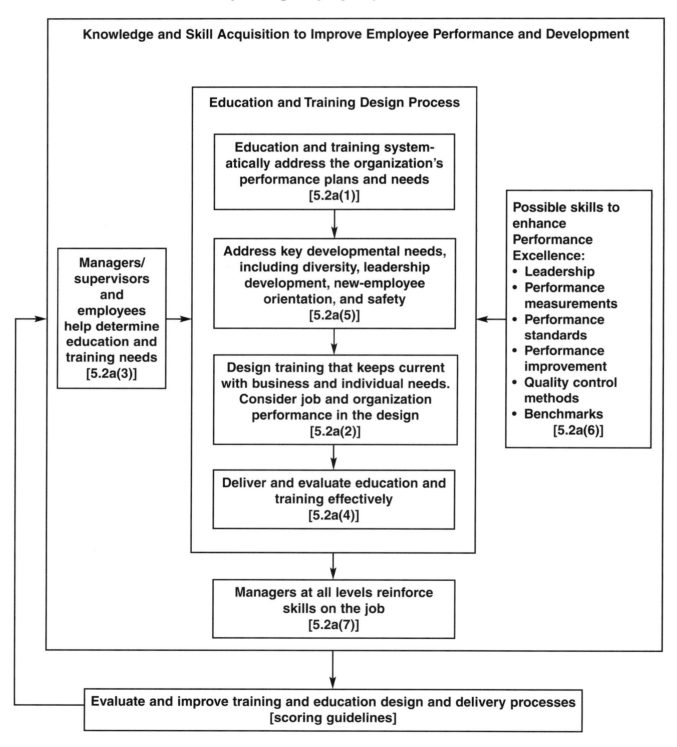

Knowledge and Skill Acquisition to Improve Employee Performance and Development

Education and Training Design Process

Education and training systematically address the organization's performance plans and needs
[5.2a(1)]

Address key developmental needs, including diversity, leadership development, new-employee orientation, and safety
[5.2a(5)]

Design training that keeps current with business and individual needs. Consider job and organization performance in the design
[5.2a(2)]

Deliver and evaluate education and training effectively
[5.2a(4)]

Managers/ supervisors and employees help determine education and training needs
[5.2a(3)]

Possible skills to enhance Performance Excellence:
- Leadership
- Performance measurements
- Performance standards
- Performance improvement
- Quality control methods
- Benchmarks
[5.2a(6)]

Managers at all levels reinforce skills on the job
[5.2a(7)]

Evaluate and improve training and education design and delivery processes
[scoring guidelines]

5.2 *Employee Education, Training, and Development Item Linkages*

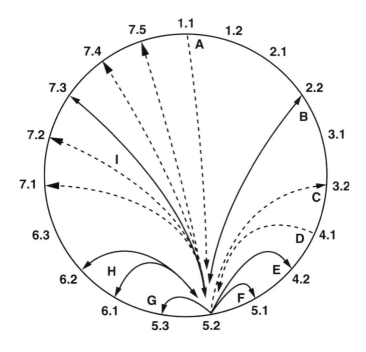

	Nature of Relationship
A	Leaders at all levels [1.1] reinforce training on the job to ensure its effectiveness [5.2].
B	Human resource development plans [2.2a] are used to help align training [5.2] to support the organizational goals [2.2b].
C	Training [5.2] can enhance capabilities of customer-contact employees and strengthen customer relationships [3.2a].
D	Key measures and benchmarking data [4.1] are used to improve training [5.2].
E	Information regarding training effectiveness [5.2] is analyzed [4.2].
F	Effective training [5.2] enables employees and managers at all levels to improve skills and their ability to manage, organize, and design better work processes [5.1].
G	Effective training [5.2] is often critical to maintaining and improving a safe, healthful work environment [5.3a].
H	Training [5.2] is essential to improving work-in-process effectiveness and innovation [6.1 and 6.2]. In addition, training requirements [5.2] are defined, in part, by process requirements [6.1 and 6.2].
I	Results of improved training and development [5.2] are reported in 7.3. In addition, customer satisfaction [7.1], financial and market [7.2], and operational performance and product and service quality results [7.5] are monitored, in part, to assess training effectiveness [5.2].

5.2 Employee Education, Training, and Development—Sample Effective Practices

A. Employee Education, Training, and Development

- Systematic needs analyses are conducted by managers and employees to ensure that skills required to perform work are routinely assessed, monitored, and maintained.
- Clear linkages exist between strategic objectives and the education and training that are provided. Skills are developed based on work demands and employee needs.
- Employee input is considered when developing training plans.
- Employee career and personal development options, including development for leadership, diversity, new-employee orientation, and safety, are enhanced through formal education and training. Some development uses on-the-job training, such as rotational assignments or job exchange programs.
- The organization uses various methods to deliver training to ensure that it is suitable for employee knowledge and skill levels.
- Training is linked to work requirements, which managers reinforce on the job. Just-in-time training is preferred (rather than just-in-case training) to help ensure that the skills will be used immediately after training.
- Employee feedback on the appropriateness of the training is collected and used to improve course delivery and content.
- The organization systematically evaluates training effectiveness on the job. Performance data are collected on individuals and groups at all levels to assess the impact of training.
- Employee satisfaction with courses is tracked.
- Training design and delivery is systematically refined and improved based on these evaluations.

5.3   Employee Well-Being and Satisfaction (25 points)
Approach/Deployment Scoring

Describe how your organization maintains a work environment and an employee support climate that contribute to the well-being, satisfaction, and motivation of all employees.

Within your response, include answers to the following questions:

a.   Work Environment
How do you address and improve workplace health, safety, and ergonomic factors? How do employees take part in identifying these factors and in improving workplace safety? Include performance measures and/or targets for each key environmental factor. Also include significant differences, if any, based on different work environments for employee groups and/or work units.

b.   Employee Support Climate
(1)   How do you enhance your employees' work climate via services, benefits, and policies? How are these enhancements selected and tailored to the needs of different categories and types of employees, and to individuals, as appropriate?

(2)   How does your work climate consider and support the needs of a diverse workforce?

c.   Employee Satisfaction
(1)   How do you determine the key factors that affect employee well-being, satisfaction, and motivation?

(2)   What formal and/or informal assessment methods and measures do you use to determine employee well-being, satisfaction, and motivation? How do you tailor these methods and measures to a diverse workforce and to different categories and types of employees? How do you use other indicators, such as employee turnover, absenteeism, grievances, and productivity to assess and improve employee well-being, satisfaction, and motivation?

(3)   How do you relate assessment findings to key business results to identify work environment and employee support climate improvement priorities?

Notes:
N1.   Approaches for enhancing your employees' work climate [5.3b(1)] might include counseling; career development and employability services; recreational or cultural activities; non–work-related education; day care; job rotation and/or sharing; special leave for family responsibilities and/or for community service; home safety training; flexible work hours; outplacement; and retiree benefits (including extended health care).

Continued on next page

N2. Specific factors that might affect your employees' well-being, satisfaction, and motivation [5.3c(1)] include effective employee problem or grievance resolution; safety factors; employee views of management; employee training, development, and career opportunities; employee preparation for changes in technology or the work organization; work environment and other work conditions; workload; cooperation and teamwork; recognition; benefits; communications; job security; compensation; and equal opportunity.

N3. Measures and/or indicators of well-being, satisfaction, and motivation [5.3c(2)] might include safety; absenteeism; turnover; turnover rate for customer-contact employees; grievances; strikes; other job actions; insurance costs; worker's compensation claims; and results of surveys. Your results relative to such measures and/or indicators should be reported in Item 7.3.

N4. Priority setting [5.3c(3)] might draw upon your human resource results presented in Item 7.3 and might involve addressing employee problems based on their impact on your organizational performance.

This Item looks at the organization's work environment, your employee support climate, and how you determine employee satisfaction, with the aim of fostering the well-being, satisfaction, and motivation of all employees, recognizing their diverse needs.

The first part of this Item [5.3a] looks at how the organization provides a safe and healthful work environment for all employees, taking into account their differing work environments and associated requirements. Employees should help identify and improve factors important to workplace safety:

- The organization should be able to show how it includes such factors in its planning and improvement activities. Important factors in this area include establishing appropriate measures and targets for employee safety and health. Organizations should also recognize that employee groups might experience very different environments and need different services to ensure workplace safety.
- Organizations should also identify appropriate measures and targets for key environmental factors so that status and progress can be tracked.

The second part of this Item [5.3b] looks at the organization's approach to enhance employee well-being, satisfaction, and motivation based upon a holistic view of employees as key stakeholders. Organizations need to consider a variety of services, facilities, activities, and opportunities to address the needs of different employee groups and to tailor these to their well-being, satisfaction, and motivation. Increasingly, the needs of a diverse workforce have to be addressed in order to reduce attrition and increase motivation.

You are asked how you enhance employee well-being, satisfaction, and motivation based upon a holistic view of this key stakeholder group. Special emphasis is placed on the variety of approaches you use to satisfy a diverse workforce with differing needs and expectations:

- Examples of services, facilities, activities, and other opportunities are personal and career counseling; career development and employability services; recreational or cultural activities; formal and informal recognition; non-work-related education; day care; special leave for family responsibilities and/or for community service; home safety training; flexible work hours; outplacement; and retiree benefits, including extended health care. Also, these services might include career enhancement activities, such as skills assessments, helping employees develop learning objectives and plans, and conducting employability assessments.

- As the workforce becomes more diverse (including employees that may work in other countries for multinational companies), it becomes more important to consider and support the needs of those employees with different services.

The last part of this Item [5.3c] looks at how the organization determines employee well-being, satisfaction, and motivation. Many factors might affect employee morale, well-being, and satisfaction. Although satisfaction with pay and promotion potential is important, these factors might not be adequate to understand the factors that contribute to the overall climate for motivation and high performance. For this reason, the high-performing organizations usually consider a variety of factors that might affect well-being, satisfaction, and motivation, such as effective employee problem or grievance resolution; safety; employee views of leadership and management; employee development and career opportunities; employee preparation for changes in technology or work organization; work environment; workload; cooperation and teamwork; recognition; benefits; communications; job security; compensation; diversity; and capability to provide required services to customers:

- In addition to direct measurement of employee satisfaction and well-being through formal or informal surveys, some other indicators of satisfaction and well-being include absenteeism, turnover, grievances, strikes, OSHA reportables, and worker's compensation claims.

- Information and data on the well-being, satisfaction, and motivation of employees are actually used in identifying improvement priorities. Priority setting might draw upon human resource results presented in Item 7.3 and might involve addressing employee problems based on impact on organizational performance. Factors inhibiting motivation need to be prioritized and addressed. Failure to address these factors are likely to result in even more problem symptoms and adversely affect the results (Item 7.3).

5.3 Employee Well-Being and Satisfaction

How the organization maintains a work environment and employee support climate that supports the well-being, satisfaction, and motivation of employees

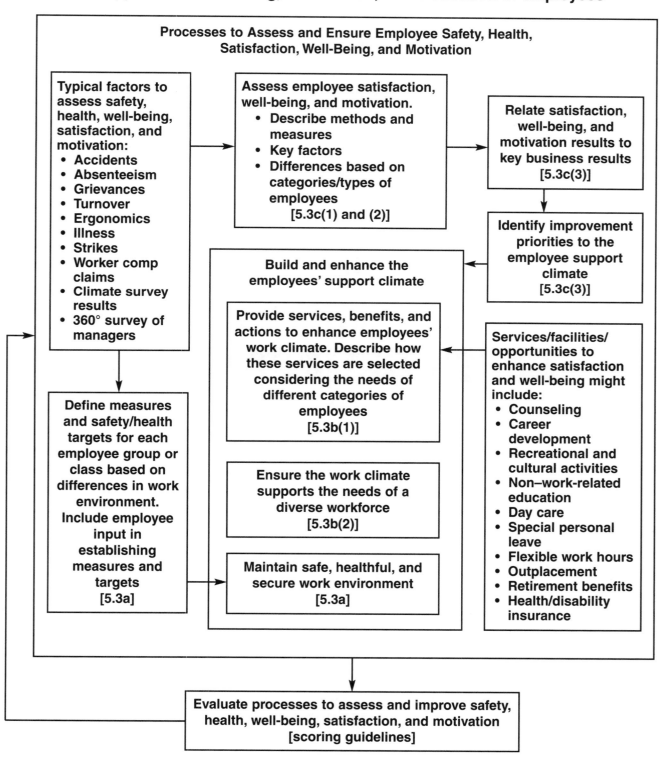

Processes to Assess and Ensure Employee Safety, Health, Satisfaction, Well-Being, and Motivation

Typical factors to assess safety, health, well-being, satisfaction, and motivation:
- **Accidents**
- **Absenteeism**
- **Grievances**
- **Turnover**
- **Ergonomics**
- **Illness**
- **Strikes**
- **Worker comp claims**
- **Climate survey results**
- **360° survey of managers**

Assess employee satisfaction, well-being, and motivation.
- **Describe methods and measures**
- **Key factors**
- **Differences based on categories/types of employees**
  [5.3c(1) and (2)]

Relate satisfaction, well-being, and motivation results to key business results [5.3c(3)]

Identify improvement priorities to the employee support climate [5.3c(3)]

Build and enhance the employees' support climate

Provide services, benefits, and actions to enhance employees' work climate. Describe how these services are selected considering the needs of different categories of employees [5.3b(1)]

Ensure the work climate supports the needs of a diverse workforce [5.3b(2)]

Maintain safe, healthful, and secure work environment [5.3a]

Define measures and safety/health targets for each employee group or class based on differences in work environment. Include employee input in establishing measures and targets [5.3a]

Services/facilities/opportunities to enhance satisfaction and well-being might include:
- **Counseling**
- **Career development**
- **Recreational and cultural activities**
- **Non–work-related education**
- **Day care**
- **Special personal leave**
- **Flexible work hours**
- **Outplacement**
- **Retirement benefits**
- **Health/disability insurance**

Evaluate processes to assess and improve safety, health, well-being, satisfaction, and motivation [scoring guidelines]

5.3 Employee Well-Being and Satisfaction Item Linkages

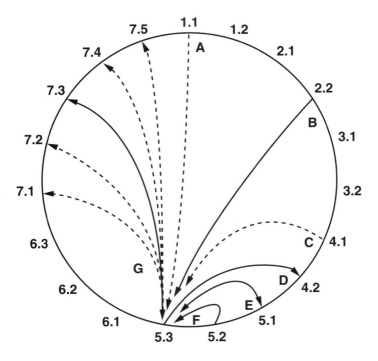

Nature of Relationship	
A	Leaders at all levels [1.1] have responsibility for enhancing employee morale and well-being [5.3].
B	Human resource development plans [2.2a] address morale and well-being concerns [5.3].
C	Key benchmarking data [4.1] are used to design processes to enhance employee morale and well-being [5.3].
D	Information regarding employee well-being and morale [5.3c] is used to gain a better understanding of problems and performance capabilities [4.2].
E	High morale [5.3] enhances employee participation, self-direction, and initiative [5.1], and vice versa.
F	Training systems [5.2] enhance employee development, leading to improved employee morale and well-being [5.3].
G	Systems that enhance employee satisfaction and well-being [5.3] can boost performance [7.2 and 7.5] and customer satisfaction [7.1]. Specific results of employee well-being and satisfaction systems are reported in 7.3.

5.3 Employee Well-Being and Satisfaction—Sample Effective Practices

A. Work Environment

- Quality activities consider issues relating to employee health, safety, and workplace environment. Plans exist to optimize these conditions and eliminate adverse conditions.
- Root causes of health and safety problems are systematically identified and eliminated. Corrective actions are communicated widely to help prevent the problems in other parts of the organization.
- Targets are set and reviewed for all key health, safety, and ergonomic factors affecting the employees' work environment.

B. Employee Support Climate

- Special activities and services are available for employees. These can be quite varied, depending on the needs of different employee categories. Examples include the following:
  - Flexible benefits plan, including health care, on-site day care, dental, portable retirement, education (both work and non–work-related), maternity, paternity, and family illness leave.
  - Group purchasing power program where the number of participating merchants is increasing steadily.
  - Special facilities for employee meetings to discuss their concerns.
- Senior leaders build a work climate that addresses the needs of a diverse workforce. Recruitment and training are tools to enhance the work climate.

C. Employee Satisfaction

- Key employee satisfaction opinion indicators are gathered periodically based on the stability of the organization (organizations in the midst of rapid change conduct assessments more frequently).
- On-demand electronic surveys are available for quick response and tabulations any time managers need employee satisfaction feedback.
- Satisfaction data are derived from employee focus groups, e-mail data, employee satisfaction survey results, turnover, absenteeism, stress-related disorders, and other data that reflect employee satisfaction. (A key employee satisfaction indicator is one that reflects conditions affecting employee morale and motivation.)

- Managers use the results of these surveys to focus improvements in work systems and enhance employee satisfaction. Actions to improve satisfaction are clearly tied to assessments, so employees understand the value of the assessment and the improvement initiative does not appear random or capricious.
- Employee satisfaction indicators are correlated with drivers of business success to help identify where resources should be placed to provide maximum business benefit.
- Methods to improve how employee satisfaction is determined are systematically evaluated and improved. Techniques to actually improve employee satisfaction and well-being are, themselves, evaluated and refined consistently.

6 *Process Management—85 Points*

> The **Process Management** category examines the key aspects of your organization's process management, including customer-focused design, product and service delivery, support, and supplier and partnering processes involving all work units.

Process management is the focal point within the Criteria for all key work processes. Built into the category are the central requirements for efficient and effective process management—effective design; a prevention orientation; linkage to suppliers and partners; operational performance; cycle time; and evaluation, continuous improvement, and organizational learning.

Flexibility, cost reduction, and cycle time reduction are increasingly important in all aspects of process management and design. In simplest terms, flexibility refers to your ability to adapt quickly and effectively to changing requirements. Depending on the nature of the organization's strategy and markets, flexibility might mean rapid changeover from one product to another, rapid response to changing demands, or the ability to produce a wide range of customized services. Flexibility might demand special strategies, such as implementing modular designs, sharing components, sharing manufacturing lines, and providing specialized training. Flexibility also increasingly involves outsourcing decisions, agreements with key suppliers, and novel partnering arrangements.

Cost and cycle time reduction often involve many of the same process management strategies as achieving flexibility. Thus, it is crucial to utilize key measures for these requirements in your overall process management.

Process management contains three Items that evaluate the management of product and service processes, support processes, and supplier and partnering processes.

Product and Service Processes
- Design, develop, and introduce products and services to meet customer requirements, operational performance requirements, and market requirements
- Ensure a rapid, efficient, trouble-free introduction
- Manage and continuously improve operating processes

Support Processes
- Design, develop, and introduce products and services to meet customer requirements, operational performance requirements, and market requirements
- Manage and continuously improve support processes

Supplier and Partnering Performance
- Ensure performance requirements are met, minimize supplier cost, and help suppliers improve performance and their ability to help you

6.1 Product and Service Processes (55 points)
Approach/Deployment Scoring

Describe how your organization manages key product and service design and delivery processes.

Within your response, include answers to the following questions:

a. Design Processes
(1) What are your design processes for products/services and their related production/delivery processes?

(2) How do you incorporate changing customer/market requirements into product/service designs and production/delivery systems and processes?

(3) How do you incorporate new technology into products/services and into production/delivery systems and processes, as appropriate?

(4) How do your design processes address design quality and cycle time, transfer of learning from past projects and other parts of the organization, cost control, new design technology, productivity, and other efficiency/effectiveness factors?

(5) How do you ensure that your production/delivery process design accommodates all key operational performance requirements?

(6) How do you coordinate and test design and production/delivery processes to ensure capability for trouble-free and timely introduction of products/services?

b. Production/Delivery Processes
(1) What are your key production/delivery processes and their key performance requirements?

Continued on next page

(2) How does your day-to-day operation of key production/delivery processes ensure meeting key performance requirements?

(3) What are your key performance measures and/or indicators used for the control and improvement of these processes? Include how real-time customer input is sought, as appropriate.

(4) How do you improve your production/delivery processes to achieve better process performance and improvements to products/services, as appropriate? How are improvements shared with other organizational units and processes, as appropriate?

Notes:

N1. Product and service design, production, and delivery differ greatly among organizations, depending upon many factors. These factors include the nature of your products and services, technology requirements, issues of modularity and parts commonality, customer and supplier relationships and involvement, and product and service customization. Responses to Item 6.1 should address the most critical requirements for your business.

N2. Responses to Item 6.1 should include how your customers and key suppliers and partners are involved in your design processes, as appropriate.

N3. Your results of operational improvements in product and service design and delivery processes should be reported in Item 7.5. Your results of improvements in product and service performance should be reported in Item 7.1.

This Item looks at the organization's key product and service design and delivery processes, with the aim of improving your marketplace and operational performance.

The first part of this Item looks at key design processes for products and services and their related production and delivery processes. Organizations must have a process to address key requirements, such as customer/market requirements and new technology:

- Your design approaches could differ appreciably depending upon the nature of your products/services—whether the products/services are entirely new, variants, or involve major or minor process changes. You should consider the key requirements for your products and services. Factors that might need to be considered in design include: safety; long-term performance; environmental impact; "green" manufacturing; measurement capability; process capability; manufacturability; maintainability; supplier capability; and documentation. Effective design also must consider cycle time and productivity of production and delivery processes. This might involve detailed mapping of manufacturing or service processes and redesigning ("reengineering") those processes to achieve efficiency, as well as to meet changing customer requirements.

- Frequently, this process includes capturing information from customer complaint data that are collected using the processes described in Item 3.2a. Immediate access to customer complaint data allows the organization to make design or production changes quickly to prevent problems from recurring.
- Many organizations need to consider requirements for suppliers and/or business partners at the design stage. Overall, effective design must take into account all stakeholders in the value chain. If many design projects are carried out in parallel, or if the organization's products utilize parts, equipment, and facilities that are used for other products, coordination of resources might be a major concern but might offer means to significantly reduce unit costs and time to market.
- Design processes should address key factors, such as cost control and cycle time. The organization should ensure or it has a mechanism in place that encourages learning from past design projects.
- To ensure the design process is efficient, all related activities should be coordinated within the organization. Coordination of design and production/delivery processes involves all work units and/or individuals who will take part in production/delivery and whose performance materially affects overall process outcome. This might include groups, such as R&D, marketing, design, and product/process engineering.
- Design processes should cover all key operational performance requirements and appropriate coordination and testing to ensure effective product/service launch.

The last part of this Item [6.1b] looks at how the organization ensures its production and delivery processes meet key performance requirements consistently:

- As part of the assessment, organizations must identify key production/delivery processes, their key performance requirements, and key performance measures. These requirements and measures are the basis for maintaining and improving your products, services, and production/delivery processes. Organizations should describe the key processes, their specific requirements, and how performance relative to these requirements is determined and maintained.
- Organization should also identify key in-process measurements and customer interactions. These measurements and interactions require the identification of critical points in processes for measurement,

observation, or interaction. These activities should occur at the earliest points possible in processes to minimize problems and costs that may result from deviations from expected performance. Expected performance frequently requires setting performance levels or standards to guide decision making. When deviations occur, corrective action is required to restore the performance of the process to its design specifications. Depending on the nature of the process, the corrective action could involve technical and/or human considerations. Proper corrective action involves changes at the source (root cause) of the deviation. Such corrective action should minimize the likelihood of this type of variation occurring again or anywhere else in the organization. When customer interactions are involved, differences among customers must be considered in evaluating how well the process is performing. This might entail specific or general contingencies, depending on the customer information gathered. This is especially true of professional and personal services.

• Finally, the organization must have a system in place to evaluate and improve production/delivery processes to achieve better processes and products/services. Better performance means not only better quality from your customers' perspective, but better financial and operational performance—such as productivity—from the organization's perspective. A variety of process improvement approaches are commonly used. These approaches include:
  –Sharing successful strategies across the organization;
  –Process analysis and research (for example, process mapping, optimization experiments, and error proofing);
  –Research and development results;
  –Benchmarking;
  –Using alternative technology; and
  –Using information from customers of the processes—within and outside of the organization.

Process improvement approaches might utilize financial data to evaluate alternatives and set priorities. Together, these approaches offer a wide range of possibilities, including complete redesign ("reengineering") of processes.

6.1 Product and Service Processes

How products and services, as well as production/delivery processes, are designed, managed, and improved

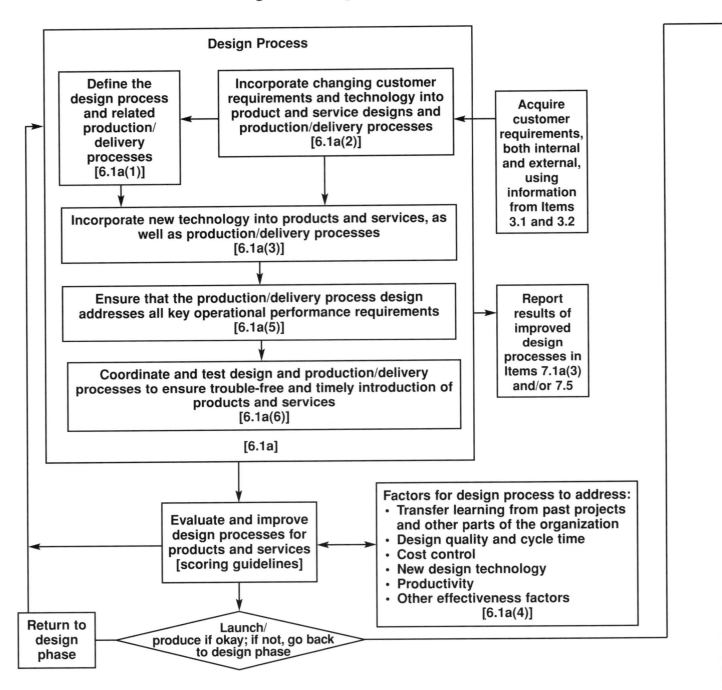

continued on next page

continued from previous page

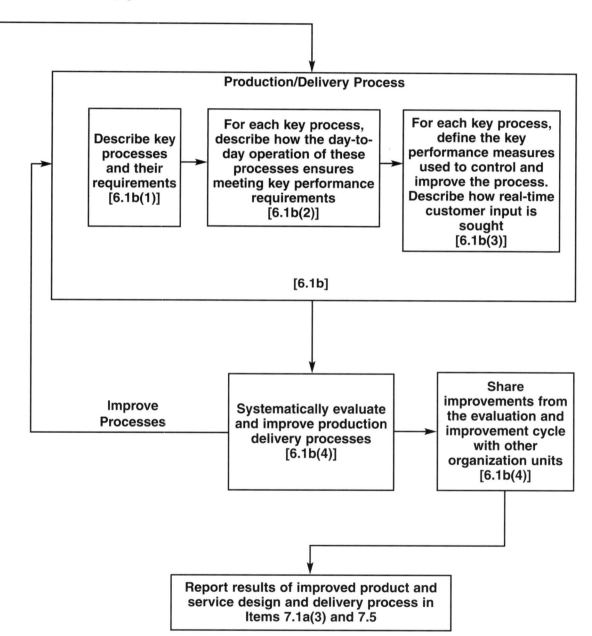

6.1 Product and Service Processes Item Linkages

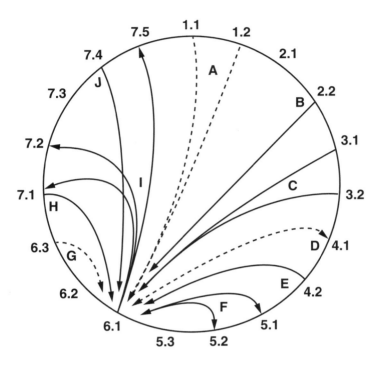

Nature of Relationship	
A	Leaders at all levels [1.1] have a responsibility for ensuring that work processes are designed [6.1a] consistent with organizational objectives, including those relating to public responsibility and corporate citizenship [1.2].
B	Goals, deployed to the workforce [2.2], are used to drive and align actions to achieve improved performance [6.1].
C	Information about customer requirements [3.1] and information from customer hot lines (complaints) through customer-contact employees [3.2a] is used to design or modify products and services to better meet requirements.
D	Critical work processes [6.1] are used to help identify and prioritize benchmarking or comparison targets [4.1]. Benchmarking and comparison data [4.1] are used to improve work processes [6.1].
Continued on next page	

	Nature of Relationship (continued)
E	Priorities for work process improvements [6.1] are set based on performance data analysis [4.2].
F	The design and delivery of new/modified products and services [6.1] often defines new flexible work systems [5.1] and skills to be acquired [5.2] and more flexible work systems [5.1] to implement them. In addition, high-performance, flexible work systems [5.1] and training [5/1] are essential to improving work processes [6.1].
G	Effective management of supplier and partner performance [6.3] can result in improved operations processes [6.1] by reducing error, rework, and delay.
H	Information about customer satisfaction [7.1] is used to target improvement efforts in product and service design and development processes [6.1].
I	Processes ensure that products and services are designed to meet customer requirements; have a trouble-free introduction [6.1a]; and address product and service production and delivery [6.1b], product and service operating performance [7.1a(3) and 7.5], and financial results [7.2].
J	Information about supplier performance [7.4] is essential to the design and implementation of new, modified, or customized products and services [6.1a].

6.1 Product and Service Processes—Sample Effective Practices

A. Design Processes

- A systematic, iterative process (such as quality function deployment) is used to maintain a focus on the voice of the customer and convert customer requirements into product or service design, production, and delivery.
- Product design requirements are systematically translated into process specifications, with measurement plans to monitor process consistency.
- The work of various functions is coordinated to bring the product or service through the design-to-delivery phases. Functional barriers between units have been eliminated organizationwide.
- Concurrent engineering is used to operate several processes (for example, product and service planning, R&D, manufacturing, marketing, supplier certification) in parallel as much as possible, rather than operating in sequence. All activities are closely coordinated through effective communication and teamwork.
- Internal process capacity and supplier capability, using such measures as C_{pk} are reviewed and considered before production and delivery process designs or plans are finalized.
- Market, design, production, service, and delivery reviews occur at defined intervals or as needed.
- Steps are taken (such as design testing or prototyping) to ensure that the production and delivery process will work as designed and will meet customer requirements.
- Design processes are evaluated, and improvements have been made so that future designs are developed faster (shorter cycle time), at lower cost, and with higher quality, relative to key product or service characteristics that predict customer satisfaction.

B. Production/Delivery Processes

- Performance requirements (from Item 6.1a, design processes, and Item 3.1, customer requirements) are set using facts and data and are monitored using statistical or other process control techniques.
- Production and service delivery processes are measured and tracked. Measures (quantitative and qualitative) should reflect or assess the extent to which customer requirements are met, as well as production consistency.

- For processes that produce defects (out-of-control processes), root causes are quickly and systematically identified, and corrective action is taken to prevent their recurrence.
- Corrections are monitored and verified. Improvements are shared throughout the organization.
- Processes are systematically reviewed to improve productivity, reduce cycle time and waste, and increase quality.
- Tools are used—such as flowcharting, work redesign, and reengineering—throughout the organization to improve work processes.
- Benchmarking, competitive comparison data, or information from customers of the process (in or out of the organization) are used to gain insight to improve processes.

6.2 Support Processes (15 points)
Approach/Deployment Scoring

Describe how your organization manages its key support processes.

Within your response, include answers to the following questions:

a. Support Processes

(1) What are your key support processes?

(2) How do you determine key support process requirements, incorporating input from internal and/or external customers, as appropriate? What are the key operational requirements (such as productivity and cycle time) for the processes?

(3) How do you design these processes to meet all the key requirements?

(4) How does your day-to-day operation of key support processes ensure meeting key performance requirements? How do you determine and use in-process measures and/or customer feedback in your support processes?

(5) How do you improve your support processes to achieve better performance and to keep them current with business needs and directions, as appropriate? How are improvements shared with other organizational units and processes, as appropriate?

Notes:

N1. Your support processes are those that support your organization's products/services design and delivery processes, and business operations. This might include information and knowledge management, finance and accounting, facilities management, research and development, administration, and sales/marketing. The key support processes to be included in Item 6.2 are unique to your organization and how you operate. Focus should be on your most important processes not addressed in Items 6.1 and 6.3.

N2. Your results of improvements in key support processes and key support process performance results should be reported in Item 7.5.

This Item looks at the organization's key support processes with the aim of improving overall operational performance. The requirements of this Item are similar to the requirements in Item 6.1.

The organization must ensure its key support processes are designed to meet all operational and customer requirements. To do this, organizations must incorporate input from internal and external customers, as appropriate:

- Support processes are those that support product and/or service delivery but are not usually designed in detail with the products and services. The support process requirements usually do not depend significantly upon product and service characteristics. Support process design requirements usually depend significantly upon internal customer requirements, and they must be coordinated and integrated to ensure efficient and effective linkage and performance.
- Support processes might include finance and accounting, software services, sales, marketing, public relations, information services, personnel, legal services, plant and facilities management, research and development, and secretarial and other administrative services.

As with core operating processes, described in Item 6.1, the organization must ensure that the day-to-day operation of its key support processes consistently meet the key performance requirements. To do this, in-process measures should be defined to permit rapid identification and correction of potential problems. Support processes should develop mechanisms to obtain and use customer feedback to help identify problems and take corrective action.

Finally, organizations should systematically evaluate and improve its key support processes to achieve better performance and to keep them current with changing business needs and directions:

- This Item calls for information on how the organization evaluates and improves the performance of your key support processes. Four approaches to evaluating and improving support processes are frequently used:
- Process analysis and research;
- Benchmarking;
- Use of alternative technology; and
- Use of information from customers of the processes—within and outside the organization.

Together, these approaches offer a wide range of possibilities, including complete redesign (reengineering) of processes.

6.2 Support Processes

How key support processes are designed, managed, and improved

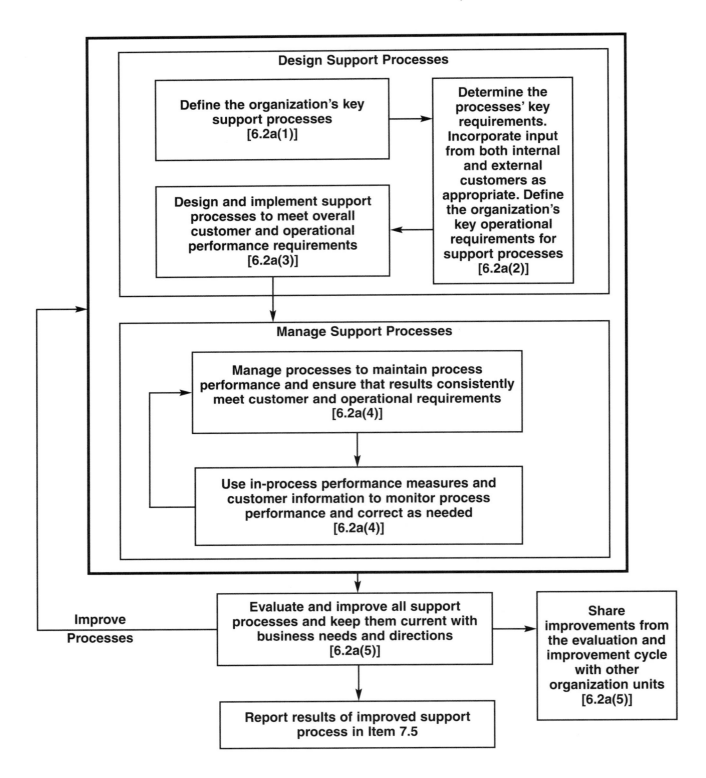

6.2 Support Processes Item Linkages

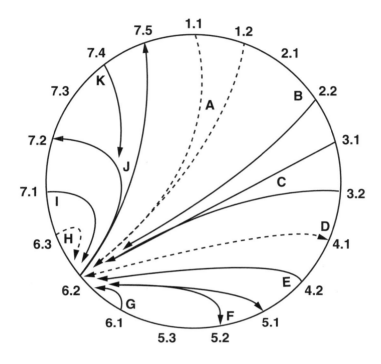

	Nature of Relationship
A	Leaders at all levels [1.1] ensure that support processes [6.2] are aligned with organization priorities, including regulatory and public responsibilities [1.2].
B	Goals deployed to the workforce [2.2] are used to drive and align actions to achieve improved support performance [6.2].
C	Information about customer requirements [3.1] and from customer-contact personnel [3.2a] is used to identify improvement opportunities in support-work processes [6.2].
D	Critical work processes in the support area [6.2] are used to help identify and prioritize benchmarking targets [4.1]. Benchmarking data [4.1] are used to improve support-work processes [6.2].
E	Priorities for support-work processes improvement [6.2] are set based on performance data and analysis [4.2] to enhance operations throughout the organization.

Continued on next page

	Nature of Relationship (continued)
F	High-performance, flexible work systems and effective recognition [5.1] and training [5.2] are essential to improving support-work processes [6.2]. In addition, design and delivery of new/modified support services [6.2] can help define new flexible work systems [5.1] and skills that need to be acquired [5.2].
G	New or modified design or delivery processes for core business areas [6.1] can help define requirements and set priorities for support services [6.2].
H	Effective management of supplier and partner performance [6.3] may be required to improve support-work processes [6.2] by reducing rework, error, and delay.
I	Information about customer satisfaction [7.1] is used to target improvement efforts in support-work processes [6.2].
J	Improved support-work processes [6.2] produce better product and service quality, operational efficiency [7.5], and financial results [7.2].
K	Supplier and partner capabilities, as indicated by performance results [7.4], are considered in the design process for support services [6.2].

6.2   Support Processes—Sample Effective Practices

A. Support Processes

- A formal process exists to understand internal customer requirements, translate those requirements into efficient service processes, and measure their effectiveness.
- Specific improvements in support services are made with the same rigor and concern for the internal and external customer as improvements in core operating processes.
- All key support services are subject to continuous review and improvements in performance and customer satisfaction.
- Systems to ensure process performance are maintained, and customer requirements are met. In-process measures are defined and monitored to ensure early alert of problem.
- Root causes of problems are systematically identified and corrected for processes that produce defects.
- Corrections are monitored and verified. Processes used and results obtained should be systematic and integrated throughout the organization.
- Support processes are systematically reviewed to improve productivity, reduce cycle time and waste, and increase quality. Ideas are shared throughout the organization.
- Work process simplification or improvement tools are used with measurable sustained results.
- Stretch goals are used to drive higher levels of performance.
- Benchmarking, competitive comparison data, or information from customers of the process (in or out of the organization) are used to gain insight to improve processes.

6.3 Supplier and Partnering Processes (15 points)
Approach/Deployment Scoring

Describe how your organization manages its key supplier and/or partnering interactions and processes.

Within your response, include answers to the following questions:

a. Supplier and Partnering Processes

(1) What key products/services do you purchase from suppliers and/or partners?

(2) How do you incorporate performance requirements into supplier and/or partner process management? What key performance requirements must your suppliers and/or partners meet to fulfill your overall requirements?

(3) How do you ensure that your performance requirements are met? How do you provide timely and actionable feedback to suppliers and/or partners? Include the key performance measures and/or indicators and any targets you use for supplier and/or partner assessment.

(4) How do you minimize overall costs associated with inspections, tests, and process and/or performance audits?

(5) How do you provide business assistance and/or incentives to suppliers and/or partners to help them improve their overall performance and to improve their abilities to contribute to your current and longer-term performance?

(6) How do you improve your supplier and/or partner processes, including your role as supportive customer/partner, to keep current with your business needs and directions? How are improvements shared throughout your organization, as appropriate?

Notes:

N1. The term *supplier* refers to other organizations and to units of your parent organization that provide you with goods and services.

N2. Your supplier and partnering processes might include processes for supply chain improvement and optimization, beyond your direct suppliers and partners.

N3. If your organization selects preferred suppliers and/or partners based upon volume of business or criticality of their supplied products and/or services, include your selection criteria in the response.

N4. Your results of improvements in supplier and partnering processes and supplier/partner performance results should be reported in Item 7.4.

This Item [6.3] looks at the organization's key supplier and partnering processes and relationships with the aim of improving suppliers' performance, which should lead to improved internal operating performance:

- Suppliers and partners are receiving increasing focus as many organizations reevaluate their core functions and the potential for better overall performance through strategic use of suppliers and partners. As a result, supply chain management is a growing factor in many organizations' productivity, profitability, and overall business success.

The organization should identify the key products and services it obtains from suppliers and partners to understand the nature and business criticality of these supplies. The organization should also define its key performance requirements and measures for suppliers and partners, and how it uses these requirements and measures to manage and improve their performance. These performance requirements and associated measures should be the principal factors used in making purchases (for example, quality, timeliness, and price):

- In identifying key suppliers and partners, the organization should consider goods and services used in the design, production, delivery, and use of the organization's products and services, that is, consider both upstream and downstream suppliers and partners.

The organization should provide actionable feedback and minimize its costs associated with acceptance testing. The organization is also expected to provide its suppliers and partners with assistance and incentives, which will contribute to improvements in their performance and, in turn, the organization's performance.

- The Item places particular emphasis on the unique relationships that lead to high performance. Electronic data and information exchange is fostering new modes of communication and new types of relationships that can support high performance on the part of suppliers and customers.
- Organizations are encouraged to focus on actions that will not only improve supplier performance, but actions that will enable it to contribute to improved performance. In addition to electronic information exchange, other actions might include:

  –Improving procurement and supplier management processes;

  –Joint planning;

  –Customer-supplier teams;

  –Training;

  –Long-term agreements; and

  –Recognition.

Supplier management planning might include changes in supplier selection, leading to a reduction in the number of suppliers and an increase in preferred supplier and partnership agreements.

Finally, the organization should systematically evaluate and improve its supplier and partnering processes. This should help both the organization and its key suppliers keep current with changing business needs and directions.

6.3 Supplier and Partnering Processes

How the supplier and partnering process, relationship, and performance are designed, managed, and improved

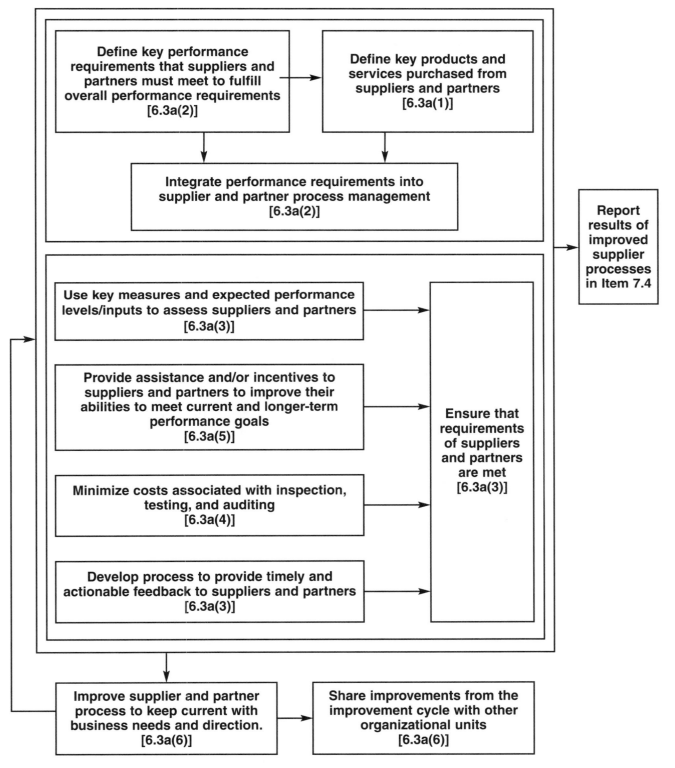

6.3   Supplier and Partnering Processes Item Linkages

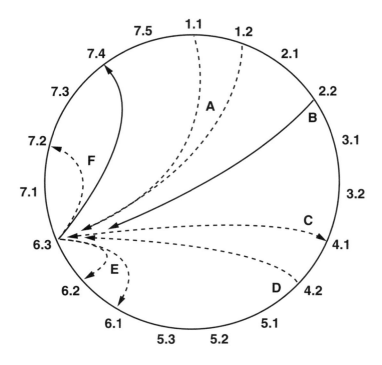

	Nature of Relationship
A	Leaders at all levels [1.1] who interact with suppliers and partners have a responsibility to ensure systematic improvement of performance on key indicators [6.3] and ensure that suppliers and partners do not act in a manner inconsistent with the organization's commitment to the public, including regulatory compliance [1.2].
B	Goals [2.2], deployed through the key supplier chain, are used to drive improved supplier performance [6.3] in critical areas.
C	Problems and issues with supplier performance [6.3] are used to help identify and prioritize benchmarking targets [4.1]. Benchmarking and comparison data [4.1] are used to improve supplier performance initiatives [6.3].
D	Data are analyzed [4.2] to help improve supplier and partner work processes and performance [6.3].
E	Improved supplier performance [6.3] may be required to, and typically helps to, improve work processes [6.1 and 6.2].
F	Improved supplier processes [6.3] result in better supplier performance [7.4] and possibly better financial performance [7.2].

6.3 Supplier and Partnering Processes—Sample Effective Practices

A. Supplier and Partnering Processes

- Performance requirements are clearly defined in measurable terms and communicated to suppliers.
- Decisions on which suppliers are selected are driven by measurable performance characteristics of the supplier's capabilities to achieve high levels of Performance Excellence and exceed requirements, rather than primarily on price.
- Measures of expected supplier performance are in place.
- Data on supplier and partner performance are provided to suppliers frequently so that they can adjust and improve performance rapidly.
- The organization has a system in place to review and improve its own procurement processes and processes for communicating with and selecting suppliers and partners.
- Procedures are in place to improve supplier and partner performance (for example, fewer defective parts, less rework and scrap, faster response time) that include training or certification programs. The organization systematically helps its key suppliers improve their own performance and capabilities. This information is shared throughout the organization.
- Actions are taken to reduce unnecessary costs—such as incoming inspection, testing, or audits—by improving the internal performance systems of suppliers and partners.

7 Business Results—450 Points

The **Business Results** category examines your organization's performance and improvement in key business areas—customer satisfaction, product and service performance, financial and marketplace performance, human resource results, supplier and partner results, and operational performance. Also examined are performance levels relative to competitors.

The Business Results category provides a results focus that encompasses customers' evaluation of the organization's products and services, overall financial and market performance, and results of all key processes and process improvement activities. Through this focus, the Criteria's dual purposes—superior value of offerings as viewed by customers and the marketplace, and superior organizational performance reflected in operational and financial indicators—are maintained. Category 7 thus provides real-time information (measures of progress) for evaluation and improvement of processes, products, and services, aligned with overall organizational strategy:

- Item 4.2 calls for analysis of business results data and information to determine overall organizational performance.

Taken together, business results presents a balanced scorecard of organizational performance. Historically, businesses have been far too preoccupied with financial performance. Many performance reviews focused almost exclusively on achieving (or failing to achieve) expected levels of financial performance. As such, the results were considered "unbalanced":

- Financial results are considered "lagging" indicators of business success. Financial results are the net of all the good processes, bad processes, satisfied customers, dissatisfied customers, motivated employees, disgruntled employees, effective suppliers, and sloppy suppliers, to name a few. By the time financial indicators become available, bad products and dissatisfied customers have already occurred.
- The second most lagging indicator is customer satisfaction. By definition, customers must experience the product or service before they

are in a position to comment on their satisfaction with that product or service. As with financial results, customer satisfaction is affected by many variables, including process performance, employee motivation and morale, and supplier performance.

- On the other hand, leading indicators help organizations predict subsequent customer satisfaction and financial performance. Leading indicators include operational effectiveness and employee well-being and satisfaction. Supplier and partner performance, because it affects an organization's own operating performance, is also a leading indicator of customer satisfaction and financial performance.

Taken together, these measures represent a balance between leading and lagging indicators and enable decision makers to identify problems early and take corrective action.

Category 7 requires organizations to report current levels and improvement trends for the following:

- Customer satisfaction and dissatisfaction and product and service quality broken out by appropriate customer groups and market segments
- Financial and marketplace performance
- Human resource performance
- Supplier and partner performance
- Operational performance

For all of these areas, organizations must include appropriate comparative data to enable examiners to define what "good" means. Otherwise, even though performance may be improving, it is difficult to determine if the level of performance is good or not.

7.1 Customer Focused Results (115 points)
Results Scoring

Summarize your organization's customer focused results, including customer satisfaction and product and service performance results. Segment your results by customer groups and market segments, as appropriate. Include appropriate comparative data.

Provide data and information to answer the following questions:

a. *Customer Focused Results*
   (1) What are your current levels and trends in key measures and/or indicators of customer satisfaction, dissatisfaction, and satisfaction relative to competitors?
   (2) What are your current levels and trends in key measures and/or indicators of customer loyalty, positive referral, customer-perceived value, and/or customer relationship building, as appropriate?
   (3) What are your current levels and trends in key measures and/or indicators of product and service performance?

Notes:

N1. Customer satisfaction and dissatisfaction results reported in this Item should relate to determination methods and data described in Item 3.2.

N2. Measures and/or indicators of customer satisfaction relative to competitors might include objective information and data from your customers and from independent organizations.

N3. Comparative performance of your products and services and product/service performance measures that serve as indicators of customer satisfaction should be included in 7.1a(3).

N4. The combination of direct customer measures/ indicators in 7.1a(1) and 7.1a(2) with product and service performance measures/indicators in 7.1a(3) provides an opportunity to determine cause and effect relationships between your product/service attributes and evidence of customer satisfaction, loyalty, positive referral, etc.

This Item looks at the organization's customer focused performance results with the aim of demonstrating how well the organization has been satisfying your customers and delivering product and service quality that lead to satisfaction and loyalty.

Organizations must provide data to demonstrate current levels, trends, and appropriate comparisons for key measures and/or indicators of:
- Customer satisfaction, dissatisfaction, and satisfaction relative to competitors;
- Customer loyalty (retention), positive referral, and customer-perceived value; and
- Product and service performance relating to key drivers of customer satisfaction and retention.

This Item focuses on the creation and use of all relevant data to determine and help predict the organization's performance as viewed by customers.
- Relevant data and information include: customer satisfaction and dissatisfaction; retention, gains, and losses of customers and customer accounts; customer complaints and warranty claims; customer-perceived value based on quality and price; and awards, ratings, and recognition from customers and independent rating organizations.
- The Item includes measures of product and service performance that serve as indicators of customers' views and decision making relative to future purchases and relationships. These measures of product and service performance are derived from customer-related information gathered in Items 3.1 and 3.2 ("listening posts"). If properly selected, improvements in the features should show a strong, positive correlation with customer and marketplace improvement indicators. The correlation between product/service performance and customer indicators is a critical management tool—a device for defining and focusing on key quality and customer requirements and for identifying product/service differentiators in the marketplace.
- Product/service performance results appropriate for recording in this Item might be based upon one or more of the following:
  - Internal (organizational) measurements;
  - Field performance;
  - Data collected by the organization or for the organization;
  - Customer surveys on product and service performance; and
  - Attributes that cannot be accurately assessed through direct measurement (for example, ease of use) or when variability in customer expectations makes the customer's perception the most meaningful indicator (for example, courtesy).

- The correlation between product/service performance and customer indicators is a critical management tool for defining and focusing on key quality and customer requirements and for identifying product/service differentiators in the marketplace. The correlation might reveal emerging or changing market segments, the changing importance of requirements, or even the potential obsolescence of offerings.

7.1 Customer Focused Results

The organization's customer satisfaction and customer dissatisfaction results using indicators of product/service performance that tend to be predictors of customer satisfaction

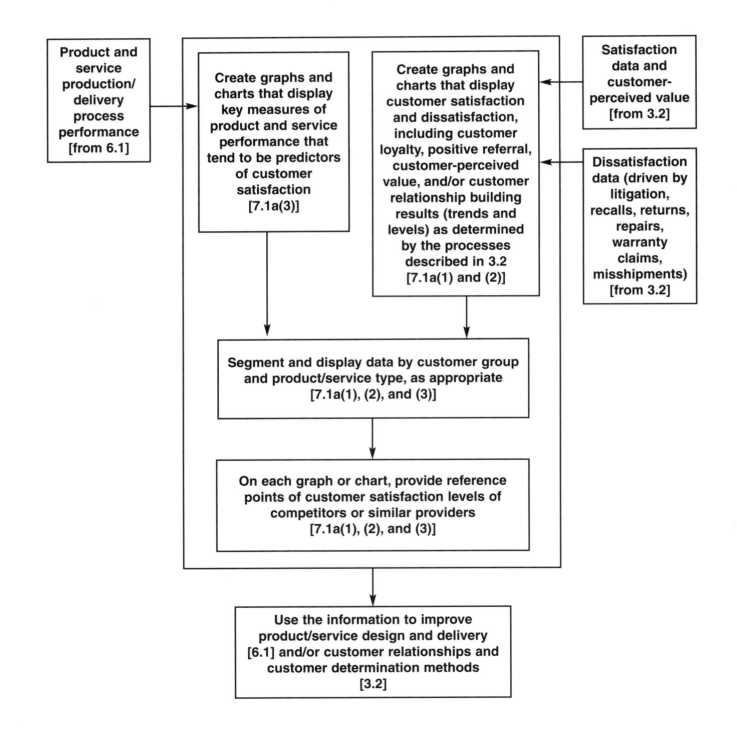

7.1 *Customer Focused Results Item Linkages*

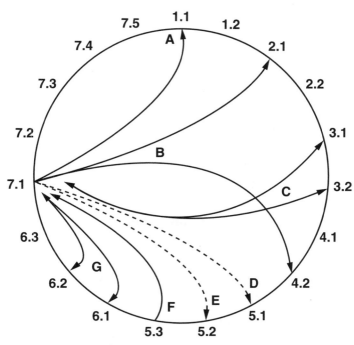

	Nature of Relationship
A	Data on levels of satisfaction of customers and indicators of product/service performance [7.1] are monitored by leaders at all levels [1.1].
B	Data on customer satisfaction and product/service performance indicators [7.1] are collected and used to analyze operational performance [4.2] and for strategic planning [2.1].
C	Processes used to gather intelligence about current customer requirements [3.1], strengthen customer relations [3.2a], and determine customer satisfaction [3.2b] are used to define and produce customer satisfaction results data [7.1]. In addition, customer satisfaction results [7.1] are used to set customer-contact requirements (service standards) [3.2a] and understand basic customer requirements [3.1].
D	Recognition and rewards [5.1b] may be based, in part, on customer satisfaction results [7.1].
E	Customer satisfaction data [7.1] are monitored, in part, to assess training effectiveness [5.2].
F	Systems to enhance employee satisfaction and well-being [5.3] can produce higher levels of customer satisfaction [7.1], especially from customer-contact employees.
G	Data on satisfaction or dissatisfaction of customers [7.1] are used to help design products and services and to improve operational [6.1] and support [6.2] processes. Design and production/delivery processes [6.1] have a direct effect on customer satisfaction/dissatisfaction results [7.1].

7.1 Customer Focused Results—Sample Effective Results

A. Customer Focused Results

- Trends and indicators of customer satisfaction and dissatisfaction (including complaint data), segmented by customer groups, are provided in graph and chart form for all key measures. Multiyear data are provided.
- All indicators show steady improvement. (Indicators include data collected in Area 3.2b, such as customer assessments of products and services, customer awards, and customer retention, and in Item 6.1, such as quality levels and on-time delivery.)
- All indicators compare favorably to competitors or similar providers.
- Graphs and information are accurate and easy to understand.
- Data are not missing.
- Results data are supported by customer feedback, customers' overall assessments of products and services, customer awards, and indicators from design and production/delivery processes of products and services.
- Data are presented concerning customer dissatisfaction for the most relevant product or service quality indicators collected through the processes described in Item 3.2b (some of which may be referenced in the business overview).
- Operational data are presented that correlate with, and help predict, customer satisfaction. These data show consistently improving trends and levels that compare favorably with competitors.

7.2 Financial and Market Results (115 points)
Results Scoring

Summarize your organization's key financial and marketplace performance results, segmented by market segments, as appropriate. Include appropriate comparative data.

Provide data and information to answer the following questions:

a. Financial and Market Results

(1) What are your current levels and trends in key measures and/or indicators of financial performance, including aggregate measures of financial return and/or economic value, as appropriate?

(2) What are your current levels and trends in key measures and/or indicators of marketplace performance, including market share/position, business growth, and new markets entered, as appropriate?

Note:

Aggregate measures, such as return on investment (ROI), asset utilization, operating margins, profitability, profitability by market/customer segment, liquidity, debt to equity ratio, value added per employee, and financial activity measures, are appropriate for responding to 7.2a(1).

This Item looks at the organization's financial and market results, with the aim of understanding marketplace challenges and opportunities.

Organizations should provide data demonstrating levels, trends, and appropriate comparisons for key financial, market, and business indicators. Overall, these results should provide a complete picture of financial and marketplace performance:

- Measures reported in this Item are those usually tracked by senior leaders to assess organization-level performance.
- Appropriate financial measures and indicators might include:
  – Revenue
  – Profits
  – Market position
  – Cash-to-cash cycle time
  – Earnings per share
- Marketplace performance measures might include:
  – Market share
  – Measures of business growth
  – New product and geographic markets entered (including exports)
  – Percent of sales from new products

7.2 Financial and Market Results

Results of improvement efforts using key measures and/or indicators of financial and market performance

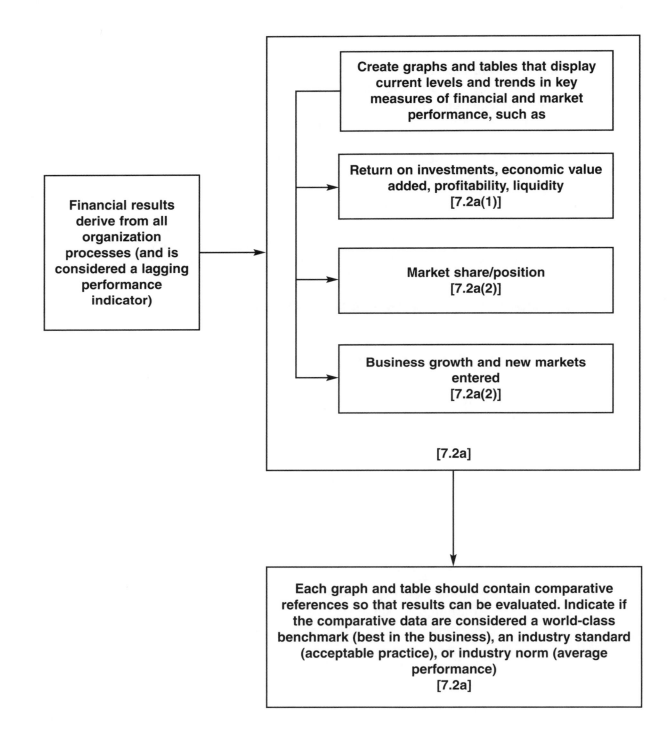

Financial results derive from all organization processes (and is considered a lagging performance indicator)

Create graphs and tables that display current levels and trends in key measures of financial and market performance, such as

Return on investments, economic value added, profitability, liquidity
[7.2a(1)]

Market share/position
[7.2a(2)]

Business growth and new markets entered
[7.2a(2)]

[7.2a]

Each graph and table should contain comparative references so that results can be evaluated. Indicate if the comparative data are considered a world-class benchmark (best in the business), an industry standard (acceptable practice), or industry norm (average performance)
[7.2a]

7.2 Financial and Market Results Item Linkages

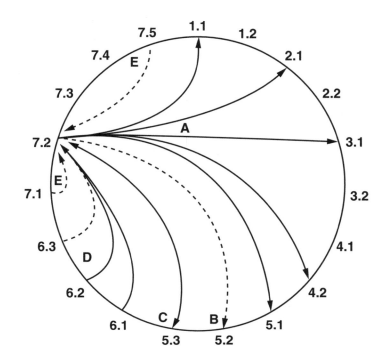

Nature of Relationship	
A	Financial and market results data [7.2] are used for strategic planning [2.1], understanding market requirements [3.1], leadership monitoring and decision making [1.1], and analysis [4.2] and may be used as a basis for compensation, recognition, and reward [5.1].
B	Financial data [7.2] are monitored, in part, to assess training effectiveness [5.2].
C	Employee morale and well-being [5.3] affect financial performance results [7.2], and vice versa.
D	Financial and market results [7.2] are enhanced by improvements in product and service processes [6.1], support processes [6.2], and supplier and partner processes [6.3].
E	Organization-specific results [7.1a(3) and 7.5] form the basis for financial and market results [7.2].

7.2 Financial and Market Results—Sample Effective Results

A. Financial and Market Results

- Key measures and indicators of organization market and financial performance address the following areas:
  - –Effective use of materials, energy, capital, and assets;
  - –Asset utilization;
  - –Market share, business growth, new markets entered, and market shifting;
  - –Return on equity;
  - –Operating margins;
  - –Pretax profit;
  - –Earnings per share;
  - –Generating enough revenue to cover expenses (not-for-profit and public sector); and
  - –Operating within budget (government sector).
- Measures and indicators show steady improvement.
- Important financial and market data are presented.
- Comparative data include industry best, best competitor, and other appropriate benchmarks.

7.3   Human Resource Results (80 Points)
Results Scoring

Summarize your organization's human resource results, including employee well-being, satisfaction, development, and work system performance. Segment your results by types and categories of employees, as appropriate. Include appropriate comparative data.

Provide data and information to answer the following questions:

a. Human Resource Results
  (1) What are your current levels and trends in key measures and/or indicators of employee well-being, satisfaction and dissatisfaction, and development?
  (2) What are your current levels and trends in key measures and/or indicators of work system performance and effectiveness?

Notes:

N1. Results reported in this Item should relate to activities described in Category 5. Your results should be responsive to key process needs described in Category 6, and your organization's action plans and related human resource plans described in Item 2.2.

N2. For appropriate measures of employee well-being and satisfaction, see notes to Item 5.3. Appropriate measures and/or indicators of employee development might include innovation and suggestion rates, courses completed, learning, on-the-job performance improvements, and cross-training.

N3. Appropriate measures and/or indicators of work system performance and effectiveness might include job and job classification simplification, job rotation, work layout, and changing supervisory ratios.

This Item looks at the organization's human resource results, with the aim of demonstrating how well the organization has created, maintained, and enhanced a positive, productive, learning, and caring work environment.

Organizations should provide data demonstrating current levels, trends, and appropriate comparisons for key measures and/or indicators of employee well-being, satisfaction, dissatisfaction, and development. The organization should also provide data and information on the organization's work system performance and effectiveness:

- Results reported might include generic or organization-specific factors.
  - Generic factors might include safety, absenteeism, turnover, satisfaction, and complaints (grievances). For some measures, such as

absenteeism and turnover, local or regional comparisons may be most appropriate.
  – Organization-specific factors related to human research results might include factors that relate to employee well-being and satisfaction. These factors might include extent of training or cross-training, and systems to promote the effectiveness of systems to promote self-directed and empowered employees.
- Results measures reported for work system performance might include improvement in job classification, job rotation, work layout, and local decision making. Results reported might include input data, such as extent of training, but the main emphasis should be on data that show effectiveness of outcomes.

7.3 Human Resource Results

Results of human resource improvement efforts using key measures and/or indicators of such performance

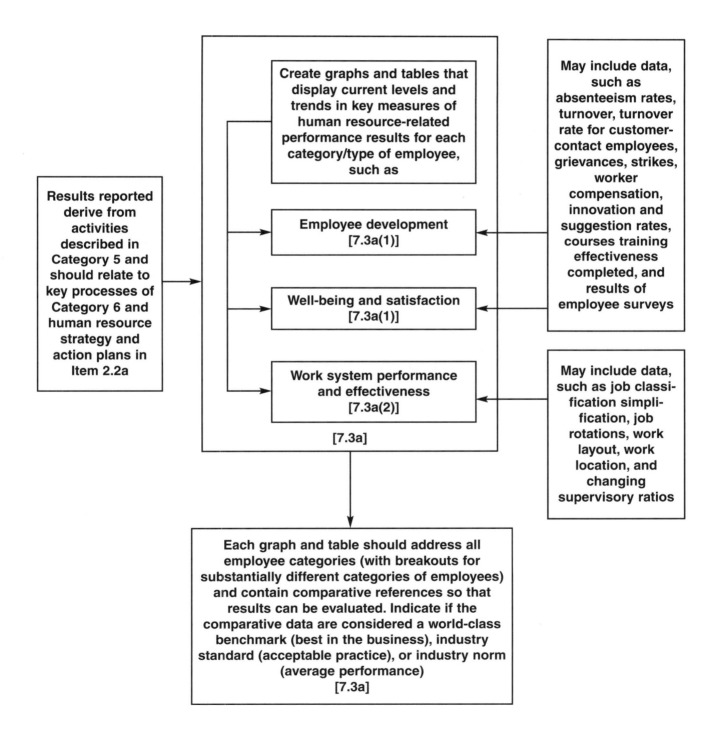

7.3 Human Resource Results Item Linkages

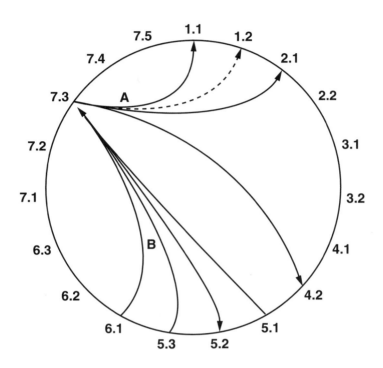

Nature of Relationship	
A	Human resource results data [7.3] are collected and used for planning [2.1], for leader decision making [1.1], to provide feedback to organizational managers [1.1], and analysis [4.2]. In addition, results in the area of employee safety [7.3] are used to ensure compliance with regulatory requirements [1.2].
B	Human resource results derive from and are enhanced by improving work systems and enhancing flexibility and by strengthening employee recognition systems [5.1], training [5.2], and well-being and satisfaction [5.3]. In addition, human resource results data [7.3] are monitored, in part, to assess training effectiveness [5.2].

7.3   Human Resource Results—Sample Effective Results

A. Human Resource Results

- The results reported in Item 7.3 derive from activities described in Category 5 and the Human Resource Plans and Goals from Item 2.2a.
- Multiyear data are provided to show sustained performance.
- All results show steady improvement.
- Data are not missing. If human resource results data are declared important, they are reported.
- Comparison data for benchmark or competitor organizations are reported.
- Trend data are reported for employee satisfaction with working conditions, safety, retirement package, and other employee benefits. Satisfaction with management is also reported.
- Trends for declining absenteeism, grievances, employee turnover, strikes, and worker compensation claims are reported.
- Data are reported for all employee categories.

7.4 Supplier and Partner Results (25 Points)
Results Scoring

Summarize your organization's key supplier and partner results. Include appropriate comparative data.

Provide data and information to answer the following question:

a. Supplier and Partner Results
What are your current levels and trends in key measures and/or indicators of supplier and partner performance? Include your performance and/or cost improvements resulting from supplier and partner performance and performance management.

Note:
Results reported in this Item should relate directly to processes and performance requirements described in Item 6.3.

This Item looks at the organization's supplier and partner results, with the aims of demonstrating how well the organization ensures the quality, delivery, and price of externally provided goods and services and how well suppliers/partners contribute to improved organizational performance.

Organizations should provide data demonstrating current levels, trends, and appropriate comparisons for key measures and/or indicators of supplier and partner performance, including how their performance affects your improved performance. Results managers should emphasize the organization's most critical requirements for business success:

- Suppliers and partners provide goods and services upstream and downstream. Data reported should reflect results by whatever means they occur—via improvements by suppliers and partners and/or through better selection of suppliers and partners.
- For purposes of this Item, providers of goods and services within your parent organization, but not in your own organization, should be included as suppliers or partners.
- Results reported might include:
  - Quality levels
  - Cost savings
  - Total supply chain management costs

- Reductions in waste caused by supplier products and services
- Reductions in inventory
- Reductions in cycle time
- Increases in productivity
- Indicators of better connection and communication, such as those achieved via electronic commerce or data exchanges
- Indicators of supplier and partner performance improvement via external compliance programs, such as ISO 9000

7.4 Supplier and Partner Results

Results of supplier and partner performance improvement efforts using key measures and/or indicators of such performance

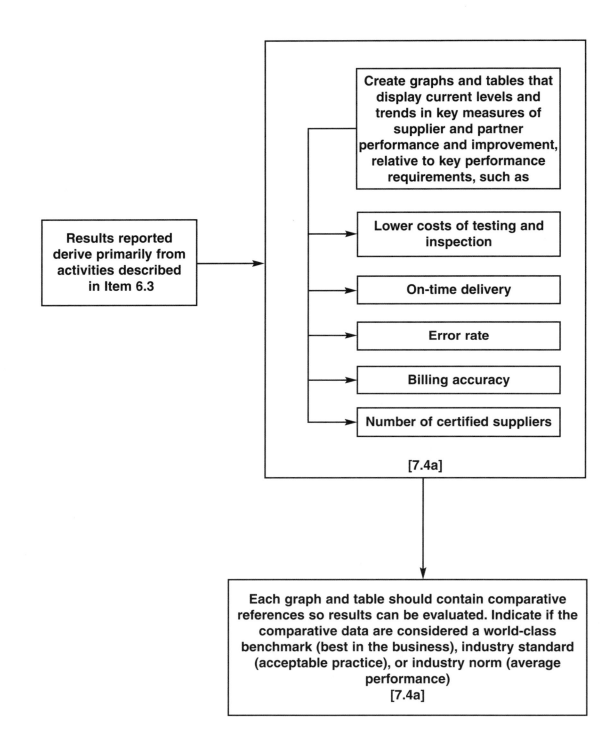

Results reported derive primarily from activities described in Item 6.3

Create graphs and tables that display current levels and trends in key measures of supplier and partner performance and improvement, relative to key performance requirements, such as

Lower costs of testing and inspection

On-time delivery

Error rate

Billing accuracy

Number of certified suppliers

[7.4a]

Each graph and table should contain comparative references so results can be evaluated. Indicate if the comparative data are considered a world-class benchmark (best in the business), industry standard (acceptable practice), or industry norm (average performance)
[7.4a]

7.4 Supplier and Partner Results Item Linkages

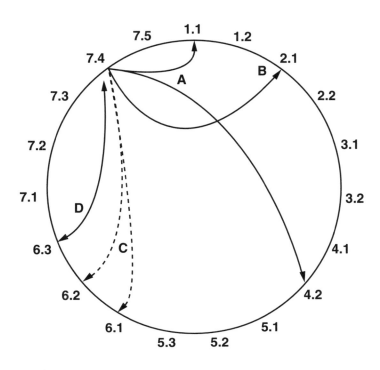

	Nature of Relationship
A	Supplier and partner performance results data [7.4] are collected and used to provide feedback to organizational managers [1.1] for analysis [4.2] relative to supplier and partner performance.
B	Supplier and partner performance results [7.4] are used to determine supplier capabilities during the strategic planning process [2.1].
C	Supplier and partner capabilities as reflected in the results data [7.4] are considered in the product and service processes [6.1] and support processes [6.2] to help determine the overall process capability of the organization to deliver products and services that meet customer requirements.
D	Processes to improve supplier and partner capability [6.3a] affect supplier and partner results [7.4].

7.4   Supplier and Partner Results—Sample Effective Results

A. Supplier and Partner Results

- Results are broken out by key suppliers or supplier types as appropriate. Data are presented using the measures and indicators of supplier performance described in the Business Overview, Item 6.3, and relevant goals in Area 2.2b.
- If the organization's supplier management efforts include factors, such as building supplier partnerships or reducing the number of suppliers, data related to these efforts are included in responses.
- Supplier performance measures include defect rate, on-time delivery, and number of certified suppliers.
- Multiyear data are provided to demonstrate steady improvement.
- Data are not missing. All data declared to be important are reported.
- Comparison data for suppliers of benchmark or competitor organizations are reported.
- Data are broken out by meaningful supplier categories to demonstrate consistent improvement in each category.

7.5   Organizational Effectiveness Results (115 Points)
Results Scoring

Summarize your organization's key operational performance results that contribute to the achievement of organizational effectiveness. Include appropriate comparative data.

Provide data and information to answer the following questions:

a. Organizational Effectiveness Results

(1) What are your current levels and trends in key measures and/or indicators of key design, production, delivery, and support process performance? Include productivity, cycle time, and other appropriate measures of effectiveness and efficiency.

(2) What are your results for key measures and/or indicators of regulatory/legal compliance and citizenship? What are your results for key measures and/or indicators of accomplishment of organizational strategy?

Notes:

N1. Results reported in Item 7.5 should address your key organizational requirements and progress toward accomplishment of your key organizational performance goals as presented in the Business Overview and in Items 1.1, 2.2, 6.1, and 6.2. Include results not reported in Items 7.1, 7.2, 7.3, and 7.4.

N2. Results reported in Item 7.5 should provide key information for analysis (Item 4.2) and review (Item 1.1) of your organizational operational performance and should provide the operational basis for customer results (Item 7.1) and financial and market results (Item 7.2).

N3. Regulatory/legal compliance results reported in Item 7.5 should address requirements described in Item 1.2.

This Item looks at the organization's other key operational performance results, with the aim of achieving organizational effectiveness and key organizational goals.

Organizations should provide data in this Item if it does not belong in Items 7.1, 7.2, 7.3, or 7.4. Results expected in Item 7.5 should report on current levels, trends, and appropriate comparisons for key measures and/or indicators of operational and strategic performance that support the ongoing achievement of results reported in Items 7.1 through 7.4:

- This Item encourages the organization to develop and include unique and innovative measures to track business development and operational improvement. However, all key areas of business and operational performance should be covered by measures that are relevant and important to the organization.
- Measures and/or indicators of operational effectiveness and efficiency might include reduced emission levels, waste stream reductions, by-product use, and recycling; internal responsiveness indicators, such as cycle times, production flexibility, lead times, set up times, and time to market; business-specific indicators, such as innovation rates, product/process yields, and delivery performance to request; third-party assessment results, such as ISO 9000 audits; and indicators of strategic goal achievement.

The organization should also provide data and information on the results of its regulatory/legal compliance and citizenship activities:

- Measures should include environmental and regulatory compliance and noteworthy achievements in these areas, as appropriate. Results also should include indicators of support for key communities and other public purposes.
- If the organization has received sanctions or adverse actions under law, regulation, or contract during the past three years, the incidents and current status should be summarized.

7.5 Organizational Effectiveness Results

**Results of improvement efforts that contribute
to achievement of operational effectiveness**

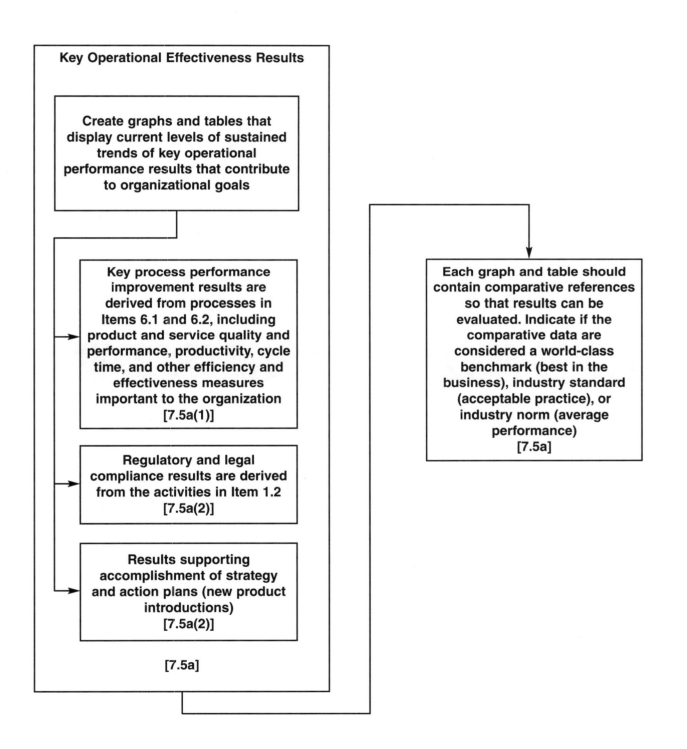

7.5 *Organizational Effectiveness Results Item Linkages*

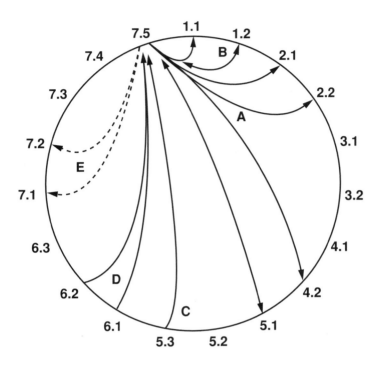

Nature of Relationship	
A	Product and service quality characteristics and operational performance results data [7.5] are collected and used for planning [2.1]; goal setting [2.2]; management; monitoring; and decision making [1.1], analysis [4.2], and reward and recognition determination [5.1]. In addition, processes to improve employee initiative and flexibility [5.1] can enhance performance results [7.5].
B	Regulatory and legal compliance resulting from the activities in Item 1.2 should be reported in 7.5. In addition, these results are monitored to determine if process changes are needed.
C	Employee morale and well-being [5.3] affect product and service quality results [7.5].
D	Designing products and services to meet customer requirements, improved operational performance [6.1], and support performance [6.2] affect product and service quality [7.5].
E	Organization effectiveness results [7.5] provide the basis for financial and market results [7.2] and customer-focused results [7.1].

7.5   Organizational Effectiveness Results—Sample Effective Results

A. Organizational Effectiveness Results

- Indices and trend data are provided in graph and chart form for all operational performance measures identified in Items 6.1, 6.2, and 1.2; relevant organizational goals (2.2); and the key business factors identified in the business overview and not reported elsewhere in Category 7. Multiyear data are reported.
- Most to all indicators show steady improvement.
- Product and service quality measures and indicators address requirements, such as accuracy, timeliness, and reliability. Examples include defect levels; repeat services; meeting product, service delivery, or response times; and availability levels. However, if these measures predict customer satisfaction, they should be moved to Item 7.1.
- Operational performance measures address:
  - Productivity, efficiency and effectiveness, such as productivity indices, human resource utilization, waste reduction, energy efficiency, and product/service design improvement measures
  - Public responsibilities, such as environmental improvements
  - Cycle time reductions
- Comparative data include industry best, best competitor, industry average, and appropriate benchmarks. Data are also derived from independent surveys, studies, laboratory testing, or other sources.
- Data are not missing. (For example, do not show a steady trend from 1992 to 1998, but leave out 1994.)
- Data are not aggregated, since aggregation tends to hide poor performance by blending it with good performance. Break out and report trends separately.

Tips on Preparing a Baldrige Award Application

Applications are put together by every conceivable combination of teams, committees, and individual efforts, including consultants. There is no "right" or "best" way to do it. There are, however, lessons that have been learned and are worth considering because they contribute to people and organizations growing and improving.

The thoughts that follow are intended to generate conversation and learning. They are not intended to present a comprehensive treatment of the subject.

Getting the Fingerprints of the Organization on the Application

How do we put together a "good" application? To be "good" from a technical perspective, it must be both accurate and respond fully to the requirements of the Criteria.

To be effective, the application must be more than technically accurate. The organization must feel a sense of commitment and ownership for the application. Ownership requires a role for people throughout the organization, as well as top leadership. The actual putting of words on paper can be accomplished in a variety of ways. However, ignoring this larger question of ownership exposes the organization to developing a sterile, disjointed, or unrecognizable document that discounts its value as a vehicle of growth.

The Spirit and Values in an Application

Like it or not, the team or individual that is responsible for developing an application will be closely watched by everyone in the organization. The people coordinating the development of the application need to be perceived as "walking the talk." They need to be seen as believers and role models for what is being written. In the midst of the pressure of putting together an application, a few values have to be continuously brought to the forefront:
  • Continuous improvement must be fully embedded in all management processes and work processes.

- The application describes the system that is actually used to run the business. This includes not just a description of the pieces but the linkages among the activities that make the organization function effectively.
- Put your best foot forward, but do not exaggerate—don't perfume the pig.

Core Values and Recurring Themes

In a document as complex and fact-filled as an application, make sure key messages are clearly communicated. There are 11 core values, and the application must address all of them. The organization needs to decide at the onset, what key factors drive business success. These key factors must pop out from each category and tie together the entire application. This is one of the reasons it becomes so important to design and write the overview early and well. Too many applicants ignore the importance of the overview as an organizing tool. The overview must clearly identify those things that are important to the business, its customers, and the future of the business. These selected themes need to serve as a constant reminder as the application is developed. We are often asked, "How many themes should an organization focus on?" The answer really depends on how many the organization actually uses. Try developing three.

Tests for Reasonableness

During the development of an application there are "tests" that need to be conducted periodically with two groups of people: the senior executive team and customer-contact employees.

With senior executive teams, the issue is the rate of growth of those Items undergoing intensive improvement efforts and under the direct sponsorship of senior executives. Every Baldrige application effort uses the occasion to drive significant business process improvements throughout the organization. The development of an application offers an opportunity to review these initiatives. Each initiative is usually an improvement on an existing process and, therefore, a candidate for inclusion in an application to demonstrate progress.

At the customer-contact of front line worker level, the issue is a "reality check." Does the application as written reflect the way the business is run? Several things happen at this level when people are given the opportunity to review a developing application:

- Customer contact and frontline people should get an opportunity to comment on how closely the write-up reflects reality. It provides the writer(s) the opportunity to calibrate their words with reality.
- It forces the customer contact and frontline employee to take a "roof top" view, which can be a learning experience in itself.
- It forces the writer to walk in the shoes of the individual contributor—again learning.

Test the Application

As an application comes together, a question asked by everyone—particularly the leadership team—is, "How well are we doing, what's the score?" Although the real value of an application is continuous improvement, the competitive nature of people also comes to the forefront. After all, it's that spirit that helps drive us to higher levels of excellence. Nurture that spirit.

The best means of getting an objective review is to have people outside the organization who are familiar with the Baldrige process examine the application. It is surprising how differently outsiders sometimes view the workings of the business we have just written about and know so well. The important aspect of this review is obviously the skill of the reviewers or examiners. The value to the organization is threefold:

- Sets expectations and eliminates surprises.
- Provides an opportunity for an early start on improvement initiatives.
- Provides a test of understandability by outsiders, which every application ultimately has to pass.

Take Time to Celebrate/Continuously Improve

Developing an application is tough work. At the end of the day it is (1) a document highlighting the accomplishments and future aspirations of the organization, (2) a plan for getting there, and (3) an operations manual for new people entering the business.

At key milestones in the development of an application, it is important to take time to celebrate the accomplishments just completed. The celebration should be immediate, inclusive, and visible. Such a celebration raises questions within the organization, it raises eyebrows, and it raises expectations—all of which are critical when trying to change and improve the overall performance of the organization. It also presents a perfect opportunity to promote improvement initiatives.

Some Closing Thoughts

In the words of David Kearns, former CEO of Xerox and one of the greatest leaders of Performance Excellence in the United States, "Quality is a journey without an end." Every company today is faced with the struggle to bring about change—and the pace quickens each year. The Baldrige Award is a mechanism that can help focus the energy for change in a most productive manner. Used properly, it can help companies break out of restrictive paradigms and continue on the journey to top levels of Performance Excellence.

The Business Overview

The Business Overview is an outline of your organization. It should address what is most important to the organization, key influences on how it operates, and where it is headed. The Business Overview is a statement of what is relevant and important to your organization and its performance. Many organizations make a mistake in preparing a superficial Business Overview. It is a statement about the organization that helps examiners understand key components of your business. It should be carefully and completely developed and fully address all the required elements. The Business Overview helps you and the examiners focus on key business performance requirements and business results. It is used by the examiners and judges in all stages of application review and during the site visit.

Guidelines for Preparing the Business Overview

The Business Overview consists of five sections:

Basic Description of Your Organization

This section should provide information on the following:
- Your products and services;
- The size and location(s) of your organization and whether it is publicly or privately owned;
- Your organizational culture: purpose, vision, mission, and values, as appropriate;
- Your major markets: local, regional, national, or international; and principal customer types, such as consumers, other businesses, and government;
- Your employee base, including number, types, educational level, bargaining units, and special safety requirements;
- Your major equipment, facilities, and technologies used; and
- Regulatory environment affecting you: occupational health and safety, environmental, financial and product, etc.

If your organization is a subunit of a larger organization, describe:
- The organizational relationship to your "parent" and percent of employees the subunit represents;

- How your products and services relate to those of your "parent" and/or other units of the "parent" organization; and
- Key support services, if any, that your "parent" organization provides.

Customer and Market Requirements

This section should provide information on:

- Key customer and market requirements (for example, on-time delivery, low defect levels, price demands, and after-sales services) for products and services.
- Briefly describe all important requirements, and note significant differences, if any, in requirements among customer groups and/or market segments. (Note any special relationships, such as partnerships, with customers or customer groups.)

Supplier and Partnering Relationships

This section should provide information on:

- Types and numbers of suppliers of goods and services;
- The most important types of suppliers, dealers, and other businesses; and
- Any limitations, special relationships, or special requirements that may exist with some or all suppliers and partners.

Competitive Situation

This section should provide information on:

- Numbers and types of competitors;
- Your position (relative size, growth) in the industry;
- Principal factors that determine competitive success, such as productivity growth, cost reduction, and product innovation; and
- Changes taking place that affect competition, such as growing global competition.

Business Directions

This section should provide information, as appropriate, on:

- Major new thrusts, such as changes in products or entry into new markets or segments;
- New business alliances;
- Introduction of new technologies;
- Changes in strategy; and
- Unique factors.

Page Limit   The Business Overview is limited to five pages.

2000 Criteria Response Guidelines

The guidelines given in this section are offered to assist Criteria for Performance Excellence users in responding most effectively to the requirements of the 19 Criteria Items. Writing an application for the Baldrige Award involves responding to these requirements in 50 or fewer pages.

The guidelines are presented in three parts:
- General Guidelines regarding the Criteria booklet, including how the Items are formatted;
- Guidelines for Responding to Approach/Deployment Items; and
- Guidelines for Responding to Results Items.

General Guidelines

Review the Item format and understand how to respond to the Item requirements.
The Item format shows the different parts of Items, the significance of each part, and where each part is placed. It is especially important to understand the Areas to Address and the Item Notes.

Item requirements are presented in question format, sometimes with modifying statements. Responses to an Item should contain answers to all questions and modifying statements; however, each question need not be separately answered. Responses to multiple questions within a single Area to Address may be grouped as appropriate to the organization. The Appendix to this book contains a restatement of the Criteria in declarative sentences, not questions. Many have found this makes it easier to understand the many different requirements that are embedded in the Criteria.

Start by preparing the Business Overview.
The Business Overview is the most appropriate starting point for writing an application. The Business Overview is intended to help everyone—including Criteria users/application writers and reviewers—to understand what is most relevant and important to the organization's business.

In addition, read the information describing the linkages, sample effective practices, and process flow diagrams presented in this book. In particular, be certain to understand how the various requirements of the Criteria are integrated into a comprehensive management system.

Guidelines for Responding to Approach/Deployment Items

The Criteria focus on key performance results. However, results by themselves offer little diagnostic value. For example, if some results are poor or are improving at rates slower than the competition's, it is important to understand why this is so and what might be done to accelerate improvement.

The purpose of Approach/Deployment Items is to permit diagnosis of the organization's most important processes—the ones that enable fast-paced performance improvement and contribute to key business results. Diagnosis and feedback depend heavily upon the processes and systems that are in place. For this reason, it is important to respond to these Items by providing key process information.

Understand the Meaning of "How"

Items requesting information on approach include questions that begin with the word *how*. Responses should outline key process information, such as methods, measures, deployment, and evaluation/improvement/learning factors. Responses lacking such information, or merely providing an example, are referred to in the Scoring Guidelines as anecdotal information and are worth little to nothing.

Show What and How

Describe your system for meeting the requirements of each Item. Ensure that methods, processes, and practices are fully described. Use flowcharts to help examiners visualize your key processes.

It is important to give basic information about what the key processes are and how they work. Although it is helpful to include who performs the work, merely stating *who* does not permit diagnosis or feedback related to the central issue of *how* the process works. For example, stating that "customer satisfaction data are analyzed by the Customer Service Department" does not permit diagnosis or feedback, because from this information, it is impossible to determine if the approach is systematic, consistently applied, evaluated, refined, or widely used. A meaningful analysis of strengths and opportunities for improvement cannot be provided.

Show That Activities Are Systematic

Ensure that the response describes a systematic approach, not merely an anecdotal example.

Systematic approaches are repeatable, predictable, and involve the systematic use of data and information for evaluation, subsequent improvement, and learning. In other words, the approaches are consistent over time, build in learning and evaluation, and show maturity. Scores above 50 percent rely on clear evidence that approaches are systematic, evaluated, and refined.

Show Deployment

Ensure that the response gives clear and sufficient information on deployment. For example, one must be able to distinguish from a response whether an approach described is used in one, some, most, or all parts of the organization.

Deployment can be shown compactly by using summary tables that outline what is done in different parts of the organization. This is particularly effective if the basic approach is described in a narrative.

Show Focus, Consistency, and Integration

The response demonstrates that the organization is focused on key processes and on improvements that offer the greatest potential to improve business performance and accomplish organization action plans.

There are four important factors to consider regarding integration:
- The Business Overview should make clear what is important;
- The Strategic Planning Category, including the strategic objectives and action plans, should highlight areas of greatest focus and describe how deployment plan and strategy alignment is accomplished;
- Descriptions of organizational-level analysis and review (Items 4.2 and 1.1) should show how the organization analyzes and reviews performance information to set priorities; and
- The Process Management Category should highlight product, service, support, and supplier processes that are key to overall performance.

Integrating systems required in the Approach/Deployment Items and tracking corresponding measures in the Results Items should improve business performance.

Respond Fully to Item Requirements

Ensure that the response fully addresses all important parts of each Item and each Area to Address. Missing information will be interpreted by examiners as a gap in approach and/or deployment. All areas should be addressed and checked in final review. Individual components of an Area to Address may be addressed individually or together.

Cross-Reference When Appropriate

Each Item response should, as much as possible, be self-contained. However, some responses to different Items might be mutually reinforcing. It is then appropriate to refer to the other responses, rather than to repeat information. In such cases, key process information should be given in the Item requesting this information. For example, employee education and training should be described in detail in Item 5.2. References elsewhere to education and training would then reference, but not repeat, this detail.

Use a Compact Format

Applicants should make the best use of the 50 application pages permitted. Use flowcharts, tables, and "bulletized" presentation of information.

Refer to the Scoring Guidelines

The evaluation of Item responses is accomplished by consideration of the Criteria Item requirements and the maturity of the organization's approaches, breadth of deployment, and strength of the improvement process relative to the scoring guidelines. Therefore, applicants need to consider both the Criteria and the scoring guidelines in preparing responses. In particular, remember that in order to score over 50 percent, organizations must demonstrate consistent evaluation and corresponding improvements. The Scoring Guidelines make this requirement applicable to *all* Items in Categories 1 through 6. Even if the details of the Item do not ask for a description of techniques, it will help the examiners give you full credit for your processes if an explanation is provided to show how the processes are evaluated and refined.

Guidelines for Responding to Results Items

The Baldrige Criteria place great emphasis on results. All Results Items remain in Category 7 for 2000. Items 7.1, 7.2, 7.3, 7.4, and 7.5 call for results related to all key requirements, stakeholders, and goals.

Focus on Reporting Critical Results

Results reported should cover the most important requirements for business success highlighted in the Business Overview and the Strategic Planning and Process Management categories, and included in responses to other Items, such as Human Resource Focus (Category 5) and Process Management (Category 6).

Four key requirements for effective presentation of results data include the following:
- Trends show directions of results and rates of change;
- Performance levels show performance on some meaningful measurement scale;
- Comparisons show how trends or levels compare with those of other, appropriately selected organizations; and
- Breadth of results show that all important results are included.

No Minimum Time

No minimum period of time is required for trend data. However, results data might span five years or more for some results. Trends might be much shorter for some of the organization's more recent improvement activities. Because of the importance of showing deployment and focus, new data should be included even if trends and comparisons are not yet well established. However, it may be better to report four quarterly measures covering a one-year period than two measures for beginning and end of year. The four measures help to demonstrate a sustained trend (if one exists).

Compact Presentation

Many results can be reported compactly by using graphs and tables. Graphs and tables should be labeled for easy interpretation. Results over time or compared with others should be "normalized"—presented in a way (such as use of ratios) that takes into account various size factors. For example, reporting safety trends in terms of lost workdays per 100 employees would be more meaningful than total lost workdays, if the number of employees has varied over the time period, or if you are comparing your results to organizations varying in size from yours.

Link Results with Text

Descriptions of results and the results themselves should be close together in the application. Trends that show a significant positive or negative change should be explained. Use figure numbers that correspond to Items. For example, the third figure for Item 7.1 should be 7.1-3. (See the example below.)

The following graph illustrates data an applicant might present as part of a response to Item 7.1, Customer Focused Results. In the Business Overview and in Item 3.1, the applicant has indicated on-time delivery as a key customer requirement.

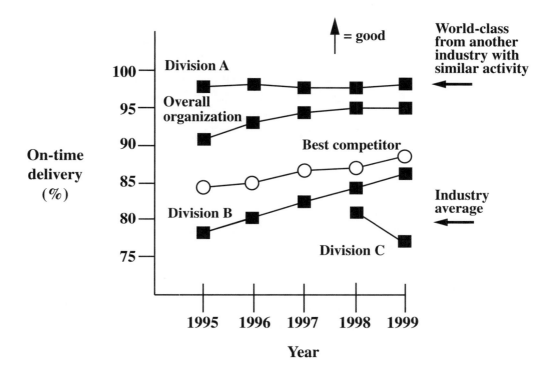

Figure 7.1-3 On-Time Delivery Performance

Using the graph, the following characteristics of clear and effective data presentation are illustrated:

- A figure number is provided for reference to the graph in the text.
- Both axes and units of measure are clearly labeled.
- Trend lines report data for a key business requirement—on-time delivery.
- Results are presented for several years.
- Appropriate comparisons are clearly shown.
- The organization shows, using a single graph, that its three divisions separately track on-time delivery.

- If different segments or components exist, show each as a separate measure. Avoid aggregating data when the segments are meaningful.
- An upward-pointing arrow appears on the graph, indicating that increasing values are "good." (A downward-pointing arrow would indicate that decreasing values are "good.")

To help interpret the scoring guidelines, the following comments on the graphed results in the sample would be appropriate:
- The current overall organization performance level is very good to excellent. This conclusion is supported by the comparison with competitors and with a world-class level.
- The organization exhibits an overall excellent improvement record.
- Division A is the current performance leader—showing sustained high performance and a slightly positive trend. Division B shows rapid improvement. Its current performance is near that of the best industry competitor, but it trails the world-class level.
- Division C—a new division—is having early problems with on-time delivery. The applicant should analyze and explain the early problems in the application text. Its current performance is not yet at the level of the best industry competitor.

Complete Data   Be sure that results data are displayed for all relevant customer, financial, market, human resource, operational performance, and supplier performance characteristics. If you identify relevant performance measures and goals in other parts of the analysis (for example, Items 1.2, 2.1, 2.2, 3.1, 3.2, 4.1, 4.2, 5.1, 5.2, 5.3, 6.1, 6.2, and 6.3), be sure to include the results of these performance characteristics in Category 7. As each relevant performance measure is identified in the assessment process, create a blank chart and label the axes. Define all units of measure, especially if they are industry-specific or unique to the applicant. As data are collected, populate the charts. If expected data are not provided in the application, examiners may assume that the trends or levels are not good. Missing data drive the score down in the same way that poor trends do.

Break Out Data This point, mentioned earlier, bears repeating: avoid aggregating the data. Where appropriate, break data into meaningful components. If you serve several different customer groups, display performance and satisfaction data for each group. As the following graph demonstrates, only one of the three trends is positive, although the average is positive. Examiners will seek component data when aggregate data are reported. Presenting aggregate data instead of meaningful component data is likely to reduce the score.

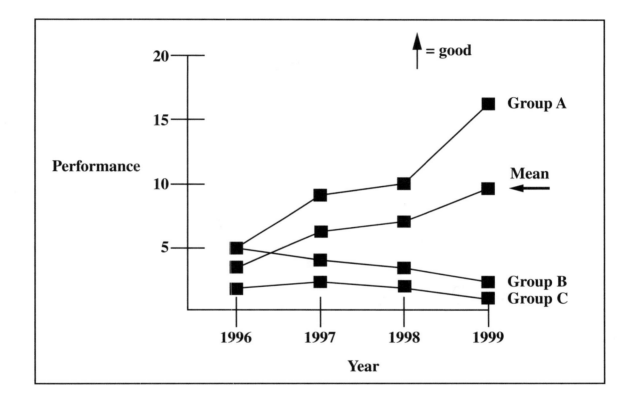

The Importance of Criteria Notes Several Items are followed by one or more notes that offer some insight and explanation about the Item. Often these notes suggest activities or measures that other organizations have used to meet the requirements of the Item. There are many ways to manage a high-performance system that are not included in the notes. Notes are considered suggestions and *not* requirements.

Data and Measures

Comparison data are required for all Items in Category 7. These data are designed to demonstrate how well the organization is performing. To judge Performance Excellence, one must possess comparison data. In the following chart, performance is represented by the line connecting the squares. Clearly, the organization is improving, but how "good" is it? Without comparison data, answering that question is difficult.

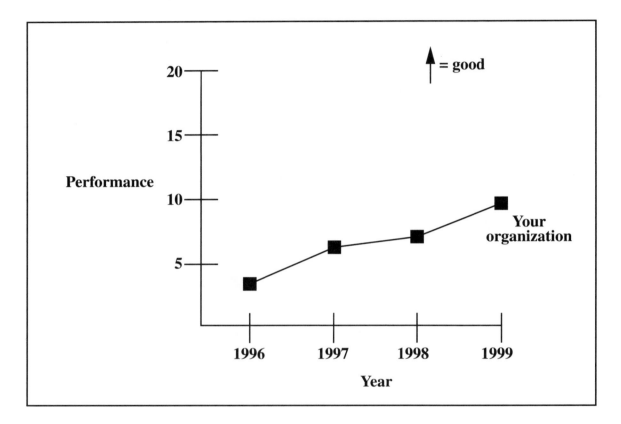

Now consider the chart with comparison data added.

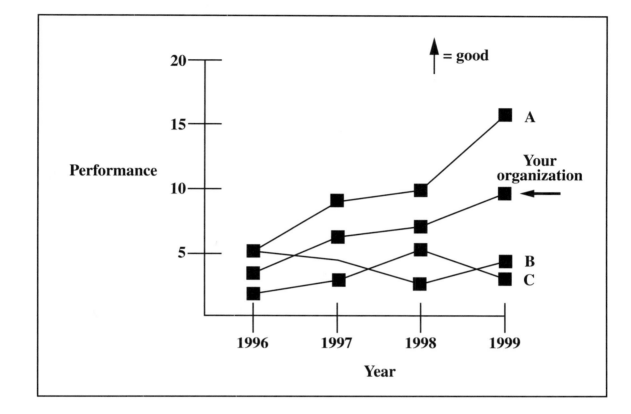

Note the position of three hypothetical comparisons, represented by the letters A, B, and C. Consider the following two scenarios:

- If **A** represents the industry average and both **B** and **C** represent area competitors, examiners would conclude that your organization's performance was substandard, even though it is improving.

- If **A** represents a best-in-class (benchmark) organization and **B** represents the industry average, examiners would conclude that your organizational performance is very good.

In both scenarios, the organizational performance remained the same, but the examiner's perception of it changed based on changes in comparison data.

Measures   Agreeing on relevant measures is a difficult task for organizations in the
early phases of quality and performance improvement. The task is easier if
the following guidelines are considered:

- Clearly define customer requirements. Clear customer requirements
  are easier to measure. Clearly defined customer requirements require
  probing and suggesting. For example, the customer of a new computer wants the equipment to be reliable. After probing to find what
  reliable means, we discover that (1) the customer expects it to
  work all of the time, and if it does stop working, the customer expects
  fast service; (2) prompt appearance at the site; (3) immediate access
  to parts; and (4) the ability to fix it right the first time.

- For each of the four requirements defined, identify a measure. For
  example, mean time between failures is one indicator of reliability, but
  it does not account for all of the variation in customer satisfaction.
  Since the customer is concerned with run time, we must assess how
  long it took the repair technician to arrive at the site, diagnose the
  problem, and fix it. Measures include *time in hours, days,* and *weeks*
  between failures; *time in minutes* between the service call and the
  computer regaining capability (time to fix); *time in minutes* waiting for
  parts; and the associated costs in terms of cash and worker effort.

- Collect and report data. Several charts might be required to display
  these factors, or one chart with several lines.

Scoring System

The scoring of responses to Criteria Items (Items) and Award applicant feedback are based on three evaluation dimensions:
- Approach,
- Deployment, and
- Results.

Criteria users need to furnish information relating to these dimensions. Specific factors for these dimensions are described as follows:

Approach
Approach refers to how you address the Item requirements—the method(s) used. The factors used to evaluate approaches include:
- Appropriateness of the methods to the requirements;
- Effectiveness of use of the methods. Degree to which the approach:
  - Is systematic, integrated, and consistently applied;
  - Embodies evaluation/improvement/learning cycles; and
  - Is based on reliable information and data.
- Alignment with organizational needs; and
- Evidence of innovation.

Deployment
Deployment refers to the extent to which your approach is applied to all requirements of the Item. The factors used to evaluate deployment include:
- Use of the approach in addressing Item requirements relevant to your organization; and
- Use of the approach by all appropriate work units.

Results
Results refers to outcomes in achieving the purposes given in the Item. The factors used to evaluate results include:
- Current performance;
- Performance relative to appropriate comparisons and/or benchmarks;
- Rate, breadth, and importance of performance improvements; and
- Linkage of results measures to key customer, market, process, and action plan performance requirements identified in the Business Overview and in Approach/Deployment Items.

Item Classification and Scoring Dimensions are classified according to the kinds of information and/or data you are expected to furnish relative to the three evaluation dimensions. The two types of Items and their designations are:

1. Approach/Deployment (for all Items in Categories 1–6)
2. Results (for all Items in Category 7)

Approach and deployment are linked to emphasize that descriptions of approach should always indicate the deployment—consistent with the specific requirements of the Item. Although approach and deployment dimensions are linked, feedback to award applicants reflects strengths and/or opportunities for improvement in either or both dimensions.

Results Items call for data showing performance levels and trends on key measures and/or indicators of organizational performance. However, the evaluation factor, "breadth" of performance improvements, is concerned with how widespread your improvement results are. This is directly related to the deployment dimension. That is, if improvement processes are widely deployed, there should be corresponding results. A score for a Results Item is thus a weighted composite based upon overall performance, taking into account the breadth of improvements and their importance. In order to evaluate the "goodness" of the result, comparative data must be provided.

Importance as a Scoring Factor

The three evaluation dimensions previously described are critical to evaluation and feedback. However, evaluation and feedback also considers the importance of your reported Approach, Deployment, and Results to your key business factors. The areas of greatest importance should be identified in the Business Overview and in the narrative for Items such as 2.1 (Strategy Development), 2.2 (Strategy Deployment), 3.1 (Customer and Market Knowledge), 3.2 (Customer Satisfaction and Relationship), 4.1 (Measurement of Organizational Performance), 5.1 (Work Systems), 5.3 (Employee Well-being and Satisfaction), 6.1 (Product and Service Processes), and 7.5 (Organizational Effectiveness Results). Your key customer requirements and key strategic objectives and action plans are particularly important.

Assignment of Scores to Your Responses

Baldrige Award examiners observe the following guidelines in assigning scores to applicants' responses:

- All Areas to Address should be included in the Item response. Also, responses should reflect what is most important to the organization.
- In assigning a score to an Item, an examiner first decides which scoring

range (for example, 50 percent to 60 percent) best fits the overall Item response. Overall "best fit" does not require total agreement with each of the statements for that scoring range. Actual score within the range depends upon an examiner's judgment of the closeness of the Item response in relation to the statements in the next higher and next lower scoring ranges.

- An Approach/Deployment Item score of 50 percent represents an approach that meets the objectives of the Item and that is deployed to the principal activities and work units covered in the Item. Higher scores reflect maturity (cycles of improvement), integration, and broader deployment.

- A Results Item score of 50 percent represents a clear indication of improvement trends and/or good levels of performance in the principal results areas covered in the Item. Higher scores reflect better improvement rates and/or levels of performance and better comparative performance, as well as broader coverage.

Approach/Deployment	Results
0%	• No systematic approach evident; anecdotal information	• No results or poor results in areas reported
10% to 20%	• Beginning of a systematic approach to the basic purposes of the Item • Major gaps exist in deployment that would inhibit progress in achieving the basic purposes of the Item • Early stages of a transition from reacting to problems to a general improvement orientation	• Some improvements and/or early good performance levels in a few areas • Results not reported for many to most areas of importance to the organization's key business requirements
30% to 40%	• An effective, systematic approach, responsive to the basic purposes of the Item • Approach is deployed, although some areas or work units are in early stages of deployment • Beginning of a systematic approach to evaluation and improvement of basic Item processes	• Improvements and/or good performance levels in many areas of importance to the organization's key business requirements • Early stages of developing trends and obtaining comparative information • Results reported for many to most areas of importance to the organization's key business requirements
50% to 60%	• An effective, systematic approach, responsive to the overall purposes of the Item • Approach is well deployed, although deployment may vary in some areas or work units • A fact-based, systematic evaluation and improvement process is in place for basic Item processes • Approach is aligned with basic organizational needs identified in the other Criteria categories	• Improvement trends and/or good performance levels reported for most areas of importance to the organization's key business requirements • No pattern of adverse trends and no poor performance levels in areas of importance to the organization's key business requirements • Some trends and/or current performance levels—evaluated against relevant comparisons and/or benchmarks—show areas of strength and/or good to very good relative performance levels • Business results address most key customer, market, and process requirements
70% to 80%	• An effective, systematic approach, responsive to the multiple requirements of the Item • Approach is well-deployed, with no significant gaps • A fact-based, systematic evaluation and improvement process and organizational learning/sharing are key management tools; clear evidence of refinement and improved integration as a result of organizational-level analysis and sharing • Approach is well-integrated with organizational needs identified in the other Criteria categories	• Current performance is good to excellent in areas of importance to the organization's key business requirements • Most improvement trends and/or current performance levels are sustained • Many to most trends and/or current performance levels—evaluated against relevant comparisons and/or benchmarks—show areas of leadership and very good relative performance levels • Business results address most key customer, market, process, and action plan requirements
90% to 100%	• An effective, systematic approach, fully responsive to all the requirements of the Item • Approach is fully deployed without significant weaknesses or gaps in any areas or work units • A very strong, fact-based, systematic evaluation and improvement process and extensive organizational learning/sharing are key management tools; strong refinement and integration, backed by excellent organizational-level analysis and sharing • Approach is fully integrated with organizational needs identified in the other Criteria categories	• Current performance is excellent in most areas of importance to the organization's key business requirements • Excellent improvement trends and/or sustained excellent performance levels in most areas • Evidence of industry and benchmark leadership demonstrated in many areas • Business results fully address key customer, market, process, and action plan requirements

Supplementary Scoring Guidelines

Author's note: Many examiners and organizations have found the official scoring guidelines to be vague, although they have been improved considerably this year. The guidelines, presented in 20 percent increments, may increase the difficulty of reaching consensus on a score and increase scoring variation. To resolve this problem, I developed the following supplemental scoring guidelines. Many state award programs have used these guidelines for several years and found that they make the consensus process easier and produce comparable scores.

Approach/
Deployment

1. For each Approach/Deployment Item, first determine the appropriate level on the approach scale. This sets the upper possible score the applicant may receive on the Item.
2. Then read the corresponding level on the deployment scale. For example, if the approach level is 40 percent, read the 40 percent standard on the deployment scale where one would expect "several work units are in the early stages of deployment," and "progress in achieving the primary purposes of the Item is not inhibited." If that is the case, the final score is 40 percent.
3. However, if the deployment score is lower than the approach score, then it establishes the lower range of possible final scores for the Item. The actual final score will be between the low and high scores. For example, if "many major gaps exist and progress is significantly inhibited," the lowest possible score would be 10 percent. This final score must be between 40 and 10 percent (for example, 10, 20, 30, or 40 percent).
4. Never increase an approach score based on better deployment.
5. Scoring Approach/Deployment Items are presented on the pages immediately following this scoring section.

Results

1. For Results Items, base your assessment only on the standards described on the results scale. *Do not consider approach or deployment standards at all.*
2. Determine the extent to which performance results are positive, complete, and at high levels relative to competitors or similar providers or an industry standard.
3. To determine the extent to which all important results are reported, examiners should develop a list of the key measures the applicant indicates are important. Start with the measures listed in the overview section. Then add to the key measures list based on key data reported in Item 2.1 and the goals in 2.2, as well as measures that may be mentioned in Categories 5 and 6. Key measures can be reported anywhere in an application.

Score	Approach	Deployment
0%	No systematic approach evident; anecdotal information.	Anecdotal, undocumented.
10%	Early beginning of a systematic approach consistent with the basic purposes of the Item is somewhat evident. Mostly reactive approach to problems. Many key requirements of the Item not addressed. In the earliest stages of transitioning from reacting to problems to a general improvement orientation.	Many major gaps exist in deployment. Progress in achieving basic purposes of Item is significantly inhibited.
20%	A partially systematic but beginning approach consistent with the basic purposes of the Item is evident. Generally reactive to problems. Some key requirements of the Item not addressed. In the early stages of transitioning from reacting to problems to a general improvement orientation.	Some major gaps exist in deployment. Progress in achieving basic purposes of Item is noticeably inhibited.
30%	An effective systematic approach responsive to the basic purposes of the Item is somewhat evident. A few key requirements of the Item not addressed. Beginning of a systematic approach to evaluation but little, if any, improvement of basic Item processes is evident. Random improvements may have been made.	The approach is generally deployed although several units are in the earliest stages of deployment. Progress in achieving primary purposes of Item is minimally inhibited.
40%	An effective systematic approach responsive to the basic purposes of the Item is clearly in place. Several minor requirements of the Item are not addressed. Beginning of a systematic approach to evaluation and improvement of basic Item processes is evident. Random improvements may have been made.	The approach is deployed, although several units are in the early stages of deployment. Progress in achieving primary purposes of Item is not inhibited.
50%	An effective systematic approach responsive to the overall purposes of the Item is fully developed. Some minor requirements of the Item are not addressed. Fact-based improvement system is in place for basic Item processes that includes process evaluation in key areas (but no refinements are in place). Random improvements may have been made. The approach is aligned with some basic organization needs identified in the other Criteria categories.	No major gaps in deployment exist that inhibit progress in achieving primary purposes of Item, although deployment may vary in some areas or work units. Some work units still in the early stages of deployment.
60%	An effective systematic approach responsive to the overall purposes of the Item is clearly in place. A few minor requirements of the Item not addressed. Fact-based improvement system is in place for the basic requirements of the Item, including at least one evaluation cycle completed, and some systematic refinement based on the evaluation in key areas. The approach is aligned with most basic organization needs identified in the other Criteria categories.	No major gaps in deployment exist that inhibit progress in achieving primary purposes of Item, although deployment may vary in some areas or work units. A few work units still in the early stages of deployment.
70%	An effective systematic approach, responsive to many of the multiple purposes of the Item is clearly in place. Organizational learning and sharing are frequently used management tools at many levels. Some systematic evaluation and evidence of refinements and improved integration result from organization-level analysis and learning. The approach is aligned and well integrated with many overall organization needs identified in the other Criteria categories.	Approach is well deployed with some work units in the middle to advanced. No significant gaps exist that inhibit progress in achieving the purposes of Item.
80%	An effective systematic approach, responsive to most of the multiple purposes of the Item is clearly in place. Organizational learning and sharing are frequently used management tools at most levels. Considerable systematic evaluation and evidence of refinements and integration result from organization-level analysis and learning. The approach is aligned and well integrated with most overall organization needs identified in the other Criteria categories.	Approach is well deployed with many work units in the advanced stages. No gaps exist that inhibit progress in achieving the purposes of Item.
90%	An effective systematic approach, responsive to all of the multiple purposes of the Item is in place. Considerable systematic evaluation and extensive refinements and improved organizational sharing and learning are key management tools at most levels. Some innovative processes are evident with strong refinement and integration supported by substantial organization-level analysis and sharing.	Approach is fully deployed with most work units in the advanced stages. No significant gaps or weaknesses exist in any areas or work units.
100%	An effective systematic approach, fully responsive to all of the multiple purposes of the Item is clearly in place. Considerable systematic evaluation and clear evidence of extensive refinements and improved organizational sharing and learning are key management tools at all levels. Many innovative processes are evident, with strong refinement and integration supported by excellent organization-level analysis and sharing.	Approach is fully deployed with most to all work units in the advanced stages. No significant gaps or weaknesses exist in any areas or work units.

Approach/Deployment Terms

Systematic   Look for evidence of a system—a repeatable, predictable process that is used to fulfill the requirements of the Item. Briefly describe the system. Be sure to explain *how* the system works. You must communicate the nature of the system to people who are not familiar with it. This is essential to achieve the 30 percent scoring threshold.

Integrated   Determine the extent to which the system is integrated or linked with other elements of the overall management system. Show the linkages across categories for key themes, such as those displayed earlier for each Item.

Consider the extent to which the work of senior leaders is integrated. For example:

1. Senior executives (Item 1.1) are responsible for shaping and communicating the organization's vision, values, and expectations throughout the leadership system and workforce.

2. They develop relationships with key customers (Item 3.2) and monitor customer satisfaction (Item 7.1) and organization performance (Items 7.2, 7.3, 7.4, and 7.5).

3. This information, when properly analyzed (Item 4.2), helps them plan better and make more informed decisions to optimize customer satisfaction and operational and financial performance.

4. With this in mind, senior executives participate in strategy development (Item 2.l) and ensure the alignment of the workplace to achieve organizational goals (Item 2.2).

5. Senior executives may also become involved in supporting new structures to improve employee performance (Item 5.1), training effectiveness (Item 5.2), and employee well-being and satisfaction (Item 5.3).

Similar relationships (linkages) exist between other Items. Highlight these linkages to demonstrate integration.

Prevention-Based   Prevention-based systems are characterized by actions to minimize or prevent the recurrence of problems. In an ideal world, all systems would produce perfect products and flawless service. Since that rarely happens, high-performing organizations are able to act quickly to recover from a problem (fight the fire) and then take action to identify the root cause of the problem and prevent it from surfacing again. The nature of the problem, its root cause, and appropriate corrective action is communicated to all relevant employees so that they can implement the corrective action in their area before the problem arises.

Continuous Improvement

Continuous improvement is a bedrock theme. It is the method that helps organizations keep their competitive edge. Continuous improvement involves evaluation and improvement of processes crucial to organizational success. Evaluation and improvement completes the high-performance management cycle. Continuous improvement evaluations can be complex, data-driven, statistical processes or as simple as a focus group discussing what went right, what went wrong, and how it can be done better. The key to optimum performance lies in the pervasive evaluation and improvement of all processes. By practicing systematic, pervasive, continuous improvement, time becomes the organization's ally. Consistent evaluation and refinement practices with correspondingly good deployment can drive the score to 60 percent or 70 percent, and higher.

Complete

Each Item contains one or more areas to address. Many areas to address contain several parts. Failure to address all areas and parts can push the score lower. If an area to address or part of an area does not apply to your organization, it is important to explain why. Otherwise, examiners may conclude that the system is incomplete.

Anecdotal

If your assessment describes a process that is essentially anecdotal and does not systematically address the Criteria, it is worth very little (0 to 10 points).

Deployment

The extent to which processes are widely used by organization units affects scoring. For example, a systematic approach that is well integrated, evaluated consistently, and refined routinely may be worth 70 percent to 90 percent. However, if that process is not in place in all key parts of the organization, the 70 percent to 90 percent score will be reduced, perhaps significantly, depending on the nature and extent of the gap.

Major gaps are expected to exist at the 0 to 20 percent level. At the 30 percent and higher levels, no major gaps exist, although some units may still be at the early stages of development. At the 70 percent to 80 percent level, no major gaps exist and the approach is well integrated with organizational needs identified in other parts of the Criteria.

Summary

For each Item examined, the process is rated as follows:
- Anecdotal: 0 to 10 percent
- Systematic: 10 percent to 30 percent
- Fully developed: 40 percent
- Prevention-based and evaluated: 50 percent
- Integrated: 50 percent to 100 percent
- Refined: 60 percent to 80 percent
- Widely used, with no gaps in deployment: 70+ percent

Systematic, integrated, prevention-based, and continuously improved systems that are widely used are generally easier to describe than undeveloped systems. Moreover, describing numerous activities or anecdotes does not convince examiners that an integrated, prevention-based system is in place. In fact, simply describing numerous activities and anecdotes suggests that an integrated system does not exist. However, by tracing critical success threads through the relevant Items in the Criteria, the organization demonstrates that its system is integrated and fully deployed.

To demonstrate system integration, pick several critical success factors and show how the organization manages them. For example, trace the leadership focus on performance:

- Identify performance-related data that are collected to indicate progress against goals (Item 4.1).
- Show how performance data are analyzed (Item 4.2) and used to set work priorities (Item 1.1).
- Show how performance effectiveness is considered in the planning process (Item 2.1) and how work at all levels is aligned to increase performance (Item 2.2).
- Demonstrate the impact of human resource management (Item 5.1) and training (Item 5.2) on performance, and show how both tie to the strategy and human resource plans (Item 2.2).
- Show how design, development, production, delivery, and support processes (Items 6.1 and 6.2) are enhanced to improve results.
- Report the results of improved performance (Items 7.1, 7.2, 7.3, 7.4, and 7.5).
- Determine how improved performance affects customer satisfaction levels (Item 7.1).
- Show how customer concerns (Item 3.1 and 3.2) are used to drive the selection of key measures (Item 4.1) and affect design and delivery processes (Item 6.1).

Note that the application is limited to 50 pages, not including the 5-page Business Overview. This may not be sufficient to describe in great detail the approach, deployment, results, and systematic integration of all of your critical success factors, goals, or key processes. Thus, you must pick the most important few, indicate them as such, then thoroughly describe the threads and linkages throughout the application.

Self-Assessments of Organizations and Management Systems

Baldrige-based self-assessments of organization performance and management systems take several forms, ranging from rigorous and time intensive, to simple and somewhat superficial. This section discusses the various approaches to organizational self-assessment and the pros and cons of each. Curt Reimann, the first director of the Malcolm Baldrige National Quality Award Office and the closing speaker for the 10th Quest for Excellence Conference, spoke of the need to streamline assessments to get a good sense of strengths, areas for improvement, and the vital few areas to focus leadership and drive organizational change. Three distinct types of self-assessment will be examined: the written narrative, the Likert scale survey, and the behaviorally anchored survey.

Full-Length Written Narrative

The Baldrige application development process is the most time-consuming organizational self-assessment process. To apply for the Baldrige Award, applicants must prepare a 50-page written narrative to address the requirements of the Performance Excellence Criteria. In the written self-assessment, the applicant is expected to describe the processes and programs it has in place to drive Performance Excellence. The Baldrige application process serves as the vehicle for self-assessment in most state-level quality awards. The process has not changed since the national quality award program was created in 1987 (except for reducing the maximum page limit from 85 to 50 pages).

Over the years, three methods have been used to prepare the full-length, comprehensive written narrative self-assessment:

- The most widely used technique involves gathering a team of people to prepare the application. The team members are usually assigned one of the seven Categories and asked to develop a narrative to address the Criteria requirements of that category. The category writing teams are frequently subdivided to prepare responses Item by Item. After the initial draft is complete, an oversight team consolidates the narrative and tries to ensure processes are linked and integrated throughout. Finally, top leaders review and scrub the written narrative to put the best spin on the systems, processes, and results reported.

- Another technique is similar to that previously described. However, instead of subdividing the writing team according to the Baldrige categories, the team remains together to write the entire application. In this way, the application may be more coherent and the linkages between business processes are easier to understand. This approach also helps to ensure the consistency and integrity of the review processes. However, with fewer people involved, the natural "blind spots" of the team may prevent a full and accurate analysis of the management system. Finally, as with the method previously described, top leaders review and scrub the written narrative.
- The third method of preparing the written narrative is the least common and involves one person writing for several days to produce the application. Considering the immense amount of knowledge and work involved, it is easy to understand why the third method is used so rarely.

With all three methods, external experts are usually involved. Baldrige Award recipients usually reported they hired consultants to help them finalize their application by sharpening its focus and clarifying linkages.

Pros:

- Baldrige-winning organizations report that the discipline of producing a full-length written self-assessment (Baldrige application) helped them learn about their organization and identify areas for improvement before the site visit team arrived. The written narrative self-assessment process clearly helped focus leaders on their organization's strengths and areas for improvement—provided that a complete and honest assessment was made.
- The written narrative self-assessment also provides rich information to help examiners conduct a site visit (the purpose of which is to verify and clarify the information contained in the written self-assessment).

Cons:

- Written narrative self-assessments are extremely time and labor intensive. Organizations that use this approach for Baldrige or state applications or for internal organizational review, report that it requires between approximately 2000 and 4000 hours of effort—sometimes much more. People working on the self-assessment are diverted from other tasks during this period.
- Because the application is closely scrutinized and carefully scrubbed and because of page limits, it may not fully and accurately describe the actual management processes and systems of the organization.

Decisions based on misleading or incomplete information may take the organization down the wrong path.

- Although the written self-assessment provides information to help guide a site visit, examiners cannot determine the depth of deployment because only a few points of view are represented in the narrative.
- Finally and perhaps most importantly, the discipline and knowledge required to write a meaningful narrative self-assessment is usually far greater than that possessed within the vast majority of organizations. Even the four 1997 Baldrige winners hired expert consultants to help them prepare and refine their written narrative.

Short Written Narrative

Two of the most significant obstacles to writing a useful full-length written narrative self-assessment are poor knowledge of the Performance Excellence Criteria and the time required to produce a meaningful assessment. If people do not understand the Criteria, it takes significantly longer to prepare a written self-assessment. In fact, the amount of time required to write an application/assessment is inversely related to the knowledge of the Criteria possessed by the writers. The difficulty associated with writing a full-length narrative has prevented many organizations from participating in state, local, or school award programs.

To encourage more organizations to begin the performance improvement journey, many state award programs developed progressively higher levels of recognition, ranging from "commitment" at the low-end, through "demonstrated progress," to "achieving excellence" of the top of the range. However, even with progressive levels of recognition, the obstacle of preparing a 50-page written narrative prevented many from engaging in the process. To help resolve this problem, several state programs permit applicants who seek recognition at the lower levels to submit a 7- to 20-page "short" written narrative self-assessment. (Most states still require applicants for the top-level award to complete a full-length written self-assessment.) The short form ranges from requiring a one-page description per category to one-page per Item (hence the 7- to 20-page range in length).

Pros:
- It clearly takes less time to prepare the short form.
- Because of the reduced effort required to complete the self-assessment, states find more organizations are beginning the process of assessing and improving their performance.

Cons:
- The short form provides significantly less information to help examiners prepare for the site visit. Although it does take less time to prepare than the full-length version, the short form still requires several hundred hours of team preparation.
- The short form is usually closely scrutinized and carefully scrubbed just as its full-length cousin. This reduces accuracy and value to both the organization and examiners.
- The knowledge required to write even a short narrative prevents organizations in the beginning stages from preparing an accurate and meaningful assessment.
- Finally, there is not enough information presented in the short form to understand the extent of deployment of the systems and processes covered by the Criteria.

The Likert Scale Survey

Just about everyone is familiar with a Likert scale survey. These surveys typically ask respondents to rate, on a scale 1 to 5, the extent to which they strongly disagree or strongly agree with a comment.

The following is an example of a simple Likert scale survey Item:

Senior leaders effectively communicate values and customer focus.				
1	**2**	**3**	**4**	**5**
Strongly Disagree				**Strongly Agree**

A variation on the simple Likert scale survey Item has been developed in an attempt to improve consistency among respondents. Brief descriptors have been added at each level as shown in the following descriptive Likert scale survey Item:

1	**2**	**3**	**4**	**5**
None	**Few**	**Some**	**Many**	**Most**
Senior leaders effectively communicate values and customer focus.				

Pros:

- The Likert scale survey is quick and easy to administer. People from all functions and levels within the organization can provide input.

Cons:

- Both the simple and the descriptive Likert scale survey Items are subject to wide ranges of interpretation. One person's rating of 2 and another person's rating of 4 may actually describe the same systems or behaviors. This problem of scoring reliability raises questions about the accuracy and usefulness of both the simple and the descriptive survey techniques for conducting organizational self-assessments. After all, a quick and easy survey that produces inaccurate data still has low value. That is the main reason why states have not adopted the Likert scale survey as a tool for conducting the self-assessments, even for organizations in the beginning stages of the quality journey.

The Behaviorally Anchored Survey

A behaviorally anchored survey contains elements of a written narrative and a survey approach to conducting a self-assessment. The method is simple. Instead of brief descriptors, such as "strongly agree/strongly disagree" or "none-few-some-many-most," a more complete behavioral description is presented for each level of the survey scale. Respondents simply identify the behavioral description that most closely fits the activities in the organization. A sample follows:

Making Improvements Based on Progress Reviews [1.1b(2 and 3)]

1F How do leaders use the results of progress reviews?

1 **Not Evident** ☑	Leaders do not use performance reviews to spot areas that need improvement.
2 **Beginning** ☐	A few leaders use performance reviews to spot areas that need improvement.
3 **Basically** **Effective** ☐	Some leaders use performance reviews to spot areas that need improvement.
4 **Mature** ☐	Many leaders use performance reviews to spot areas that need improvement. They sometimes check the accuracy of their reviews.
5 **Advanced** ☐	Most leaders use performance reviews to spot areas that need improvement. They sometimes share findings with key suppliers, business partners, and customers to help them improve. They regularly check the accuracy of their reviews. They constantly make improvements.
6 **Role Model** ☐	Nearly all leaders use performance reviews to spot areas that need improvement. They regularly share findings with key suppliers, business partners, and customers to help them improve. They regularly check the accuracy of their reviews. They constantly make improvements.
Not **Applicable** ☐	I do not have enough information to answer this question.

Describe how your leaders use progress review findings to improve organizational performance. Suggest ways they can improve.

Improving Leadership and Management [1.1b(4)]

1G How well do leaders and managers use performance data and employee feedback to improve their own effectiveness?

1 **Not Evident** ☐	Leaders only use financial and budget results, not employee feedback, to improve their own effectiveness.
2 **Beginning** ☑	Leaders mostly use financial and budget results, and very little employee feedback, to improve their own effectiveness. Sometimes they use this information to set personal improvement goals. They have made few, if any, actual improvements in their effectiveness.
3 **Basically Effective** ☐	Some leaders use some key performance results, as well as employee feedback, to evaluate their own effectiveness. Some use this information to set personal improvement goals. Some actually make improvements in their own effectiveness.
4 **Mature** ☐	Many leaders use many key performance results, as well as employee feedback, to evaluate their own effectiveness. Many use this information to set personal improvement goals. Sometimes they make improvements in their own effectiveness.
5 **Advanced** ☐	Most leaders use most key performance results, as well as employee feedback, to evaluate their own effectiveness. Most use this information to set personal improvement goals. Usually they make improvements in their own effectiveness.
6 **Role Model** ☐	Nearly all leaders use all key performance results, as well as employee feedback, to evaluate their own effectiveness. They nearly all use this information to set personal improvement goals. They constantly make improvements in their own effectiveness.
Not Applicable ☐	I do not have enough information to answer this question.

Describe ways that your leaders and managers use employee feedback or performance results to improve their own effectiveness. Suggest ways they can improve.

Since the behavioral descriptions in the survey combine the requirements of the Criteria with the standards from the scoring guidelines, it is possible to produce accurate Baldrige-based scores for Items and categories for the entire organization and for any subgroup or division.

The following tables provide sample scores for the entire organization and for two job classifications. The following bar graph shows the percent scores, on a 0 to 100 scale, for each Item. This helps users determine at a glance the relative strengths and weaknesses.

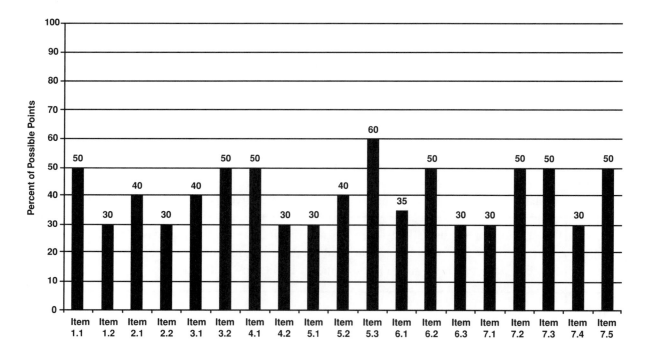

**Sample Organization
Overall Percent Scores by Item**

The following chart shows the ratings by subgroup, in this case, position of senior managers and supervisors. On the previous graph, Item 1.1, Leadership System reflected a rating of 50 percent. However, according to the following breakout, senior managers believe the processes are much stronger (over 60 percent) than supervisors (less than 35 percent). This typically indicates incomplete systems development or poor deployment of existing systems and processes required by the Item.

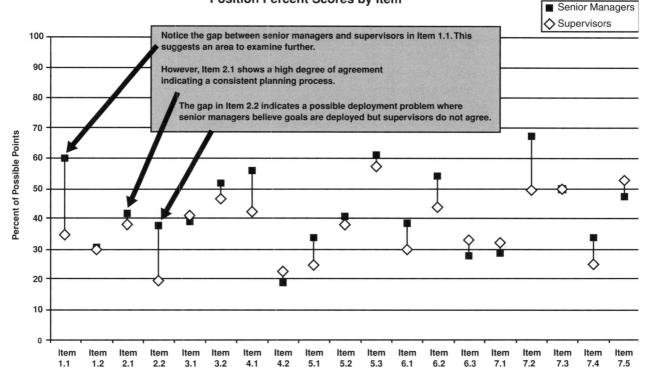

Sample Organization
Position Percent Scores by Item

■ Senior Managers
◇ Supervisors

Notice the gap between senior managers and supervisors in Item 1.1. This suggests an area to examine further.

However, Item 2.1 shows a high degree of agreement indicating a consistent planning process.

The gap in Item 2.2 indicates a possible deployment problem where senior managers believe goals are deployed but supervisors do not agree.

The following Pareto diagram presents data reflecting the areas respondents believed were most in need of improvement. Continuing with the leadership example, it is clear that respondents believe that leaders need to do a better job of setting clear high-performance expectations (Theme D), communicating vision and performance expectations (Theme E), and assessing and improving leadership performance and accountability (Theme G). This helps examiners focus on which areas in leadership may be the most important opportunities for improvement.

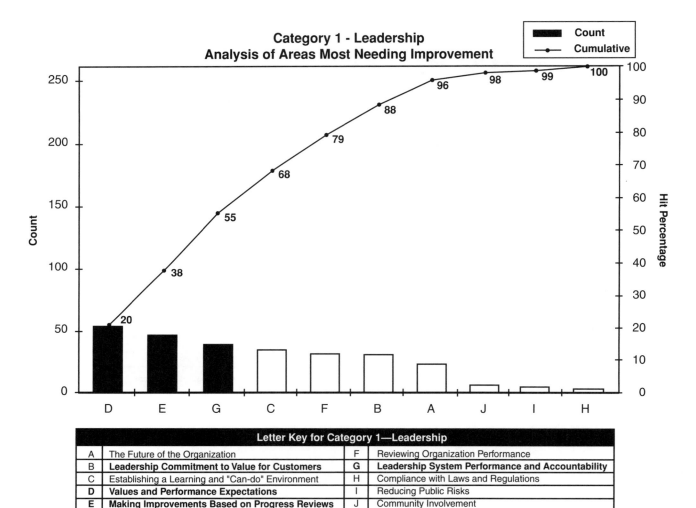

Letter Key for Category 1—Leadership			
A	The Future of the Organization	F	Reviewing Organization Performance
B	**Leadership Commitment to Value for Customers**	G	**Leadership System Performance and Accountability**
C	Establishing a Learning and "Can-do" Environment	H	Compliance with Laws and Regulations
D	**Values and Performance Expectations**	I	Reducing Public Risks
E	**Making Improvements Based on Progress Reviews**	J	Community Involvement

The following chart allows examiners to determine what type of employee (in this case administrator or faculty staff) identified the various improvement priorities. Look at D and G, and you will see that faculty/staff identified the need to improve these areas by a 3-to-1 margin. This tends to indicate a deployment gap and suggests that administrators are not perceived as effective as they believe themselves to be.

Priority Improvement Counts and Percentages — By Position for Leadership Category

1. **Leadership**

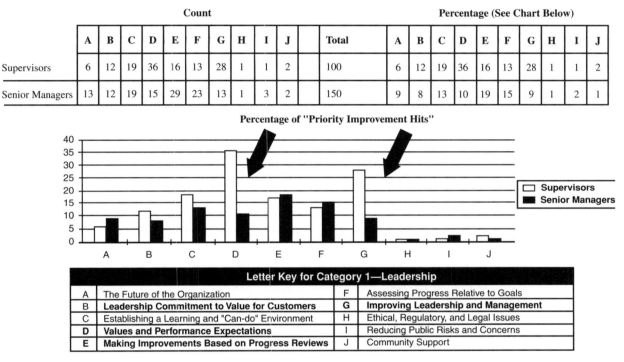

	Count											Percentage (See Chart Below)									
	A	B	C	D	E	F	G	H	I	J	Total	A	B	C	D	E	F	G	H	I	J
Supervisors	6	12	19	36	16	13	28	1	1	2	100	6	12	19	36	16	13	28	1	1	2
Senior Managers	13	12	19	15	29	23	13	1	3	2	150	9	8	13	10	19	15	9	1	2	1

Percentage of "Priority Improvement Hits"

□ Supervisors
■ Senior Managers

	Letter Key for Category 1—Leadership		
A	The Future of the Organization	F	Assessing Progress Relative to Goals
B	**Leadership Commitment to Value for Customers**	G	**Improving Leadership and Management**
C	Establishing a Learning and "Can-do" Environment	H	Ethical, Regulatory, and Legal Issues
D	**Values and Performance Expectations**	I	Reducing Public Risks and Concerns
E	**Making Improvements Based on Progress Reviews**	J	Community Support

Finally, a complete report of the comments and explanations of the respondents can be prepared and used by examiners and organization leaders for improvement planning.

Pros:

- Descriptive behavioral anchors increase the consistency of rating. That is, one respondent's rating of 2 is likely to be the same as another respondent's rating of 2.

- Although completing a behaviorally anchored survey requires more reading than a Likert scale survey, the amount of time and cost required to complete it is still less than 20 percent of the time and cost required to prepare even a short written narrative.
- Because it is easy and simple to use, the behaviorally anchored survey does not impose a barrier to participation as does the written narrative. States and companies who use surveys with properly written behavioral anchors find the accuracy of the assessment to be as good and, in many cases, better than that achieved by the narrative self-assessment, and significantly better than Likert scale assessments. By obtaining input from a cross-section of functions and levels throughout the organization, a performance profile can be developed which not only identifies strengths and areas for improvement, but deployment gaps as well—something the written narrative assessments rarely provide.
- For organizations doing business throughout the world, the behaviorally anchored survey—translated into the native language of respondents—permits far greater input than the written narrative.
- Modern techniques involving surveying through Internet access created an easy way to survey a large, global company.
- Accurate survey data, based on behavioral anchors, can be used to compare or benchmark organizations within and among industries, and can also support longitudinal performance studies.
- Finally, examiners report that the effort required to analyze survey data and plan a site visit is about 50 percent less than the amount of effort required to analyze and prepare for a site visit based on a written narrative. Moreover, they report better information regarding deployment.

Cons:

- Organizations with highly developed performance management systems that seek to apply for top state or national recognition may prefer to practice developing the full-length narrative self-assessment because it is usually required.
- Examiners who are comfortable with the Baldrige application review process, which requires 25 or more hours to conduct an individual review of a full-length narrative self-assessment, initially find it disconcerting to develop comments and plan a site visit based on data gathered from a survey. Different training for examiners is required to develop skills at using survey data to prepare feedback and plan site visits.

NOTE: The preceding report of a behaviorally anchored self-assessment survey is administered by the National Council for Performance Excellence, Winooski, Vermont. Readers may contact them by calling Wendy Steager at (800) 655-1922 or by writing to NCPE, One Main Street, Winooski, Vermont 05404. The Vermont Council for Quality, Minnesota Council for Quality, and Florida Sterling Award and their boards of examiners use this survey technique to assess schools, government agencies, and businesses. The behaviorally anchored survey has completely replaced the written narrative self-assessment as the application for the Vermont Quality Award, as well as the Aruba National Quality Award. Examiners successfully use survey data to plan and conduct site visits in numerous companies as well. At the same time, organization leaders use survey data for improvement planning. The Florida Sterling Award and the Minnesota Quality Award use the behaviorally anchored survey approach for organizations in the early stages of developing Performance Excellence systems. In addition, many private sector organizations are using this type of assessment for internal business evaluations.

In conclusion:

- The full-length written narrative self-assessment is costly. It provides useful information both to examiners and the organizations completing it. The process of completing the written self-assessment can help more advanced organizations to focus and work together as a team.
- The usefulness of the short form written self-assessment is marginal especially for beginning organizations; little useful information is provided to examiners and managers/employees of the organization. However, because it takes less time to complete, one of the barriers to participation is lowered.
- Concerns over the accuracy and interrater reliability of the simple and descriptive Likert scales make their use in conducting effective organizational assessments of management systems questionable.
- The behaviorally anchored survey combines the benefits of survey speed with the accuracy and completeness of a well-developed written narrative self-assessment. In addition, the behaviorally anchored survey can identify gaps in deployment unlike the written narrative self-assessment and is less costly and faster to administer than the written narrative.

A complete copy of business, education, and health-care surveys can be obtained from the National Council for Performance Excellence, One Main Street, Winooski, Vermont 05404 (802-655-1922). Following are two sample surveys:

1. A behaviorally anchored survey
2. A modified Likert scale survey

Baldrige Business

Organizational Self-Assessment
Modified Likert Scale
Version

2000

Customized Demographic Profile

Each participating organization completes a customized demographic profile (a generic sample follows). In this way, survey data can be analyzed by these variables to help pinpoint specific areas needing improvement. This allows the extent of use (deployment) of management systems to be examined.

Position	Location	Function	Org.	Years of Service
_ Executive	_ North	_ Engineering	_ 1	_ 0 < 1
_ Manager	_ South	_ Sales	_ 2	_ 1 < 3
_ Supervisor	_ East	_ Human Resources	_ 3	_ 3 < 5
_ Technician	_ West		_ 4	_ 5 < 10
_ Individual Contributor	_ HQ	_ Finance	_ 5	_ 10+
		_ Quality	_ Other	
		_ Marketing		
		_ Materials Planning		
		_ Manufacturing		
		_ Supply Management		
		_ Info. Technology		
		_ Other		

Instructions

This sample form of the Quantum Performance Group Baldrige organizational self-assessment survey consists of seven themes or questions that relate to the 2000 Baldrige Criteria for Performance Excellence. It is organized into seven "sections," one for each of the seven Baldrige categories. Note that the theme reference numbers on this sample survey (for example, 1B–**Leadership Commitment to Value for Customers**) refers to the theme on the Full-Length Survey form:

- To the best of your knowledge, select a rating (1 to 6) that describes the level of development in your organization. **Note that <u>all</u> of the elements of a statement must be true before you can select that level.** If one or more is not true, you must go to a lower level. After you have selected the rating level, circle the number next to the statement.

- **If you do not know an answer, select NA (Not Applicable) or (?). If your answer is less than one (1), you may enter zero (0).**

- Continue the same way to complete all seven categories.

Summary of Category 1: Leadership

This sample assessment looks at two (2) questions in the Leadership category. The full-length assessment of Leadership contains 10 questions covering the following themes:

- The first part (questions 1A through 1G) looks at how your senior leaders set directions and seek future opportunities to help guarantee the long-term success of your organization. Your senior leaders should express clear values and set high performance expectations that address the needs of all stakeholders:
  - You are asked how your senior leaders set directions, communicate and deploy values and performance expectations, and take into account the expectations of customers and other stakeholders. This includes how leaders create an environment for innovation, learning, and knowledge sharing. You also are asked how your senior leaders review organizational performance, what key performance measures they regularly review, and how review findings are used to drive improvement and change, including your leaders' effectiveness.

- The second part (questions 1H through 1J) looks at how well your organization meets its responsibilities to the public and how your organization practices good citizenship:
  - You are asked how your organization addresses current and future impacts on society in a proactive manner and how it ensures ethical business practices in all stakeholder interactions. The impacts and practices are expected to cover all relevant and important areas—products, services, and operations. You also are asked how your organization, your senior leaders, and your employees identify, support, and strengthen key communities as part of good citizenship practices.

1B How well do top leaders demonstrate that they are serious about providing maximum value to customers?

Not Evident

1   They don't do it.

Beginning

2   A few do it but not well.

Basically Effective

3   Some do this well.

Mature

4   Many do it well. They sometimes check their effectiveness.

Advanced

5   Most do it well. They usually check their effectiveness and sometimes improve.

Role Model—Best in Class

6   Nearly all do it well. They regularly check their effectiveness and constantly improve.

NA   Not Applicable

      I do not have enough information to answer this question.

Comments: Describe how your leaders commit to providing value to their customers. How widely is this done? Suggest ways to improve this process. [Baldrige ref.: 1.1a(1)]

Summary of Category 2: Strategic Planning

This sample assessment looks at one question in the Strategic Planning category. The full-length assessment of Strategic Planning contains six questions covering the following themes:

- The first part (questions 2A through 2B) looks at how the organization develops its strategic plans. The category stresses that customer-driven quality and operational Performance Excellence are key strategic issues that need to be integral parts of your organization's overall planning. Specifically:
  - Customer-driven quality is a strategic view of quality. The focus is on the drivers of customer satisfaction, customer retention, new markets, and market share—key factors in competitiveness, profitability, and business success. Operational performance improvement contributes to short-term and longer-term productivity, growth, and cost/price competitiveness. Building operational capability—including speed, responsiveness, and flexibility—represents an investment in strengthening your competitive fitness.

- The second part (questions 2C through 2F) looks at the way work processes support your organization's strategic directions to help make sure that priorities are carried out.
  - Your organization must translate its strategic objectives into action plans to accomplish the objectives. You must also be able to assess the progress of your action plans. The aim is to ensure that your strategies are understood and followed by everyone in the organization to help achieve goals.

2C How well do all parts of the organization work to create action plans that pull together (align) to carry out its strategic objectives?

Not Evident
1   They don't do it.

Beginning
2   A few do it, but not well.

Basically Effective
3   Some do this well.

Mature
4   Many do it well. They sometimes check their effectiveness.

Advanced
5   Most do it well. They usually check their effectiveness and sometimes improve.

Role Model—Best in Class
6   Nearly all do it well. They regularly check their effectiveness and constantly improve.

NA   Not Applicable
I do not have enough information to answer this question.

Comments: Describe how action plans are created to carry out strategic objectives. How widely is this done? Suggest ways to improve this process. [Baldrige ref.: 2.2a(1)]

Summary of Category 3: Customer and Market Focus

This sample assessment looks at one question in the Customer and Market Focus category. The full-length assessment of Customer and Market Focus contains eight questions covering the following themes:

- The first part (questions 3A through 3B) looks at how your organization tries to understand what the customers and the marketplace wants. Your organization must learn about your customers and markets to help make sure you understand new customer requirements, offer the right products and services, and keep pace with changing customer demands and increasing competition:
  - You are asked how you determine key customer groups and how you segment your markets.
  - You are asked how you determine the most important product/service features.
  - Finally, you are asked how you improve the way you listen and learn from customers so that you can keep current with your changing business needs.

- The second part (questions 3C through 3H) looks at how well the organization builds good relationships with customers to get repeat business and positive referrals. You are also asked how you get data on customer satisfaction and dissatisfaction for your customers and your competitors' customers:
  - You are asked how you make it easy for customers and potential customers to get information or assistance and/or to comment and complain.
  - You are asked how your organization gathers, analyzes, and learns from complaint information to increase customer satisfaction and loyalty.
  - You are asked how you build relationships with your customers since success depends on maintaining close relationships with your customers.
  - You also are asked how you determine the satisfaction and dissatisfaction for different customer groups because satisfied customers are a requirement for loyalty, repeat business, and positive referrals.
  - Finally, you are asked how you follow up with customers and how you determine the customers' satisfaction relative to competitors so that you may improve future performance.

3B How well does your organization identify the most important requirements of its customers? Are factors that influence purchase decisions defined for current, past, and potential customers?

Not Evident

1   They don't do it.

Beginning

2   A few units do this, but only identify a few needs.

Basically Effective

3   Some units do this well.

Mature

4   Many units do this well. They sometimes check their effectiveness.

Advanced

5   Most units do this well. They usually check their effectiveness and sometimes improve.

Role Model—Best in Class

6   Nearly all units do this well. They regularly check their effectiveness and constantly improve.

NA   Not Applicable

I do not have enough information to answer this question.

Comments: Describe how you know what is most important to your customers. How widely is this done? Suggest ways to improve this process. [Baldrige ref.: 3.1a(3 and 4)]

Summary of Category 4: Information and Analysis

This sample assessment looks at one question in the Information and Analysis category. Information and analysis is the "brain center" to effectively measure performance and manage your organization to achieve Performance Excellence. Effective measures help align your organization's operations to achieve its strategic goals.

The full-length assessment of Customer and Market Focus contains five questions covering the following themes:

- The first part (questions 4A through 4D) looks at the selection, management, and use of data and information to support effective decision making at all levels. This serves as a key foundation every high-performing organization:
  - You must build an effective performance measurement system. You must select and use the right measures for tracking daily operations and use those measures for monitoring overall organizational performance. You must also make sure data and information are accurate and reliable.
  - You should use competitive comparisons and benchmarking (best practices) information to help drive performance improvement.
  - Finally, you should evaluate and improve the performance measurement system to keep it current with changing business needs.

- The second part (questions 4E through 4G) looks at how your organization analyzes its data and information to guide your organization's process management toward the achievement of key business results and strategic objectives.
- You must analyze data and information from all parts of your organization to support your senior leaders' assessment of overall organizational health, organizational planning, and daily operations.

4A How well do all parts of the organization collect complete and accurate data to track performance and improve daily decision making?

Not Evident

1 They don't do it.

Beginning

2 A few do it, but not well.

Basically Effective

3 Some do this well.

Mature

4 Many do it well. They sometimes check their effectiveness.

Advanced

5 Most do it well. They usually check their effectiveness and sometimes improve.

Role Model—Best in Class

6 Nearly all do it well. They regularly check their effectiveness and constantly improve.

NA Not Applicable

I do not have enough information to answer this question.

Comments: Describe how you determine what data need to be collected to tract performance and ensure effective decision making. How widely is this done? Suggest ways to improve this process. [Baldrige ref.: 4.1a(1-i, 1-ii, and 2)]

Summary of Category 5: Human Resource Focus

This sample assessment looks at one question in the Human Resource Focus category. The full-length assessment of Human Resource Focus contains nine questions covering the following themes:

- The first part (questions 5A through 5D) looks at how well your systems for work and job design, compensation, motivation, recognition, and hiring help all employees reach peak performance.
- You are asked how you design work and jobs to empower employees to exercise discretion and decision making, resulting in high performance.
- You are asked how you compensate, recognize, and reward employees to support your organization's high-performance objectives (strategic objectives).
- Finally, you are asked how you recruit and hire employees who will meet your expectations and needs. The right workforce is an enabler of high performance.

- The second part (questions 5E through 5F) looks at how well education and training meets the needs of employees:
  - You are asked how education and training are designed, delivered, reinforced on the job, and evaluated.
  - You are also asked about how well you provide training in Performance Excellence, which includes succession planning and leadership development at all levels.

- The third part (questions 5G through 5I) looks at your organization's work environment, your employee support climate, and how you determine employee satisfaction, with the aim of fostering the well-being, satisfaction, and motivation of all employees.
- You are asked how your work environment for all employees is safe and healthful.
- You are asked how you enhance employee well-being, satisfaction, and motivation for all employee groups.
- Finally, you are asked how you assess employee well-being, satisfaction, and motivation, and how you relate assessment findings to key business results to set improvement priorities.

5B How well do managers and supervisors at all levels provide feedback to employees and make sure pay, reward, and recognition support Performance Excellence goals?

Not Evident

1   They don't do it.

Beginning

2   A few do it, but not well.

Basically Effective

3   Some do this well.

Mature

4   Many do it well. They sometimes check their effectiveness.

Advanced

5   Most do it well. They usually check their effectiveness and sometimes improve.

Role Model—Best in Class

6   Nearly all do it well. They regularly check their effectiveness and constantly improve.

NA   Not Applicable

    I do not have enough information to answer this question.

Comments: Describe how managers and supervisors make sure pay, reward, and recognition are aligned to support performance goals and objectives. How widely is this done? Suggest ways to improve this process. [Baldrige ref.: 5.1a(3 and 4)]

Summary of Category 6: Process Management

This sample assessment looks at one question in the Process Management category. The full-length assessment of Process Management contains eight questions covering the following themes:

- Process management is the focal point for all key work processes. The first part (questions 6A through 6C) looks at your organization's product and service design and delivery processes:
  - You are asked how you address customer/market requirements in the design process. You are also asked how you address cost control, cycle time, and learning from past design projects. You should make sure that design processes actually work as expected.
  - You should be sure that production/delivery processes work consistently. You should define performance measures to get an early alert of potential problems so you can take prompt action to correct the problem.
  - Finally, you are asked how you improve your production/delivery processes to achieve better processes and products/services.

- The middle part of this survey chapter (questions 6D through 6E) examines your organization's key support processes, with the aim of improving your overall operational performance:
  - You are asked how your key support processes are designed to meet all the requirements of internal and external customers.
  - You should be sure that the day-to-day operation of your key support processes meets the key requirements. You should use in-process measures and/or customer feedback to get an early alert of problems.
  - Finally, you are asked how you improve your key support processes to achieve better performance.

- The last part of this survey chapter (questions 6F through 6G) examines your organization's key supplier and partnering processes and relationships, with the aim of improving your performance and your suppliers' performance.
- You are asked how you define key performance requirements and measures for suppliers and partners, and how you use these requirements and measures in managing and improving performance. These performance requirements (for example, quality, timeliness, and price) should play an important role in making purchases.
- You are asked how you provide actionable feedback to suppliers. You also are asked how you provide your suppliers and partners with assistance and incentives, which will contribute to improvements in their performance and your performance.
- Finally, you are asked how you improve your supplier and partnering processes so that you and your suppliers can keep current with your changing business needs.

6A How well do all parts of the organization design both core business and support products and services, as well as production and delivery systems that meet current and changing customer requirements?

Not Evident

1   They don't do it.

Beginning

2   A few do it, but not well.

Basically Effective

3   Some do this well.

Mature

4   Many do it well. They sometimes check their effectiveness.

Advanced

5   Most do it well. They usually check their effectiveness and sometimes improve.

Role Model—Best in Class

6   Nearly all do it well. They regularly check their effectiveness and constantly improve.

NA   Not Applicable

I do not have enough information to answer this question.

Comments: Describe how the organization designs products and services and makes sure current and changing customer requirements are included. How widely is this done? Suggest ways to improve this process. [Baldrige ref.: 6.1a(1, 2, and 3) and 6.2a(2 and 3)]

Summary of Category 7: Business Results

This sample assessment looks at one overall theme in the Business Results category. The full-length assessment of Business Results contains five questions covering the following themes:

- The Business Results category looks for the results that your management system produces. Results range from final performance (lagging) outcomes, such as customer satisfaction, market share, and financial performance to predictive (leading) outcomes, such as internal operating measures, human resource results, and supplier performance. Together, these lagging and leading results create a set of balanced indicators of organizational health, commonly called a "balanced scorecard."
- The first theme (question 7A) looks at how well your organization has been satisfying your customers and delivering product and service quality that lead to satisfaction and loyalty.
- The second theme (question 7B) looks at the strength of your organization's financial and market results.
- The third theme (question 7C) looks at how well your organization has been creating and maintaining a positive, productive, learning, and caring work environment.
- The fourth theme (question 7D) looks at how well your organization ensures the quality, delivery, and price of externally provided goods and services and how your suppliers/partners contribute to your improved performance.
- The fifth theme (question 7E) looks at your organization's other key operational performance results, to determine the strength of its organizational effectiveness.

7 How well does the organization achieve trends and results in areas important for business success?

Not Evident

1   No results or poor results.

Beginning

2   Most key results not reported. Good performance levels and improvement in a few areas.

Basically Effective

3   Many key results are reported and address many areas important to the business. Good performance levels or improvement in some areas. Beginning to develop trends and get comparison data.

Mature

4   Most key results are reported and address most areas important to the business. Good performance levels or improvement in many areas when compared to industry average.

Advanced

5   Most key results are reported and address most key customer, market, and process requirements. No adverse trends or poor performance in key areas. Good to very good performance levels or improvement in most areas when compared to benchmarks or industry average.

Role Model—Best in Class

6   Most key results are reported and address most key customer, market, process, and action plan requirements. Good to excellent performance levels and sustained improvement in most areas when compared to benchmarks. Leads the industry in some areas.

NA   Not Applicable

I do not have enough information to answer this question.

Comments: Give examples of your key customer satisfaction, loyalty, and product/service performance results. [Baldrige ref.: 7.1–7.5]

2000
Baldrige Business

Organizational
Self-Assessment
Behaviorally
Anchored Version

Customized Demographic Profile

Each participating organization completes a customized demographic profile (a generic sample follows). In this way, survey data can be analyzed by these variables to help pinpoint specific areas needing improvement. This allows the extent of use (deployment) of management systems to be examined.

Position	Location	Function	Org.	Years of Service
_ Executive	_ North	_ Engineering	_ 1	_ 0 < 1
_ Manager	_ South	_ Sales	_ 2	_ 1 < 3
_ Supervisor	_ East	_ Human Resources	_ 3	_ 3 < 5
_ Technician	_ West	_ Finance	_ 4	_ 5 < 10
_ Individual Contributor	_ HQ	_ Quality	_ 5	_ 10+
		_ Marketing	_ Other	
		_ Materials Planning		
		_ Manufacturing		
		_ Supply Management		
		_ Info Technology		
		_ Other		

Instructions

This sample form of the Quantum Performance Group Baldrige organizational self-assessment survey consists of seven themes or questions that relate to the 2000 Baldrige Criteria for Performance Excellence. It is organized into seven "chapters," one for each of the seven Baldrige categories. Note that the theme reference numbers on this sample survey (for example, 1B–**Leadership Commitment to Value for Customers**) refers to the theme on the In-Depth Survey form.

- To the best of your knowledge, select a rating (1 to 6) that describes the level of development in your organization. **Note that <u>all</u> of the elements of a statement must be true before you can select that level.** If one or more is not true, you must go to a lower level. After you have selected the rating level, circle the number next to the statement.

- **If you do not know an answer, select NA (Not Applicable) or (?). If your answer is less than one (1), you may enter zero (0).**

- Continue in the same way to complete all seven chapters.

   Time Saving Tip: Start reading at row 3. If all parts of the statement are true, go to row 4; if not, drop back to read row 2. After a few answers, save even more time by starting at the number you select most often. Don't waste time by reading from row 1 each time (unless most of your answers are 1).

Summary of Category 1: Leadership

This sample assessment looks at one question in the Leadership category. The full-length assessment of Leadership contains 10 questions covering the following themes:

- The first part (questions 1A through 1G) looks at how your senior leaders set directions and seek future opportunities to help guarantee the long-term success of your organization. Your senior leaders should express clear values and set high performance expectations that address the needs of all stakeholders:
  - You are asked how your senior leaders set directions, communicate and deploy values and performance expectations, and take into account the expectations of customers and other stakeholders. This includes how leaders create an environment for innovation, learning, and knowledge sharing. You also are asked how your senior leaders review organizational performance, what key performance measures they regularly review, and how review findings are used to drive improvement and change, including your leaders' effectiveness.

- The second part (questions 1H through 1J) looks at how well your organization meets its responsibilities to the public and how your organization practices good citizenship:
  - You are asked how your organization addresses current and future impacts on society in a proactive manner and how it ensures ethical business practices in all stakeholder interactions. The impacts and practices are expected to cover all relevant and important areas—products, services, and operations. You also are asked how your organization, your senior leaders, and your employees identify, support, and strengthen key communities as part of good citizenship practices.

Leadership Commitment to Value for Customers

1B How committed are top leaders to providing value to customers?

Not Evident

1   Top leaders focus on short-term business issues, *not on value* for customers.

Beginning

2   *A few* top leaders are just beginning to focus on value for customers.

Basically Effective

3   *Some* top leaders focus occasionally on value for customers through their written and verbal communication.

Mature

4   *Many* top leaders and managers get the organization to focus on providing maximum value to customers. They *sometimes* talk with customers. They *sometimes* check on the effectiveness of activities to focus on customer value.

Advanced

5   *Most* top leaders and managers focus on providing maximum value to customers. They *usually* talk with customers. They *usually* check on the effectiveness of activities to focus on customer value. They *sometimes* make improvements.

Role Model

6   *Nearly all* top leaders and managers focus on providing maximum value to customers. They *frequently* talk with customers. They regularly check on the effectiveness of activities to focus on customer value. They constantly make improvements.

NA   Not Applicable

    I do not have enough information to answer this question.

Summary of Category 2: Strategic Planning

This sample assessment looks at one question in the Strategic Planning category. The full-length assessment of Strategic Planning contains six questions covering the following themes:

- The first part (questions 2A through 2B) looks at how the organization develops its strategic plans. The category stresses that customer-driven quality and operational Performance Excellence are key strategic issues that need to be integral parts of your organization's overall planning. Specifically:
  - Customer-driven quality is a strategic view of quality. The focus is on the drivers of customer satisfaction, customer retention, new markets, and market share—key factors in competitiveness, profitability, and business success; and
  - Operational performance improvement contributes to short-term and longer-term productivity growth and cost/price competitiveness. Building operational capability—including speed, responsiveness, and flexibility—represents an investment in strengthening your competitive fitness.

- The second part (questions 2C through 2F) looks at the way work processes support your organization's strategic directions, to help make sure that priorities are carried out:
  - Your organization must translate its strategic objectives into action plans to accomplish the objectives. You must also be able to assess the progress of your action plans. The aim is to ensure that your strategies are understood and followed by everyone in the organization to help achieve goals.

Action Plans Based on Strategic Objectives
2C How well do the organization's action plans support its strategic objectives?

Not Evident

1   The organization's action plans *do not* support strategic objectives.

Beginning

2   The organization's action plans support *a few* strategic objectives.

Basically Effective

3   The organization's action plans support *some* strategic objectives for its key products and services.

Mature

4   The organization's action plans support *many* strategic objectives for its key products and services. The action plans are *sometimes* checked to see how well they support objectives.

Advanced

5   The organization's action plans support *most* strategic objectives for its key products and services. The action plans are *usually* checked to see how well they support objectives. They are *sometimes* improved.

Role Model

6   The organization's action plans support *all* strategic objectives for its key products and services. The action plans are *regularly* checked to see how well they support objectives. They are *constantly* improved to strengthen key products and services.

NA   Not Applicable

I do not have enough information to answer this question.

Summary of Category 3: Customer and Market Focus

This sample assessment looks at one question in the Customer and Market Focus category. The full-length assessment of Customer and Market Focus contains eight questions covering the following themes:

- The first part (questions 3A through 3B) looks at how your organization tries to understand what the customers and the marketplace wants. Your organization must learn about your customers and markets to help make sure you understand new customer requirements, offer the right products and services, and keep pace with changing customer demands and increasing competition:
  - You are asked how you determine key customer groups and how you segment your markets.
  - You are asked how you determine the most important product/service features.
  - Finally, you are asked how you improve the way you listen and learn from customers so that you can keep current with your changing business needs.

- The second part (questions 3C through 3H) looks at how well the organization builds good relationships with customers to get repeat business and positive referrals. You are also asked how you get data on customer satisfaction and dissatisfaction for your customers and your competitors' customers:
  - You are asked how you make it easy for customers and potential customers to get information or assistance and/or to comment and complain.
  - You are asked how your organization gathers, analyzes, and learns from complaint information to increase customer satisfaction and loyalty.
  - You are asked how you build relationships with your customers since success depends on maintaining close relationships with your customers.
  - You also are asked how you determine the satisfaction and dissatisfaction for different customer groups, because satisfied customers are a requirement for loyalty, repeat business, and positive referrals.
  - Finally, you are asked how you follow up with customers and how you determine the customers' satisfaction relative to competitors so that you may improve future performance.

Important Service and Product Features to Customers

3B How well does your organization understand what is most important to its customers?

Not Evident

1   The organization *does not know* which of its product and service features are most important to customers.

Beginning

2   The organization knows a *few* key product and service features that are most important to customers.

Basically Effective

3   The organization knows *some* product and service features that are most important to its customers. It has started to use this information for product planning and marketing.

Mature

4   *Many* parts of the organization know which product and service features are most important to customers. Sometimes it uses this information to support product planning, marketing, and future business development. It *sometimes* checks the accuracy of this information.

Advanced

5   *Most* parts of the organization know which product and service features are most important to customers. It uses the information to support product planning, marketing, and future business development. It *usually* checks the accuracy of this information. It *sometimes* improves the process for using it.

Role Model

6   *Nearly all* parts of the organization know which product and service features are most important to customers. Priorities for each customer segment are clearly defined and up to date. It uses the information fully to support product planning, marketing, and future business development. It *regularly* checks the accuracy of this information. It *constantly* improves the process for using it.

NA   Not Applicable

I do not have enough information to answer this question.

Summary of Category 4: Information and Analysis

This sample assessment looks at one question in the Information and Analysis category. Information and analysis is the brain center to effectively measure performance and manage your organization to achieve Performance Excellence. Effective measures help align your organization's operations to achieve its strategic goals.

The full-length assessment of Customer and Market Focus contains five questions covering the following themes:

- The first part (questions 4A through 4D) looks at the selection, management, and use of data and information to support effective decision making at all levels. This serves as a key foundation every high-performing organization:
  - You must build an effective performance measurement system. You must select and use the right measures for tracking daily operations and use those measures for monitoring overall organizational performance. You must also make sure data and information are accurate and reliable.
  - You should use competitive comparisons and benchmarking (best practices) information to help drive performance improvement.
  - Finally, you should evaluate and improve the performance measurement system to keep it current with changing business needs.

- The second part (questions 4E through 4G) looks at how your organization analyzes its data and information to guide your organization's process management toward the achievement of key business results and strategic objectives:
  - You must analyze data and information from all parts of your organization to support your senior leaders' assessment of overall organizational health, organizational planning, and daily operations.

Selection and Use of Measures

4A How does the organization know it is collecting data that will assist in daily decision making?

Not Evident

1   The organization *does not* collect data to track how well it performs.

Beginning

2   The organization collects data to track financial and market performance but very *few* other areas of business performance. Data support decision making at the top levels of the organization.

Basically Effective

3   The organization collects data to understand *some* areas of organizational performance, such as financial, market, customer satisfaction, and operational. Data support decision making in *some* parts of the organization in addition to the top levels.

Mature

4   The organization collects data to understand *many* areas of organizational performance, such as financial, market, customer satisfaction, operational, human resources, and supplier effectiveness. Data support decision making in *many* parts of the organization in addition to the top levels. The organization *sometimes* checks how well the data support decision making at the different levels.

Advanced

5   The organization collects data to understand *most* areas of organizational performance, such as financial, market, customer satisfaction, operational, human resources, and supplier effectiveness. Data support decision making in *most* parts of the organization in addition to the top levels. The organization *usually* checks how well the data support decision making at the different levels. It *sometimes* makes improvements.

Role Model

6   The organization collects data to understand *nearly all* areas of organizational performance, including financial, market, customer satisfaction, operational, human resources, and supplier effectiveness. Data support decision making in *nearly all* parts of the organization in addition to the top levels. The organization *regularly* checks how well the data support decision making throughout the organization. It *constantly* makes improvements.

NA   Not Applicable

I do not have enough information to answer this question.

Summary of Category 5: Human Resource Focus

This sample assessment looks at one question in the Human Resource Focus category. The full-length assessment of Human Resource Focus contains nine questions covering the following themes:

- The first part (questions 5A through 5D) looks at how well your systems for work and job design, compensation, motivation, recognition, and hiring help all employees reach peak performance:
  - You are asked how you design work and jobs to empower employees to exercise discretion and decision making, resulting in high performance.
  - You are asked how you compensate, recognize, and reward employees to support your organization's high-performance objectives (strategic objectives).
  - Finally, you are asked how you recruit and hire employees who will meet your expectations and needs. The right workforce is an enabler of high performance.

- The second part (questions 5E through 5F) looks at how well education and training meets the needs of employees:
  - You are asked how education and training are designed, delivered, reinforced on the job, and evaluated.
  - You are also asked about how well you provide training in Performance Excellence, which includes succession planning and leadership development, at all levels.

- The third part (questions 5G through 5J) looks at how your organization's work environment, your employee support climate, and how you determine employee satisfaction, with the aim of fostering the well-being, satisfaction, and motivation of all employees:
  - You are asked how your work environment for all employees is safe and healthful.
  - You are asked how you enhance employee well-being, satisfaction, and motivation for all employee groups.
  - Finally, you are asked how you assess employee well-being, satisfaction, and motivation, and how you relate assessment findings to key business results to set improvement priorities.

Feedback, Compensation, and Recognition

5B How well does the organization provide feedback to employees and ensure pay, reward, and recognition support Performance Excellence goals?

Not Evident

1   The organization *does not* provide effective feedback to employees or tie pay or recognition to its Performance Excellence goals and strategies.

Beginning

2   The organization provides effective feedback about performance to a *few* employees. It ties pay and recognition to a *few* Performance Excellence goals and strategies.

Basically Effective

3   The organization provides effective feedback about performance to *some* employees. It ties pay and recognition to *some* Performance Excellence goals and strategies.

Mature

4   The organization provides effective feedback about performance to *many* employees. It ties pay and recognition to *many* Performance Excellence goals and strategies. The process is *sometimes* checked to see if it is effective.

Advanced

5   The organization provides effective feedback about performance to *most* employees. It ties pay and recognition to *most* Performance Excellence goals and strategies. The process is *usually* checked to see if it is effective. It *sometimes* makes improvements.

Role Model

6   The organization provides effective feedback about performance to *nearly all* employees. It ties pay and recognition to *nearly all* Performance Excellence goals and strategies. The process is *regularly* checked to see if it is effective. It *constantly* makes improvements.

NA   Not Applicable

    I do not have enough information to answer this question.

Summary of Category 6: Process Management

This sample assessment looks at one question in the Process Management category. The full-length assessment of Process Management contains eight questions covering the following themes:

- Process management is the focal point for all key work processes. The first part (questions 6A through 6C) looks at your organization's product and service design and delivery processes:
    - You are asked how you address customer/market requirements in the design process. You are also asked how you address cost control, cycle time, and learning from past design projects. You should make sure that design processes actually work as expected.
    - You should be sure that production/delivery processes work consistently. You should define performance measures to get an early alert of potential problems so you can take prompt action to correct the problem.
    - Finally, you are asked how you improve your production/delivery processes to achieve better processes and products/services.

- The middle part of this survey chapter (questions 6D through 6E) examines your organization's key support processes, with the aim of improving your overall operational performance:
    - You are asked how your key support processes are designed to meet all the requirements of internal and external customers.
    - You should be sure that the day-to-day operation of your key support processes meets the key requirements. You should use in-process measures and/or customer feedback to get an early alert of problems.
    - Finally, you are asked how you improve your key support processes to achieve better performance.

- The last part of this survey chapter (questions 6F through 6G) examines your organization's key supplier and partnering processes and relationships, with the aim of improving your performance and your suppliers' performance:
    - You are asked how you define key performance requirements and measures for suppliers and partners, and how you use these requirements and measures in managing and improving performance. These performance requirements (for example, quality, timeliness, and price) should play an important role in making purchases.
    - You are asked how you provide actionable feedback to suppliers. You also are asked how you provide your suppliers and partners with assistance and incentives, which will contribute to improvements in their performance and your performance.
    - Finally, you are asked how you improve your supplier and partnering processes so that you and your suppliers can keep current with your changing business needs.

Designing Products and Services for Core Business Activities *and* Support Services

6A/D How well does the organization design products and services that meet customer requirements for core business and support services?

Not Effective

1   The organization *does not* have a standard design process.

Beginning

2   The organization uses a standard design process for a *few* key products and services. The design process does not include customer input.

Basically Effective

3   The organization uses a standard design process for *some* key products and services. The design process for *some* products/services uses customer input.

Mature

4   The organization has a standard design process for *many* key products and services. The design process for *many* products/services uses customer input. The organization *sometimes* checks the effectiveness of these processes to make sure they meet many operational requirements.

Advanced

5   The organization has a standard design process for *most* key products and services. The design process for *most* products/services uses customer input. The organization usually checks the effectiveness of these processes to make sure they meet most operational requirements. It *sometimes* makes improvements.

Role Model

6   The organization has a standard design process for *nearly all* key products and services. The design process for *nearly all* products/services uses customer input. The organization *regularly* checks the effectiveness of these processes to make sure they meet *nearly all* operational requirements. It *constantly* makes improvements.

NA   **Not Applicable**

     I do not have enough information to answer this question.

Summary of Category 7: Business Results

This sample assessment looks at one overall theme in the Business Results category. The full-length assessment of Business Results contains five questions covering the following themes:

- The Business Results category looks for the results that your management system produces. Results range from final performance (lagging) outcomes, such as customer satisfaction, market share, and financial performance to predictive (leading) outcomes, such as internal operating measures, human resource results, and supplier performance. Together, these lagging and leading results create a set of balanced indicators of organizational health, commonly called a "balanced scorecard."
  - The first theme (question 7A) looks at how well your organization has been satisfying your customers and delivering product and service quality that lead to satisfaction and loyalty.
  - The second theme (question 7B) looks at the strength of your organization's financial and market results.
  - The third theme (question 7C) looks at how well your organization has been creating and maintaining a positive, productive, learning, and caring work environment.
  - The fourth theme (question 7D) looks at how well your organization ensures the quality, delivery, and price of externally provided goods and services, and how your suppliers/ partners contribute to your improved performance.
  - The fifth theme (question 7E) looks at your organization's other key operational performance results to determine the strength of its organizational effectiveness.

Business Results

7 What are the trends and results in areas important to business success?

Not Evident

1   The organization's results trends *have not* improved.

Beginning

2   The organization's results trends are *mixed.* These include *limited* positive results.

Basically Effective

3   The organization's results trends show *some* improvement over time across *some* areas important to business success.

Mature

4   The organization's results trends show *good* improvement over time. This is across *many* areas important to business success. Limited competitive comparisons are available.

Advanced

5   The organization's results trends show *very good* improvement over time. The organization's results are similar to those of competitors and better than average. This is across *most* areas important to business success.

Role Model

6   The organization's results trends show *excellent* improvement. The organization's results exceed those of the better competitors. This is across *nearly all* areas important to business success.

NA   Not Applicable

I do not have enough information to answer this question.

Comments: Describe your customer satisfaction, dissatisfaction, and loyalty results data and trends. Suggest ways they can improve.

The Site Visit

Introduction

Many people and organizations have asked about how to prepare for site visits. This section is intended to help answer those questions and prepare the organization for an on-site examination. It includes rules of the game for examiners and what they are taught to look for. As we all know, the best preparation for this type of examination is to see things through the eyes of the trained examiner.

Before an organization can be recommended to receive the Malcolm Baldrige National Quality Award, it must receive a visit from a team of business assessment experts from the National Board of Examiners. Approximately 25 percent to 30 percent of organizations applying for the Baldrige Award in recent years have received these site visits.

The Baldrige Award site visit team usually includes two senior examiners—one of whom is designated as team leader—and four to seven other examiners. In addition, the team is accompanied by a representative of the National Quality Award Office and a representative of ASQ, which provides administrative services to the Baldrige Award Office under contract.

The site visit team usually gathers at a hotel near the organization's headquarters on the Sunday morning immediately preceding the site visit. During the day, the team makes final preparations and plans for the visit.

Each team member is assigned lead responsibility for one or more categories of the award Criteria. Each examiner is usually teamed with one other examiner during the site visit. These examiners usually conduct the visit in pairs to ensure the accurate recording of information.

Site visits usually begin on a Monday morning and last one week. By Wednesday or Thursday, most site visit teams will have completed their on-site review. They retire to the nearby hotel to confer and write their reports. By the end of the week, the team must reach consensus on the findings and prepare a final report for the panel of judges.

Purpose of Site Visits

Site visits help clarify uncertain points and verify self-assessment (that is, application) accuracy. During the site visit, examiners investigate areas most difficult to understand from self-assessments, such as the following:

- **Deployment.** How widely a process is used throughout the organization;
- **Integration.** Whether processes fit together to support Performance Excellence;
- **Process ownership.** Whether processes are broadly owned, simply directed, or micromanaged;
- **Employee involvement.** Whether the extent to which employees' participation in managing processes of all types is optimized; and
- **Continuous improvement maturity.** The number and extent of improvement cycles and resulting refinements in all areas of the organization and at all levels.

Characteristics of Site Visit Issues

Examiners look at issues that are an essential component of scoring and role model determination. They have a responsibility to:

- Clarify information that is missing or vague;
- Verify significant strengths identified from the self-assessment; and
- Verify deployment of the practices described in the self-assessment.

Examiners will:

- Concentrate on cross-cutting issues;
- Examine data, reports, and documents;
- Interview individuals and teams; and
- Receive presentations from the applicant organization.

Examiners are not permitted to conduct their own focus groups or surveys with customers, suppliers, or dealers or disrupt work processes. Conducting focus groups or surveys would violate the confidentiality agreements, as well as be statistically unsound.

Typically Important Site Visit Issues

- Role of senior management in leading and serving as a role model
- Degree of involvement and self-direction of employees below upper management
- Comprehensiveness and accessibility of the information system
- Utility and validity of available data
- Extent that facts and data are used in decision making
- Degree of emphasis on customer satisfaction
- Extent of systematic approaches to work processes
- Deployment and integration of quality principles and processes
- Training effectiveness
- Use of compensation, recognition, and rewards to promote key values
- Extent that strategic plans align organizational work
- Extent of the use of measurable goals at all levels in the organization
- Evidence of evaluation and improvement cycles in all work processes and in system effectiveness
- Improvement levels in cycle times and other operating processes
- Extent of integration of all processes—operational and support
- Level of maturity of improvement initiatives
- Extent of benchmarking effort
- Level of supplier involvement in performance improvement activities
- Uncovering improvements since the submission of the application (self-assessment) and receiving up-to-date business results

Discussions with the Applicant Prior to the Site Visit

Prior to the site visit, all communication between the applicant organization and its team must be routed through their respective single points of contact. Only the team leader may contact the applicant on behalf of the site visit team prior to the site visit. This helps ensure consistency of message and communication for both parties. It prevents confusion and misunderstandings.

The team leader should provide the applicant organization with basic information about the process. This includes schedules, arrival times, and equipment and meeting room needs.

Applicant organizations usually provide the following information prior to the site visit team's final site visit planning meeting at the hotel on the day before the site visit starts:
- List of key contacts
- Organization chart
- Facility layout
- Performance data requested by examiners

The team leader, on behalf of team members, will ask for supplementary documentation to be compiled (such as results data brought up to date) to avoid placing an undue burden on the organization at the time of the site visit.

The site visit team will select sites that allow them to examine key issues and check deployment in key areas. This information may or may not be discussed with the applicant prior to the site visit. Examiners will need access to all areas of the organization.

Conduct of Site Visit Team Members (Examiners)

Examiners are not allowed to discuss findings with anyone but team members. Examiners may not disclose the following to the applicant:
- Personal or team observations and findings
- Conclusions and decisions
- Observations about the applicant's performance systems, whether in a complimentary or critical way

Examiners may not discuss the following with anyone:
- Observations about other applicants
- Names of other award program applicants

Examiners may not accept trinkets, gifts, or gratuities of any kind (coffee, cookies, rolls, breakfast, and lunch are okay), so applicant organizations should not offer them. At the conclusion of the site visit, examiners are not permitted to leave with any of the applicant's materials including logo Items or catalogs—not even Items usually given to visitors.

Examiners will dress in appropriate business attire unless instructed otherwise by the applicant organization.

Opening Meeting

An opening meeting will be scheduled to introduce all parties and set the structure for the site visit. The meeting is usually attended by senior executives and the self-assessment writing team. The opening meeting usually is scheduled first on the initial day of the site visit (8:30 or 9:00 A.M.). The team leader generally starts the meeting, introduces the team, and opens the site visit. Overhead slides and formal presentations are usually unnecessary.

The applicant organization usually has one hour to present any information it believes important for the examiners to know. This includes time for a tour, if necessary.

Immediately after the meeting, examiners are likely to want to meet with senior leaders and those responsible for preparing sections of the self-assessment (application).

Conducting the Site Visit

The team will follow the site visit plan, subject to periodic adjustments according to its findings.

The site visit team will need a private room to conduct frequent caucuses. Applicant representatives are not present at these caucuses. The team will also conduct evening meetings at the hotel to review the findings of the day, reach consensus, write comments, and revise the site visit report.

If, during the course of the site visit, someone from the applicant organization believes the team or any of its members are missing the point, the designated point of contact should inform the team leader or the Baldrige Award Office monitor. Also, someone who believes an examiner behaved inappropriately should inform the designated point of contact, who will inform the team leader or the award office monitor.

Employees should be instructed to mark every document given to examiners with the name and work location of the person providing the document. This will ensure that it is returned to the proper person. Records should be made of all material given to team members.

Organizational personnel may not ask examiners for opinions and advice. Examiners are not permitted to provide any information of this type during the site visit.

Team Leader's Site Visit Checklist

This checklist provides a summary of activities required of site visit team leaders.

Preparation

- Size of team and length of visit determined, with starting and ending date and time selected
- All team members receive copies of consensus report
- Team notified of starting/ending times and locations
- Background information on new team members (if any) received
- Category lead and team pairing assignments made for each team member
- New team members complete review of narrative
- Site visit notebooks prepared
- Individual team members prepare assigned site visit issues
- Subteam members exchange site visit issues for comments
- Revised site visit issues received from subteams
- Site visit issues reviewed by team leader and comments sent to subteams
- Team asked to revise site visit themes or issues (as appropriate)

Previsit Meeting

- Examiner introductions/reintroductions
- Site visit issues and themes reviewed and approaches outlined
- Sites selected to visit and logistics reviewed
- Specific requests for first day listed (interviews and data)
- Caucus plans established

Continued on next page

Team Leader's Site Visit Checklist—continued

Conduct of Visit

- Opening presentation conducted
- Followed site visit plan
- Revised plan as required
- Caucused frequently
- Maintained records of findings
- Maintained records of applicant documents received
- Answered all selected site issues; developed information on site visit themes
- Closing meeting conducted

Site Visit Report

- Team completed site visit issues
- Team completed Item and category summary forms
- Completed overall summary form
- Team initiated report
- Report copied; original given to award office representative before leaving site
- Leader kept copy, narrative, and other notes (or a back-up person has material)
- Collected and returned all applicant material prior to leaving site
- Collected all narratives, materials, and notes; sent or given to award office

Feedback Report

- Senior examiner/feedback author collected feedback points during site visit
- Senior examiner/feedback author reviewed feedback points with team during site visit report writing session
- Reviewed feedback report completed before leaving site and sent to award office

Generic Site Visit Questions

Examiners must verify or clarify the information contained in an application, whether or not the examiners have determined a process to be a strength or an area for improvement. Examiners must verify the existence of strengths as well as clarify the nature of each significant area for improvement.

Before and during the site visit review process, examiners formulate a series of questions based on the Baldrige Performance Excellence Criteria. Because the site visit must verify or clarify all significant aspects of the organization's performance management systems against the Criteria, it is possible to identify a series of generic questions that examiners are likely to ask during the site visit process. These questions are presented in the following section to help prepare applicants for the assessment process.

Category 1—Leadership

1. Describe the process your organization used in developing your mission, vision, and values. To top leaders: Who was involved in that process? How do you set direction and guide the organization? How do you seek future opportunities for your organization?
   - Please share with us the mission, vision, and values of this organization.
   - What are your organization's top priorities?
   - How do you ensure that all your employees know this?
   - How do you know how effective you are at communicating your commitment to the vision and values?
2. How do you, as a leader, see your role in supporting processes to ensure Performance Excellence?
   - How do you role model the behaviors you want your managers and other employees to emulate?
   - What do the leaders personally do to lead this organization? What do you do that visibly displays to employees throughout the organization your personal involvement and commitment to the vision and values? How do you promote innovation?
   - What percentage of your time is spent on performance review and improvement activities? How do you review performance to assess the organization's health, competitive performance, and progress? What key performance measures do senior leaders regularly review?
   - How do you ensure the organization has the capabilities to remain competitive?
   - How do top priorities and opportunities for innovation reflect organizational review findings? How do you ensure that these

priorities and opportunities for innovation are used throughout the organization? To what extent are these priorities and innovation opportunities used with key customers, suppliers and/or partners?

- What is your process for evaluating the effectiveness of the leadership system? How do you include or use employee feedback in the evaluation?
- Please identify specific examples where the senior leadership improved the leadership system as a result of these evaluations. How do managers evaluate and improve their personal leadership effectiveness? How is employee feedback used here?

3. What are the criteria for promoting managers within the organization?
   - How are you making managers accountable for performance improvement, employee involvement, and customer satisfaction objectives?
   - What measures do you personally use to track progress toward achieving the organization's key business drivers? How often do you monitor these measures?
   - Can we see a copy of a manager's evaluation form?
   - How have you improved the process over the years of evaluating managers?

4. Share with us what you feel are the most important requirements of your key customers:
   - (Pick one of the requirements.) Which department is responsible for delivering this?
   - Please show us evidence of continuous improvement within that department.

5. What is the process used to monitor the performance of your organization? How does it relate to the organization's strategic business plan?
   - Do measurable goals exist?
   - How were the goals established?
   - How are they monitored? How often?
   - How are they key to your stakeholders' primary needs and expectations?
   - What are the key success factors (or key result areas, critical success factors, key business drivers) for your organization, and how do you use them to drive Performance Excellence?

6. As a corporate citizen, what is your process for contributing to and improving the environment and society?
   - What do you do to anticipate public concerns over the possible impact of your organization? What are some examples? How do you measure progress?
   - What are some ways your organization ensures that employees act in an ethical manner in all business transactions? How is this monitored to ensure compliance?

- Do you have any plans or processes for systematic evaluation and improvement in place?

Category 2—Strategic Planning

1. When was the last time the strategic plan was updated? How recent is it? Can we review a copy?
2. How did you develop this plan? What factors did you consider in the development of your strategic plan?
    - How does your strategic plan address supplier and/or partner capabilities? The competitive environment?
    - What role do your stakeholders play in the development of the strategic plan?
    - How do you identify resources needed to prepare for new opportunities and requirements? How are wishes addressed?
    - Are the strategic objectives for your organization derived from this plan? If not, from where do they come? May I see a list of your strategic objectives?
3. How do you plan for the development, education, and training needs of the organization? What are the organization's human resource plans (long/short term)?
    - Summarize the organization's plans related to work design, innovation, rapid response, compensation and recognition, employee development and training, recruitment, health, safety, ergonomics, special services, and employee satisfaction.
    - How do these plans optimize the use of human resources?
    - How do these plans align with the strategic plan?
    - What are examples of changes to the human resource plans based on inputs from the strategic planning in the following areas: recruitment, training, compensation, rewards, incentives, fringe benefits, programs?
4. How do you deploy these goals, objectives, and action plans throughout the organization to ensure that work is aligned and action is taken to achieve the plan?
    - How do you ensure that organizational, work unit, and individual goals and plans are aligned?
    - How do you ensure that supplier and/or partner goals are aligned with your strategic plan?
5. What is (summarize) your process for evaluation and improvement of the strategic planning and plan deployment process, including the human resource planning process?
    - What are examples of improvements made as a result of this evaluation process? Where did they occur?
6. How has your performance relative to plan been tracked?

7. Who do you consider to be your top competitors, and how does your planned performance compare to theirs and/or similar providers?
   - How do you determine who your top competitors are?
8. What are your specific goals and objectives? Please provide a copy of your long-range performance projections. How did you go about establishing these projections? How do these projections compare with your competitors' projections for the same time period?

Category 3—Customer and Market Focus

1. How do you know what your former, current, and potential customers expect of you? How does your organization determine short- and long-term customer requirements? What are they?
   - How do you differentiate key requirements from less important requirements?
   - How do you anticipate requirements and prepare to meet them?
   - How do you evaluate and improve processes for determining customer requirements?
2. How do you provide easy access for your customers to obtain information and assistance or complain? What do you expect to learn from customer complaints?
   - What is your process of handling customer complaints? Do you monitor or track complaint data? What do you do with the information?
   - What percent of complaints are resolved at first contact? Describe the training you provide to customer-contact employees.
   - Describe your process for follow-up with customers. What do you do with feedback from customers regarding products and services? What triggers action?
   - What are the customer-contact requirements or service standards? How were they determined? How do you know if standards are being met?
   - How do you evaluate and improve the customer relationship process?
   - What are some improvements you've made to the way you determine customer requirements? How did you decide they were important to make, and when were they made?
3. How often do senior managers talk to customers?
   - What do they do with this information?
4. What are your key measures for customer satisfaction and dissatisfaction? How do these measures provide information on likely future market behavior (loyalty, repurchase, and referrals)?
   - How do you measure customer satisfaction and dissatisfaction? Do you measure satisfaction/dissatisfaction for all key customer

groups/segments? What are your customer groups or segments? How do you determine them? How do you differentiate them in regard to products and services you offer? What process do you use to ensure the objectivity and validity of customer satisfaction data? What do you do with the information?

- What customer satisfaction information do you have about your competitors or benchmarks? What do you do with this information?
- How do you disseminate satisfaction/dissatisfaction information to your employees? What action do they take as a result?
- How do you know appropriate action is taken?
- How do you go about improving the way you determine customer satisfaction? Please provide some examples of how you have improved it over the past several years? When were the requirements made?

5. What processes do you use to build loyalty, positive referral, and lasting relationships with customers?
    - How do you differentiate these processes according to customer group?

6. How do you evaluate the effectiveness of processes for customer satisfaction determination and relationship enhancement? What requirements have resulted from this evaluation? When did they occur?

Category 4—Information and Analysis

1. What are the major performance indicators critical to running your organization?

2. How do you determine whether the information you collect and use for decision making is complete, timely, reliable, accessible, and accurate? What is the process you use to determine the relevance of the information to organizational goals and action plans?
    - What criteria do you use for data selection? How do you ensure that all data collected meet these criteria?
    - Describe how you obtain feedback from the users of the information. How is this feedback used to make improvements?

3. You have told us what your top priorities are. How do you benchmark against these? Please describe how needs and priorities for selecting comparisons and benchmarking are determined. Share an example of the process of prioritization:
    - How do you use competitive or comparative performance data generally?
    - How are the results of your benchmarking efforts used to set stretch targets?
    - How are the results of your benchmarking efforts used to improve work processes?

- How do you evaluate and improve your benchmarking processes?
- Show us samples of comparative studies. Picking some at random, determine: Why was the area selected? How were comparison data selected and obtained? How were data in the example used?

4. Please share with us an example of analysis of information important to your customers and your own organization's success:
    - How are data analyzed to determine relationships between customer information and financial performance; operational data and financial performance; or operational data and human resource?
    - What data and analyses do you use to understand your people, your customers, and your market?
    - How widely are these analyses used for decision making? What actions are you taking to extend the analysis across all parts of the organization?
    - What are you doing to improve the analysis process?

Category 5—Human Resource Focus

1. Do employees know and understand organization/work unit priorities? How do you determine this?
    - What do you do to ensure effective communication among employees and work units?
    - What do you do to encourage initiative and self-directed responsibility? What authority do employees have to direct their own actions and make business decisions?
    - (To employees.) What authority do you have to make decisions about resolving problems, changing process steps, and communications across departments?
    - How do you empower employees? What are some examples of processes you have used to evaluate and enhance opportunities for employees to take individual initiative and demonstrate self-directed responsibility in designing and managing their work? Show examples of actions taken and improvements made. When were they made?

2. How does the organization link recognition, reward, and compensation to achieve Performance Excellence objectives (for example, customer satisfaction, performance improvement, and organization learning)? Describe your approach to employee recognition and compensation. How does your approach reinforce achievement of goals and objectives?
    - (General question for employees.) Do you feel that your contributions to the organization are recognized? How have you been recognized for contributing to achieving organization action plans?
    - What specific reward and recognition programs are utilized?

3. How do you take into account diversity in your community and fair hiring practices in your hiring and recruitment?

4. What ongoing training is provided for your employees?
    -   How is your training curriculum designed and delivered? How do you integrate employee, supervisor, and manager feedback into the design of your training program? What methods are used?
    -   How does your training program affect operational performance goals? How do you know your training improves your business results? Show examples.
    -   What training and education do you provide to ensure that you meet the needs of all categories of employees? What training does a new employee receive to obtain the knowledge and skills necessary for success and high performance, including leadership development of employees?
    -   How do you address key development needs, such as new employee orientation, safety, and diversity training?
    -   How does training and education address Performance Excellence skills needed, such as quality control, benchmarking, and performance measurement?
    -   If applicable, how do employees in remote locations participate in training programs?
    -   What is your system for improving training? Please give us some examples of improvements made and when they were made?
    -   How do you identify skills and knowledge that will be needed by your future employees?
    -   How are these skills and characteristics reflected in recruitment and hiring practices?
5. What are your standards for employee health and safety? Does your approach to health and safety address the needs of all employee groups?
    -   How do you determine that you have a safe and healthy work environment? How do you measure this?
    -   How are you performing against those standards? How were they derived?
    -   What are your procedures for systematic evaluation and improvement?
6. How do your senior leaders, managers, and supervisors encourage employees to develop and put to use their full potential?
7. How is employee satisfaction measured? What do you do with the information?
    -   What are the key areas of concern? To employees, ask: What does the organization do to enhance your career development?
    -   What special services, facilities, activities, and opportunities does your organization provide employees?
    -   What do you do to improve employee satisfaction systematically? Please give us some examples of improvements.

Category 6—Process Management

1. What is your process for designing new or revised products and services to ensure that customer requirements are met?
   - How do suppliers, partners, customers, and support organizations participate in the design process?
   - How are design changes handled and methods used to ensure that all changes are included?
   - How do you test new products or services before they are introduced to be sure they perform as expected?
   - How do you evaluate and improve the process for designing new products/services, including reductions in cycle time? Please provide some examples of improvements and when they were made.

2. What are your key production and delivery processes and their requirements, including quality indicators and performance?
   - What steps have you taken to improve the effectiveness/efficiency of key work processes, including cycle time?
   - What are the processes by which you deliver these products and services to ensure that customer expectations will be met or exceeded?
   - Once you determine that a process may not be meeting measurement goals or performing according to expectations, what process do you use to determine root cause and to bring about process improvement?

3. Please give an example of how a customer request or complaint resulted in an improvement of a current process or the establishment of a new process?

4. Please share with us your list of key support processes, requirements, and associated process measures, including in-process measures:
   - How is performance of support services systematically evaluated and refined? Please provide some examples.
   - What are the steps you have taken to design your key support processes? How do you determine the types of services needed? How do your support services interact with and add value to your operational processes?
   - How does your organization maintain the performance of key support services? Share some examples of processes used to determine root causes of support problems and how you prevent recurrence of problems.

5. Who are your most important (key) suppliers and partners?
   - How do you determine critical characteristics your key suppliers and/or partners must meet so that your needs are met? What are the key performance requirements? What type of assistance do you provide your suppliers and/or partners to help them meet your

requirements? Please explain how you measure your supplier's and/or partner's performance and provide feedback.

- Show how you systematically help your key suppliers and/or partners improve their performance and deliver better products and services to you at a lower cost. Please provide some examples.
- What are your supplier/partner management or procurement department goals and objectives? How do you support your suppliers and/or partners to keep products and services current with your needs? How do you measure and improve their performance? Please share with us some examples.

Category 7—Business Results

1. What are the customer satisfaction trends and performance levels at this time? [Links to Item 3.2 and 6.1]:
   - Please show a breakout of data by customer group or segment.
   - How do these customer satisfaction trends and levels compare with those of your competitors or similar providers?
   - What are your current levels and trends for customer loyalty, positive referral, customer-perceived value, and relationship building?
   - What are your current levels and trends for how customers perceive your products and service performance?

2. What are the current levels and trends showing financial or marketplace performance or economic value?
   - Please provide data on key financial measures, such as return on investment (ROI), operating profits (or budget reductions as appropriate), or economic value added.
   - Please provide data on market share or business growth, as appropriate. Identify new markets entered and the level of performance in those markets.
   - How do these trends compare with those of your competitors or similar providers?

3. What are the current levels and trends showing the effectiveness of your human resource practices? [Links to Category 5]:
   - Please provide data on key indicators, such as safety/accident record, absenteeism, turnover by category and type of employee/manager, grievances, and related litigation.
   - How do these trends compare with those of your competitors or similar providers?

4. Please show us your supplier/partner performance data trends and current levels for each key indicator, such as on-time delivery, error rate, and reducing costs. [Links to Item 6.3]:

- How does performance on these key indicators compare to your competitors, other providers, or benchmarks?

5. How do you measure the quality of your products and services? [Links to Item 6.1]:
   - Please show us your performance data.
   - What are current levels and trends for key design, production, delivery and support process performance?
   - What are current level and trends for production and cycle time for design, delivery, and production?
   - How do you know which factors are most important to your customers? [Links to Item 3.1]
   - How does your performance on these key indicators compare to your competitors, other providers, or benchmarks?

6. How do you measure support service effectiveness and efficiency? [Links to Item 6.2]:
   - Please show us your performance data.
   - How do you know what the key performance indicators should be?
   - How does your performance on these key indicators compare to your competitors, other providers, or benchmarks?

7. How do you measure operating effectiveness and efficiency?
   - Please show us your performance data.
   - How do you know what the key performance indicators should be? [Links to Items 6.1 and 6.2]
   - How does your performance on these key indicators compare to your competitors, other providers, or benchmarks?
   - What are your results for regulatory/legal compliance and citizenship? [Links to Item 1.2]
   - What are your results on accomplishment of your organizational strategy?

General Cross-Cutting Questions to Ask Employees

- Who are your customers?

- What are the organization's mission, vision, and quality values? What are your goals?

- What is the strategic plan for the organization? What are the organization's goals, and what role do you play in helping to achieve the goals?

- What kind of training have you received? Was it useful?

- How are you involved in the work and decision making of the organization?

- Is this a good place to work? Why (or why not)?

- What activities are recognized or rewarded?

Summary of Business Eligibility Categories and Restrictions

Basic Eligibility Public Law 100-107 establishes the three business eligibility categories of the Baldrige Award: manufacturing, service, and small business. Any for-profit business and some subunits headquartered in the United States or its territories, including U.S. subunits of foreign companies, may apply for the Baldrige Award. Eligibility is intended to be as open as possible. For example, publicly or privately owned, domestic or foreign-owned entities, joint ventures, corporations, sole proprietorships, and holding companies may apply. Not eligible in the business category are local, state, and federal government agencies; trade associations; professional societies; and not-for-profit organizations.

Business Award Eligibility Categories and Terms

Manufacturing Companies or some subunits that produce and sell manufactured products or manufacturing processes, and producers of agricultural, mining, or construction products.

Service Companies or some subunits that sell services.

Small Business Companies engaged in manufacturing and/or the provision of services that are comprised of 500 or fewer employees.

Subunits A subunit is a unit or division of a larger (parent) company. Subunits of companies in the manufacturing and service eligibility categories might be eligible. The subunit must have more than 500 employees, or have more than 25 percent of the employees of the parent, or have been independent prior to being acquired by its parent. In the last case, it must continue to operate largely independently under its own identity.

The subunit must be self-sufficient enough to be examined in all seven Criteria categories, and it must be a discrete business entity that is readily distinguishable from other parts of the parent organization. It cannot be primarily an internal supplier to other units in the parent company or a business support function (sales, distribution, legal services, etc.).

Note: Subunits of "chain" organizations (where each unit performs a similar function or manufactures a similar product) are no longer categorically ineligible. Their eligibility is now determined by the same rules as other subunits.

Other Restrictions on Eligibility

Location

Although an applicant may have facilities outside the United States or its territories or receive support from its parent, in the event of a site visit, the applicant must ensure that the appropriate people and materials are available for examination in the United States to document the operational practices associated with all of its major business functions. In the event that the applicant receives the Baldrige Award, it must be able to share information on the seven Criteria categories at the Quest for Excellence Conference and at its U.S. facilities. Sharing beyond the Quest for Excellence Conference is on a voluntary basis.

Multiple-Application Restrictions

A subunit and its parent may not both apply for Baldrige Awards in the same year. In addition, only one subunit of a company may apply for a Baldrige Award in the same year in the same business eligibility category.

Future Eligibility Restrictions

If an organization or a subunit that has more than 50 percent of the total employees of the parent receives a Baldrige Award, the organization and all its subunits are ineligible to apply for another award for a period of five years. If a subunit receives an award, that subunit and all its subunits are ineligible to apply for another award for a period of five years. After five years, Baldrige Award recipients are eligible to reapply for the award or to reapply "for feedback only."

Eligibility Determination

To ensure that Baldrige Award recipients meet all reasonable requirements and expectations in representing the award throughout the United States, potential applicants must have their eligibility approved prior to applying for the award. Potential applicants for the 2000 Baldrige Award are encouraged to submit their Eligibility Determination Forms as early as possible after they are available but no later than April 15, 2000. This form is contained in the *2000 Application Forms & Instructions for Business, Education, and Health Care.*

Fees for the 2000 Award Cycle

Eligibility Determination Fees

The eligibility determination fee is $100 for all potential applicants. This fee is nonrefundable.

Application Fees

Manufacturing company category—$4500
Service business category—$4500
Small business category—$1500
Supplemental sections—$1500 (Note: Supplemental sections fees are charges to companies that want a business unit reviewed as part of the application process and that business unit falls under another eligibility sector. For example, assume that manufacturing is the core business of an automaker. However, the automaker also operates a chain of service stations and a car rental system—both service sector companies. A supplemental section fee could be charged for this review.)

These fees cover all expenses associated with distribution and review of applications and development of feedback reports.

Site Visit Review Fees

Site visit review fees will be set when the visits are scheduled. Fees depend upon the number of examiners assigned and the duration of the visit. Site visit review fees for applicants in the small business category will be charged at one-half of the rate charged for companies in the manufacturing and service categories.

Site visit fees cover all expenses and travel costs associated with site visit participation and development of site visit reports. These fees are paid only by those applicants reaching the site visit stage.

Feedback

All applicants receive a feedback report at the conclusion of the review process. The feedback report—a tool for continuous improvement—is:
- An assessment written by a team of leading U.S. quality and performance experts
- An applicant-specific listing of strengths and opportunities for improvement based on the Baldrige Criteria for Performance Excellence
- Used by organizations as part of their strategic planning processes to focus on their customers and to improve productivity
- A pathway for continuous improvement

The report does not provide suggestions or ideas on how to improve.

The feedback report contains the Baldrige Award evaluation team's response to the written application. Length varies according to the detail presented in the written responses to the Baldrige Award Criteria. The report includes the following components:

- Background
- Application review process
- Scoring
- Distribution of numerical scores for all applicants
- Overall scoring summary of applicant
- Criteria category scoring summary of applicant
- Details of the applicant's strengths and areas for improvement (feedback reports often contain more than 150 strengths and areas for improvement)

Strict confidentiality is observed at all times and in every aspect of application review and feedback.

A survey of 1993 and 1994 Baldrige Award applicants conducted by the National Quality Award Office showed that more than 90 percent of respondents used the feedback report in their strategic and business planning processes.

Information about current and past winners and their achievements was drawn from the award office web page. General information on the National Institute of Standards and Technology is available on the World Wide Web at *http://www.nist.gov* and on the Baldrige Award program at *http://www.quality.nist.gov.*

Malcolm Baldrige National Quality Award Winners

1999 Winners
- BI, Minneapolis, Minnesota (Service)
- The Ritz-Carlton Hotel Company, L.L.C., Atlanta, Georgia (Service)
- STMicroelectronics, Inc. - Region Americas, Carrollton, Texas (Manufacturing)
- Sunny Fresh Foods, Monticello, Minnesota; (Small Business/ Manufacturing).

BI provides training to help improve the performance of people. In this way, it helps its customers achieve their business goals. BI designs and delivers performance improvement programs that integrate communications, training, measurement, and rewards. These programs benefit customers' distributors, employees, and consumers. BI designs training, it helps customers with organizational change and strategic planning, customer loyalty programs, and sales incentive programs. Over five years, BI's revenue has grown 47 percent. Its successful strategy has been to target strategic accounts to create a much higher rate of customer satisfaction in these accounts rather than target growth in overall market share. Its products and services have resulted in customer loyalty that outperforms its top two competitors. It has retained an average of 73 percent of customers and an average of 96.3 percent of revenue.

The Ritz-Carlton Hotel Company, L.L.C. manages 36 luxury hotels worldwide. It is the only service company to receive a Baldrige Award twice. The Ritz-Carlton holds the top position in complete satisfaction with a score of 70 Percent compared to 56 percent for its closest competitor on a recent nationwide survey. Since 1995, pretax return on investment has nearly doubled. Training is key to employee retention and the company's customer-focused culture. First year managers and employees receive 250 to 310 hours of training. It has developed an innovative customer database to record guests' preferences and customize services to meet these preferences.

STMicroelectronics, Inc. designs, develops, manufactures, and markets semiconductor integrated circuits for consumer electronics and automotive, medical, telecommunications, and computer applications in the United States and around the world. ST has earned a "Best in Class" measured against major semiconductor companies based on 19 standard benchmark areas in the most recent industry report. It has performed better than key competitors in many financial and growth areas during a very volatile decade in its market. Its revenue has grown from $493 million to $937 million from 1994 to 1998, which exceeded the average of seven competitors. Its market share has increased from 1.88 percent (1991) to 2.36 percent (1998). Employee empowerment is widespread. Its employee satisfaction survey results exceeded the industry composite in 8 of 10 factors.

Sunny Fresh Foods is the first food manufacturer to receive the Baldrige Award. It manufactures further processed egg products, including pasteurized refrigerated, and frozen egg products; fat-free products; peeled hard-cooked eggs; and precooked egg products, such as omelets, french toast, and frozen scrambled eggs. This company has increased market share in U.S. markets from fourteenth in 1988 to second in 1999. It has received numerous awards form its customers. Its return on gross investment, has tripled in the last several years. All of Sunny Fresh Foods' facilities score in the excellent range on sanitation. It has many innovative work system designs that create a safe facility and minimize injuries.

1998 Winners
- Boeing Airlift and Tanker Programs, Long Beach, California (Manufacturing)
- Solar Turbines, Inc., San Diego, California (Manufacturing)
- Texas Nameplate Co., Inc., Dallas, Texas (Manufacturing)

Boeing Airlift and Tanker Programs—known as A&T, Boeing Airlift, and Tanker Programs—designs, manufactures, and supports military transport aircraft. One of its major products is the C-17, designed to airlift large, heavy cargo to locations around the world. Based in Long Beach, California, A&T has 8700 employees. In addition to other awards, A&T received the California Governor's Golden State Quality Award for management in 1996, and its Macon, Georgia, facility received the Georgia Governor's Employer of the Year Award in 1998. In addition to California and Georgia, A&T also has sites in St. Louis, Missouri; Seattle, Washington; and San Antonio, Texas; as well as at Air Force bases in Oklahoma, California, and South Carolina.

Solar Turbines, Inc. is based in San Diego, California. Solar Turbines designs and manufactures industrial gas turbines for power generation, natural gas compression, and pumping systems for sale in the United States and worldwide. Solar Turbines is one of the 50 largest exporters in the United States. A subsidiary of Caterpillar, Inc., Solar Turbines has 6200 staff at 15 U.S. sites and in 23 foreign nations. In 1995, Solar Turbines received a "Best in Class" California U.S. Senate Productivity Award in large manufacturing.

Texas Nameplate Company, Inc. was founded in 1946. Texas Nameplate manufactures and sells identification and information labels used on a variety of products, including oil field equipment, truck and trailer vehicles, and electronic and computer equipment. With 66 employees, Texas Nameplate is the smallest company ever to receive the Baldrige Award. The company has two locations in Dallas, Texas. TNC received the Texas Quality Award in 1996.

1988–1999 Baldrige Award Winners and Contact Information

This section contains a list of Baldrige Award winners and key contact personnel from 1988 to 1999 as reported by NIST and the Office of Quality Programs. First, the 1999 winners are presented, then the others in alphabetical order.

BI—1999 (Service)
Betsy Schneider, Director of Marketing Services
Telephone: (612) 844-4655
E-mail: schneide@biperf.com

STMicroelectronics –1999 (Manufacturing)
J. P. Rossomme, Manager Public Affairs and Communications
Telephone: (602) 485-2262
E-mail: Jean-Pierr.Rossomme@st.com

The RITZ-CARLTON HOTEL COMPANY—1999 (Service)
Stephanie Platt, Corporate Director of Communications
Telephone: (404) 237-5500
E-mail: Stephanie.Platt@ritzcarlton.com

SUNNY FRESH FOODS—1999 (Small Business Category)
Laura Huston, Manager of Business Process Improvement
Telephone: (612) 745-2918
E-mail: Laura_Huston@cargill.com

BOEING AIRLIFT AND TANKER PROGRAMS—1998 (Manufacturing)
Rick Fuller, Director of Communications
2401 Wandlow Road
Long Beach, CA 90807
Telephone: (562) 496-5195
E-mail: richard.l.fuller@boeing.com

SOLAR TURBINES, INC.—1998 (Manufacturing)
Larry Winegrad, Director, Process and Quality Improvement

9330 Sky Park Court
San Diego, CA 92123
Telephone: (619) 715-7777
E-mail: lwinegrad@cat.e-mail.com

TEXAS NAMEPLATE COMPANY, INC.—1998 (Manufacturing)
Scott Weber, Director of Administration
P.O. Box 150499
Dallas, TX 75315-0499
Telephone: (214) 421-8206; (800) 546-4161
E-mail: sweber@nameplate.com

3M DENTAL PRODUCTS DIVISION—1997 (Manufacturing)
Jim Wilson, Quality Specialist
3M Center; Building 260-2A-11
St. Paul, MN 55144
Telephone: (800) 449-1476; Fax: (612) 737-6049
Web site: www.mmm.com/dental/baldrige

ADAC LABORATORIES—1996 (Manufacturing)
Doug Keare, Vice President of Quality
540 Alder Drive
Milpitas, CA 95035
Telephone: (408) 321-9100; Fax: (408) 321-9686
Web site: www.adaclabs.com/pressrel/1996/101696.html

AMES RUBBER CORPORATION—1993 (Small Business)
Charles A. Roberts, Vice President, Total Quality
23-47 Ames Boulevard
Hamburg, NJ 07419
Telephone: (201) 209-3200; Fax: (201) 827-8893
Web site: www.amesrubber.com/totalqlt.htm

ARMSTRONG WORLD INDUSTRIES, INC. BUILDING PRODUCTS
OPERATIONS—1995 (Manufacturing)
Nancy D. Hann, Baldrige Coordinator
Armstrong Building Products Operations
2500 Columbia Avenue
Lancaster, PA 17604
Telephone: (717) 396-2540; Fax: (717) 396-6330
E-mail: ndhann@armstrong.com

AT&T CONSUMER COMMUNICATIONS SERVICES—1994 (Service)
John Braseli, District Manager
AT&T Consumer Markets Division
Room 6356F1
292 North Maple Avenue
Basking Ridge, NJ 07920
Telephone: (800) 473-5047; Fax: (908) 221-3015
As of 1/1/97, AT&T Consumer Communications Services became part of the new Consumer & Small Business Division of AT&T.

AT&T NETWORK SYSTEMS GROUP TRANSMISSION SYSTEMS BUSINESS UNIT—1992 (Manufacturing)
Jim Beauregard, Manager, Quality Engineering Assurance
Lucent Technologies, Inc. (including what was formerly TSBU)
1600 Osgood Street
North Andover, MA 01845
Telephone: (978) 960-4309; Fax: (978) 960-1660

AT&T UNIVERSAL CARD SERVICES—1992 (Service)
James Selzer, Vice President
8787 Baypine Road
Jacksonville, FL 32256
Telephone: (904) 954-8896; Fax: (904) 954-8720

CADILLAC MOTOR CAR COMPANY—1990 (Manufacturing)
Joseph R. Bransky, Director, Quality and Reliability
General Motors Corporation
30007 Van Dyke Ave., Room 142-37
Warren, MI 48090
Telephone: (810) 492-7704; Fax: (810) 492-7943
Tom Klipstine, Communications Staff
NAO Headquarters, Building 1-8
30400 Mound Road
Warren, MI 48090
Telephone: (810) 986-6132; Fax: (810) 986-9253

CORNING INCORPORATED TELECOMMUNICATIONS PRODUCTS DIVISION—1995 (Manufacturing)
Barbara Nazarczyk, Manager, Business Systems
Telecommunications Products Division
35 West Market Street
Corning, NY 14831
Telephone: (607) 974-8473; Fax: (607) 754-7517

CUSTOM RESEARCH, INC.—1996 (Small Business)
Beth Rounds, Senior Vice President
8401 Golden Valley Road
Minneapolis, MN 55427
Telephone: (612) 542-0882; Fax: (612) 542-0864

DANA COMMERCIAL CREDIT CORPORATION—1996 (Service)
Teressa Herbert, Director of Quality
P.O. Box 906
Toledo, OH 43697-0906
Telephone: (419) 322-7500; Fax: (419) 322-7721

EASTMAN CHEMICAL COMPANY—1993 (Manufacturing)
Christa Haynes, Coordinator, Corporate Information Center
431 Building 471
Kingsport, TN 37662
Telephone: (423) 229-1925; Fax: (423) 224-0323
Web site: www.eastman.com/corp/qual/nistemn.shtml

FEDERAL EXPRESS CORPORATION—1990 (Service)
Quality Questions and Information
Glenn Pearson, Manager, Quality and Process Improvement
1980 Nonconnah Boulevard
Memphis, TN 38132
Telephone: (901) 224-2362; Fax: (901) 224-2350

GLOBE METALLURGICAL, INC.—1988 (Small Business)
Norman Jennings, Quality Director
P.O. Box 157
Beverly, OH 45715
Telephone: (740) 984-2361; Fax: (770) 984-8635

GRANITE ROCK COMPANY—1992 (Small Business)
Dave Franceschi, Quality Services Manager
P.O. Box 50001
Watsonville, CA 95077-5001
Telephone: (408) 768-2000; Fax: (408) 768-2201

GTE DIRECTORIES CORPORATION—1994 (Service)
Bruce Rosenstie, Quality Service Manager
GTE Place, West Airfield Drive
P.O. Box 619810
D/FW Airport, TX 75261-9810

Telephone: (972) 453-0172; Fax: (972) 453-6758
Web site: www.gte.com

IBM ROCHESTER—1990 (Manufacturing)
IBM Rochester, Quality Manager
3605 Highway 52 North
Rochester, MN 55901-7829
Telephone: (507) 253-4434; Fax: (507) 253-4461
Web site: www.as400.ibm.com/quality/as400.htm

MARLOW INDUSTRIES—1991 (Small Business)
Ms. Tiki Miller, Baldrige Award Coordinator
10451 Vista Park Road
Dallas, TX 75238-1645
Fax: (214) 341-5212
Web site: www.marlow.com/quality.htm

MERRILL LYNCH CREDIT CORPORATION—1997 (Service)
Lee Lomax, Director of Quality & Business Improvement
4802 Deer Lake Drive East
Jacksonville, FL 32246
Telephone: (904) 218-6242; Fax: (904) 218-6124
Wendell Collins, Vice President-Publicity
800 Scudders Mill Road
Plainsboro, NJ 08536
Telephone: (609) 282-3121; Fax: (609) 282-1295
Web site: www.ml.com/woml/press_release/19971015-1.htm

MILLIKEN & COMPANY—1989 (Manufacturing)
Craig Long, Director of Quality
P.O. Box 1926, M-186
Spartanburg, SC 29304
Telephone: (864) 503-2003; Fax: (864) 503-2505
Web site: www.milliken.com/quality.html

MOTOROLA, INC.—1988 (Manufacturing)
Dennis Sester, Vice President and Director of Corporate Quality
1303 East Algonquin Road
Schaumburg, IL 60196
Telephone: (847) 576-5516; Fax: (847) 538-2663
Web site: www.mot.com

THE RITZ-CARLTON HOTEL COMPANY—1992 (Service)
Patrick Mene, Vice President of Quality
3414 Peachtree Road N.E., Suite 300
Atlanta, GA 30326
Telephone: (404) 237-5500; Fax: (404) 240-9771

SOLECTRON CORPORATION—1991 and 1997 (Manufacturing)
Denise Co, Quality Assurance Associate
847 Gilbraltar Drive
Milpitas, CA 95035
Telephone: (408) 956-6963; Fax: (408) 957-2645
Web site: www.solectron.com/quality/index.html
Michael Donner, Director, Corporate Communications
847 Gilbraltar Drive
Milpitas, CA 95035
Telephone: (408) 956-6688; Fax: (408) 956-7699

TEXAS INSTRUMENTS INCORPORATED DEFENSE SYSTEMS &
ELECTRONICS GROUP—1992 (Manufacturing)
Karen Hollingsworth, Director of Business Excellence
Raytheon Systems Company Sensor and Electronics Systems
P.O. Box 405, Mail Station 3461
Lewisville, TX 75067
Telephone: (972) 462-4455; Fax: (972) 462-5155

TRIDENT PRECISION MANUFACTURING, INC.—1996 (Small
Business)
April Lusk
734 Salt Road
Webster, NY 14580-9796
Telephone: (716) 265-1009; Fax: (716) 265-0126
Web site: www.tridentprecision.com/quality/index.html

WAINWRIGHT INDUSTRIES, INC.—1994 (Small Business)
Michael Simms, Plant Manager
P.O. Box 640
St. Peters, MO 63376
Telephone: (314) 278-5850; Fax: (314) 278-8806
David A. Robbins, Vice President
P.O. Box 640
St. Peters, MO 63376
Telephone: (314) 278-5850; Fax: (314) 278-8806

WALLACE COMPANY—1990 (Small Business)
Assets of the Wallace Company have been acquired by Wilson Industries.

WESTINGHOUSE ELECTRIC CORP. COMMERCIAL NUCLEAR FUEL
DIVISION—1988 (Manufacturing)
Ms. Meens Mutuala, Director of Quality and Environmental Systems
Westinghouse CNFD
P.O. Box 355
Pittsburgh, PA 15230
Telephone: (412) 374-2292; Fax: (412) 374-2334

XEROX BUSINESS SERVICES—1997 (Service)
Genny Craver
70 Linden Oaks Parkway
Rochester, NY 14625
Telephone: (716) 383-6758; Fax: (716) 264-5701
Web site: www.xerox.com/XBS/baldrige

XEROX CORPORATION BUSINESS PRODUCTS & SYSTEMS—1989
(Manufacturing)
Genny Craver
Xerox Corporation
Xerox Square—18B
100 Clinton Avenue South
Rochester, NY 14644
Telephone: (716) 383-6758; Fax: (716) 423-6041

ZYTEC CORPORATION—1991 (Manufacturing)
Karen Scheldroup, Baldrige Office
7575 Market Place Drive
Eden Prairie, MN 55344
Telephone: (612) 941-1100 x. 104; Fax: (612) 903-9688

State Quality Award Contacts

Alabama

Alabama Quality Award
Linda Vincent
Director
Alabama Productivity Center
P.O. Box 870318
Tuscaloosa, AL 35487-0318
Telephone: (205) 348-8956
Fax: (205) 348-9391
E-mail: linda@proctr.cba.ua.edu
Applicant Categories: Manufacturing, Small Business, Service, Health Care,
    Education

Arizona

Arizona State Quality Awards
Tim Jones
Executive Director
Arizona Quality Alliance
7510 E. Main St., Suite 3
Scottsdale, AZ 85251-7768
Telephone: (602) 481-3454
Fax: (602) 481-3097
E-mail: aqa@tqm.com

Arkansas

Arkansas Quality Award
Barbara Harvel
Executive Director
Arkansas Quality Award
1111 W. Capitol, Room 1013
Little Rock, AR 72201-3005
Telephone: (501) 373-1300
Fax: (501) 373-1976
E-mail: arkansasquality@compuserve.com
Applicant Categories: Quality Interest, Quality Commitment, Quality
    Achievement, Governor's Quality Award

California
California Awards for Performance Excellence (CAPE)
Administered by the: California Council for Excellence
(formerly CCQS and CalQED)
P.O. Box 1235
Poway, CA 92074-1235
Telephone: (858) 486-0400
Fax: (858) 486-8595
E-mail: cape@ccqs.org

Colorado
The Chapman Group
Michael Chapman, President
1750 Hawthorn Place
Boulder, CO 80304
Telephone: (303) 442-0715
Fax: (303) 546-0616
E-mail: mchappy@attglobal.net

Better Business Bureau's Excellence in Customer Service Award
Leslie Schwager
Executive Director
Better Business Bureau of the Pikes Peak Region, Inc.
3022 N. El Paso
Colorado Springs, CO 80907
Telephone: (719) 636-5076 x111
Fax: (719) 636-5078
E-mail: info@coloradosprings.bbb.org
Applicant Categories: Small, medium, and large businesses

Connecticut
Connecticut Award for Excellence
Brian Will
Executive Director
Connecticut Award for Excellence
52 Marjorie Lane
Vernon, CT 06066
Telephone: (860) 872-4891
Fax: (860) 872-1371
E-mail: BrianRWill@aol.com
Applicant Categories: Business, Government, Education, Health Care

Delaware
Delaware Quality Award
Zena Tucker
Delaware Quality Consortium, Inc.
Delaware Economic Development Office
99 Kings Highway
P.O. Box 1401
Dover, DE 19903
Telephone: (904) 922-5316
Fax: (904) 487-0801

Florida
Governor's Sterling Award
John Pieno, Jr.
Chairman
Florida Sterling Council
P.O. Box 13907
Tallahassee, FL 32317-3907
Telephone: (850) 922-5316
Fax: (850) 488-7579
E-mail: lowmand@eog.state.fl.us
Applicant Categories: All sectors (not multilevel)

Georgia
Georgia Oglethorpe Award
Victoria Taylor
100 Lambets Way
Alpharetta, GA 30202
Telephone: (770) 889-4011
Fax: (770) 889-6821

Hawaii
Hawaii State Award of Excellence
Norm Baker
Chamber of Commerce of Hawaii
1132 Bishop St., Suite 402
Honolulu, HI 96813
Telephone: (808) 545-4394
Fax: (808) 545-4369
E-mail: nbaker@chamberofcommercehi.org
Applicant Categories: All organizations operating in Hawaii

Idaho
Idaho Quality Award
Roland B. Smith
Director
c/o Idaho Total Quality Institute
10332 Fairview Ave., Suite 202-B
Boise, ID 83704
Telephone: (208) 364-4017
Fax: (208) 364-4035
E-mail: roland@uidaho.edu

Illinois
Lincoln Award for Business Excellence
Marie Sinioris
President, The Lincoln Foundation
Lincoln Foundation for Business Excellence
820 W. Jackson Blvd., 5th Fl.
Chicago, IL 60607
Telephone: (312) 258-5185
Fax: (312) 258-4066

Barbara Graham
Executive Director, The Lincoln Foundation for Business Excellence
820 W. Jackson Blvd., 7th Fl.
Chicago, IL 60607
Telephone: (312) 258-4055
Fax: (312) 258-4066
E-mail: rcrane@lincolnaward.org

Indiana
Indiana Quality Improvement Award
Bob Fryer
Indiana Business Modernization & Technology Corp.
One North Capitol Ave., Suite 925
Indianapolis, IN 46204-2242
Telephone: (317) 636-3058 x246
Fax: (317) 231-7095

Iowa
Iowa Award for Competitive Excellence
Dr. James L. Melsa
IA Award for Competitive Excellence
College of Engineering
Iowa State University
Ames, IA 50011
Telephone: (515) 294-5935
Fax: (515) 294-9273
E-mail: melsa@iastate.edu
Award will not start until at least 2000

Kansas   Kansas Award for Excellence
                    John Shoemaker
                    Kansas Award for Excellence
                    151 North Volutsia
                    Wichita, KS 67214
                    Telephone: (316) 978-3376
                    Fax: (316) 976-3667
                    E-mail: John_Shoemaker@qof.com
                    Applicant Categories: Three levels; all categories

Kentucky   Commonwealth of Kentucky Quality Award
                    Joe Walters
                    Program Director
                    Kentucky Quality Award
                    167 W. Main Street, Suite 500
                    Lexington, KY 40507
                    Telephone: (606) 255-9458
                    Fax: (606) 252-7900
                    E-mail: jwalters@kts-inc.org
                    Applicant Categories: Quality Interest, Quality Commitment, Quality
                        Achievement, Governor's Gold Quality Award

Maine   Margaret Chase Smith Maine State Quality Award
                    Andrea Jandebeur
                    MCS Quality Association
                    7 Community Drive
                    Augusta, ME 04330
                    Telephone: (207) 621-1988
                    Fax: (207) 282-6081
                    E-mail: mqc@Maine-Quality.org
                    Applicant Categories: Level 1: Commitment; Level 2: Progress; Level 3:
                        Excellence

Maryland   Maryland Senate Productivity Award/Maryland
                    Excellence Award
                    Amit Gupta
                    Maryland Center for Quality & Productivity
                    College of Business & Management
                    University of Maryland
                    College Park, MD 20742-7215
                    Telephone: (301) 405-7099
                    Fax: (301) 314-9119

Massachusetts	Massachusetts Performance Excellence Award
	Tyler Fairbank
	President
	MassExcellence
	600 Suffolk St., 5th Floor
	Lowell, MA 01854
	Telephone: (978) 934-2733
	Fax: (978) 934-4035
	E-mail: anne@massexcellence.com
	Applicant Categories: Three levels in Manufacturing, Service, Small Business, Nonprofit

Michigan
Michigan Quality Leadership Award
Bill Kalmar
Oakland University
525 O'Dowd Hall
Rochester, MI 48309-4401
Telephone: (248) 370-4552
Fax: (248) 370-4228
E-mail: kalmar@oakland.edu
Applicant Categories: Lighthouse (self-assessment), Navigator (Baldrige at Item level), Honor Roll (full application), Leadership Award (50-page Baldrige application)

Minnesota
Minnesota Quality Award
Patricia Fryer Billings
President
Minnesota Council for Quality
2850 Metro Drive, Suite 519
Bloomington, MN 55425
Telephone: (612) 851-3181
Fax: (612) 851-3183
E-mail: MC4quality@aol.com
Applicant Categories: Manufacturing, Service, Education, Government, Health Care, Nonprofit

Mississippi
Mississippi Quality Award
Duane Hamill
SBCJC Mississippi Quality Awards
3825 Ridgewood Road
Jackson, MS 39211
Telephone: (601) 982-6349
Fax: (601) 982-6363
E-mail: dhamill@sbcjc.cc.ms.us
Applicant Categories: Any publicly or privately held organization of any size in the state of Mississippi may apply.

Missouri

Missouri Quality Award
John J. Politi
Director
Missouri Quality Award
P.O. Box 1085
Jefferson City, MO 65102
Telephone: (573) 526-1725
Fax: (573) 526-1729
E-mail: jkuesler@mail.state.mo.us
Applicant Categories: Manufacturing, Service, Health Care, Education, Public Sector

Nebraska

The Edgerton Quality Award
Jack Ruff
Program Director
The Edgerton Quality Award Program
Nebraska Dept. of Economic Development
Existing Business Assistance Div.
P.O. Box 94666
301 Centennial Mall South
Lincoln, NE 68509
Telephone: (402) 471-4167
Fax: (402) 471-4374
E-mail: jruff@ded1.ded.state.ne.us
Applicant Categories: Two categories, three levels

Nevada

U.S. Senate Productivity Awards for Nevada
Katrina Ekedahl
Program Administrator
Quality & Productivity Institute
P.O. Box 93416
Las Vegas, NV 89193-3416
Telephone: (702) 798-7292
Fax: (702) 798-8653

New Hampshire

Granite State Quality Council
Thomas Raffio
Granite State Quality Council
P.O. Box 29
Manchester, NH 03105-0029
Telephone: (603) 223-1312
Fax: (603) 223-1299
E-mail: quality@gsqc.com

New Jersey	Governor's Award for Performance Excellence
	Rich Serfass
	Executive Director
	Quality New Jersey
	20 West State Street
	P.O. Box 827
	Trenton, NJ 08625-0827
	Telephone: (609) 777-0940
	Fax: (609) 777-2798
	E-mail: rserfass@recom.com
	Applicant Categories: All organizations; five recognition levels

New Mexico New Mexico Quality Award
Julia Gabaldon
President
Quality New Mexico
P.O. Box 25005
Albuquerque, NM 87125
Telephone: (505) 944-2001
Fax: (505) 944-2002
E-mail: qnm@quality-newmexico.org
Applicant Categories: Three levels; NM organizations with at least five
employees

New York Empire State Advantage: Excellence at Work
Barbara Ann Harms
Executive Director
Empire State Advantage
11 Computer Drive W., Suite 212
Albany, NY 12205
Telephone: (518) 482-1747
Fax: (518) 482-2231
E-mail: ESAProgram@aol.com
Applicant Categories: Two programs: Governor's Award for Excellence and
ESA Certification program; all sectors eligible

North Carolina NC Performance Excellence Process
Pryor Gibson
President and Executive Director
4904 Professional Court, Suite 100
Raleigh, NC 27609
Telephone: (800) 207-5485
Fax: (919) 872-8199
E-mail: ncqlf@aol.com
Applicant Categories: Four steps: Involvement, Commitment, Advancement,
Leadership

Oklahoma	Oklahoma Quality Award Mike Strong Director Oklahoma Quality Award Foundation, Inc. P.O. Box 26980 Oklahoma City, OK 73126-0980 Telephone: (405) 815-5295 Fax: (405) 815-5205 E-mail: mike_strong@odoc.state.ok.us Applicant Categories: Manufacturing, Service, Health Care, Education, Government—in three sizes by number of employees
Oregon	Oregon Quality Award Carolyn Mark Program Director The Performance Center 18640 NW Walker Rd., Suite 1027 Beaverton, OR 97006 Telephone: (503) 725-2805 Fax: (503) 725-2801 E-mail: cmark@performancecenter.org
Rhode Island	Rhode Island Governor's Award for Competitiveness & Excellence Lynne C. Couture RACE for Quality Management P.O. Box 6766 Providence, RI 02940 Telephone: (401) 454-3030 Fax: (401) 454-0056 E-mail: racequal@idt.net Applicant Categories: All sectors
South Carolina	South Carolina Governor's Quality Award Jeanette Reeves University of South Carolina at Spartanburg 800 University Way Spartanburg, SC 29303 Telephone: (864) 503-5990 Fax: (864) 503-5995 E-mail: jreeves@gw.uscs.edu Applicant Categories: All sectors

Tennessee
Tennessee Quality Award
Marie Williams
President and CEO
Tennessee Quality Award
Tennessee Economic Development
333 Commerce St.
Nashville, TN 37201-3300
Telephone: (800) 453-6474
Fax: (615) 214-8933
E-mail: tqa@bellsouth.net
Applicant Categories: All sectors

Texas
Texas Quality Award
Jim Carmichael
Quality Texas
P.O. Box 684157
Austin, TX 78768-4157
Telephone: (512) 477-8137
Fax: (512) 477-8137
E-mail: qualtex@swbell.net
Applicant Categories: Small Business, Manufacturing, Service, Public
    Sector, Health Care, Education

Vermont
Vermont Performance Excellence Award
Wendy Steager
President, Vermont Council for Quality
One Main Street
Champlain Mill
Winooski, VT 05404
Telephone: (802) 655-1910
Fax: (802) 655-1932
E-mail: wsteager@aol.com

Virginia
U.S. Senate Productivity and Quality Award for VA
Wanda Hylton
820 University City Blvd., MC 0364
Virginia Tech
Blacksburg, VA 24061
Telephone: (540) 231-9617
Fax: (540) 231-9886
E-mail: whylton@vt.edu
Applicant Categories: Private Sector Manufacturing and Service; Public
    Sector State, Federal, and Local Agencies

Washington

Washington State Quality Award
Bob Concannon
Washington Quality Award
8294 S. Sunset Vista Lane
Clinton, WA 98236
Telephone: (360) 579-7244
Fax: (360) 579-7244
Applicant Categories: Government, Private, Not for Profit, Education
(all categories are further divided by large (201+ employees) and small
(less than 201 employees))

Wisconsin

Wisconsin Forward Award
Sheryl Billups
Forward Award Coordinator
Wisconsin Forward Award
201 E. Washington Ave.
P.O. Box 7972
Madison, WI 53702
Telephone: (608) 266-9615
Fax: (608) 267-0330
E-mail: billupsh@dwd.state.wi.us
Applicant Categories: Commitment, Proficiency, Mastery, Excellence

Glossary

Action Plans

Action plans refer to principal organization-level drivers, derived from short- and long-term strategic planning. In simplest terms, action plans are set to accomplish those things your organization should do well for your strategy to succeed. Action plan development represents the critical stage in planning when general strategies and goals are made specific so that effective organizationwide understanding and deployment are possible. Deployment of action plans requires analysis of overall resource needs and creation of aligned measures for all work units. Deployment might also require specialized training for some employees or recruitment of personnel.

An example of an action plan element for a supplier in a highly competitive industry might be to develop and maintain a price leadership position. Action plans could entail design of efficient processes, analysis of resource and asset use, and creation of a cost accounting system, aligned for the organization as a whole. They might also involve use of a cost-accounting system that provides activity-level cost information to support day-to-day work. Unit and/or team training should include priority setting based on costs and benefits. Organization-level analysis and review should emphasize overall productivity growth. Ongoing competitive analysis and planning should remain sensitive to technological and other changes that might greatly reduce operating costs for the organization or its competitors.

Alignment

Alignment refers to consistency of plans, processes, information, resource decisions, actions, results, analysis, and learning to support key organizationwide goals.

Effective alignment requires common understanding of purposes and goals and use of complementary measures and information for planning, tracking, analysis, and improvement at three levels: the organizational level, the key process level, and the work unit level.

Analysis

Analysis refers to assessments performed by an organization or its work units to provide a basis for effective decisions. Overall organizational analysis guides process management toward achieving key business results and toward attaining strategic objectives.

Despite their importance, individual facts and data do not usually provide an effective basis for actions or setting priorities. Actions depend upon understanding cause-effect relationships. Understanding such relationships comes from analysis of facts and data.

Approach

Approach refers to how an organization addresses the Baldrige Criteria Item requirements—the methods and processes used by the organization. Approaches are evaluated on the basis of the appropriateness of the approach to the Item requirements; effectiveness of use of the approach; and alignment with organizational needs.

Asset Productivity

The productive use that is made of an organization's assets. An overall measure of asset productivity could be made by dividing the total sales/revenue/budget by total asset value. In addition, specific asset productivity can be determined by making similar calculations against a specific asset or set of assets, such as a specific plant, production line, or even the productivity of land assets (acreage).

Benchmarking

One process by which an organization compares its performance against that of other organizations, determines how those organizations achieved higher performance levels, and uses the information to improve its own performance. Although it is difficult to benchmark some processes directly in some businesses, many of the things one organization does are very similar to things that others do. For example, most organizations move information and tangible products, pay people, train them, appraise their performance, and more. A key to successful benchmarking is to identify the process elements of work and find others who are the best at that process.

Continuous Improvement

The ongoing improvement of products, programs, services, or processes by small increments or major breakthroughs.

Customer

An organization or person who receives or uses a product or service. The customer may be a member or part of another organization or the same organization, or an end user.

Cycle Time

Cycle time refers to time performance—the time required to fulfill commitments or to complete tasks.

Time measurements play a major role in the Criteria because of the great importance of time performance to improving competitiveness. In the Criteria booklet, cycle time refers to all aspects of time performance. Other time-related terms in common use are *setup time, lead time, order fulfillment time, changeover time, delivery time and time to market,* and other key process times.

Data

Numerical information used as a basis for reasoning, discussion, determining status, decision making, and analysis.

Effectiveness

The extent to which a work process produces intended results.

Efficiency

The effort or resources required to produce desired results. More-efficient processes require fewer resources than do less-efficient processes.

Employee Involvement

A practice within an organization whereby employees regularly participate in making decisions on how their work is done, including making suggestions for improvement, planning, goal setting, and monitoring performance.

High-Performance Work

High-performance work is a term used in the Item descriptions and comments. It refers to work approaches systematically pursuing ever-higher levels of overall organizational and human performance, including quality, productivity, innovation rate, and time performance. High-performance work results in improved service for customers and other stakeholders.

Approaches to high-performance work vary in form, function, and incentive systems. Effective approaches generally include cooperation between management and the workforce, including workforce bargaining units; cooperation among work units, often involving teams; self-directed responsibility (sometimes called empowerment); input to planning; individual and organizational skill building and learning; learning from other organizations; flexibility in job design and work assignments; a flattened organizational structure where decision making is decentralized and decisions are made closest to the front line; and effective use of performance measures, including comparisons. Many high-performance work systems use monetary and nonmonetary incentives based upon such factors as organizational performance, team and/or individual contributions, and skill building. Also, high-performance work approaches usually seek to align the design of organizations, work, jobs, employee development, and incentives.

Indicator

When two or more measurements are required to provide a more complete picture of performance, the measurements are called *indicators*. For example, the number of complaints is an indicator of dissatisfaction, not an exclusive measure of it. Cycle time is a discrete measure of the time it takes to complete a process. However, it is only one indicator of process effectiveness. Other indicators may include measures of rework, waste, and defects.

Innovation

Innovation refers to making meaningful change to improve products, services, and/or processes and create new value for stakeholders. Innovation involves the adoption of an idea, process, technology, or product that is considered new or new to its proposed application.

Successful organizational innovation is a multistep process that involves development and knowledge sharing, a decision to implement, implementation, evaluation, and learning. Although innovation is often associated with technological innovation, it is applicable to all key organizational processes that would benefit from breakthrough improvement and/or change.

Integrated

Refers to the interconnections between the processes of a management system. For example, to satisfy customers, an organization must understand their needs, convert those needs into designs, produce the product or service required, deliver it, assess ongoing satisfaction, and adjust the processes accordingly. People need to be trained or hired to do the work, and data must be collected to monitor progress. Performing only a part of the required activities is disjointed and not integrated.

Interrater Reliability

The degree to which multiple raters, observing the same phenomenon, will give it the same rating. If they do, it has high interrater reliability; if not, it has low interrater reliability.

Measures

Measures refer to numerical information that quantifies (measures) input, output, and performance dimensions of processes, products, services, and the overall organization.

Performance

Performance refers to output results information obtained from processes, products, and services that permits evaluation and comparison relative to goals, standards, past results, and to others. Performance might be expressed in nonfinancial and financial terms.

Operational performance refers to organizational, human resource, and supplier performance relative to effectiveness and efficiency measures and indicators. Examples include cycle time, productivity, waste reduction, and regulatory compliance. Operational performance might be measured at the work unit level, the key process level, and the organization level.

Product and service quality refers to operational performance relative to measures and indicators of product and service requirements derived from customer preference information. Product and service quality measures should correlate with, and allow the organization to predict, customer satisfaction. Examples of product and service quality include reliability, on-time delivery, defect levels, and service response time. For example, consider a coffee shop that serves breakfast coffee. Product and service quality indicators and measures may include time to serve; time to process payment; freshness (time between brewing and serving); bitterness (acidity measured by pH level); temperature; and ratio of coffee to water and grind coarseness. Taken together, these measures can predict customer satisfaction. In 2000, these results are evaluated as part of Item 7.1.

Customer-focused performance refers to performance relative to measures and indicators of customers' perceptions, reactions, and behaviors, and to measures and indicators of product and service characteristics important to customers. Examples include customer retention, complaints, customer survey results, product reliability, on-time delivery, defect levels, and service response time.

Financial and marketplace performance refers to performance using measures of cost and revenue, including asset utilization, asset growth, and market share. Examples include returns on investments, value added per employee, debt to equity ratio, returns on assets, operating margins, cash-to-cash cycle time, and other profitability and liquidity measures. Financial measures are generally tracked throughout the organization.

Supplier and partner performance refers to processes and requirements of Item 6.3. The performance of suppliers and partners usually includes factors, such as cost reduction, on-time delivery, error or defect rates, and specialized measures important to the customer.

Human resource performance relates to the activities in Category 5. Human resource performance measures usually include absenteeism, employee satisfaction ratings, safety incidents, turnover rates, strikes, worker grievances, and compensation claims.

Prevention-Based

Seeking the root cause of a problem and preventing its recurrence rather than merely solving the problem and waiting for it to happen again (a reactive posture).

Process

Process refers to linked activities with the purpose of producing a product or service for a customer (user) within or outside the organization. Generally, processes involve combinations of people, machines, tools, techniques, and materials in a systematic series of steps or actions. In some situations, processes might require adherence to a specific sequence of steps, with documentation (sometimes formal) of procedures and requirements, including well-defined measurement and control steps.

In many service situations, particularly when customers are directly involved in the service, process is used in a more general way—to spell out what must be done, possibly including a preferred or expected sequence. If a sequence is critical, the service needs to include information to help customers understand and follow the sequence.

Service processes involving customers also require guidance to the providers of those services on handling contingencies related to customers' likely or possible actions or behaviors.

Some organizations do not recognize the importance of the services they provide. Consider the coffee shop again. If the focus is only on making the best coffee and the service is poor—making customers wait too long—the coffee shop will lose customers. Delivering service value must be considered as important to success as delivering product value.

In knowledge work, such as strategic planning, research, development, and analysis, process does not necessarily imply formal sequences of steps. Rather, process implies general understandings regarding competent performance, such as timing, options to be included, evaluation, and reporting. Sequences might arise as part of these understandings.

Productivity

Productivity refers to measures of efficiency of the use of resources. Although the term is often applied to single factors, such as staffing (labor productivity), machines, materials, energy, and capital, the productivity concept applies as well to total resources used in producing outputs. Overall productivity—sometimes called *total factor productivity*—is determined by combining the productivities of the different resources used for an output. The combination usually requires taking a weighted average of the different single factor productivity measures, where the weights typically reflect costs of the resources. The use of an aggregate measure of overall productivity allows a determination of whether or not the net effect of overall changes in a process—possibly involving resource trade-offs—is beneficial.

Effective approaches to performance management require understanding and measuring single factor and overall productivity, particularly in complex cases with a variety of costs and potential benefits.

Refinement

The result of a systematic process to analyze performance of a system and improve it.

Results

Results refer to outcomes achieved by an organization in addressing the purposes of a Baldrige Criteria Item. Results are evaluated on the basis of current performance; performance relative to appropriate comparisons; rate, breadth, and importance of performance improvements; and relationship of results measures to key organizational performance requirements.

Root Cause

The original cause or reason for a condition. The root cause of a condition is that cause which, if eliminated, guarantees that the condition will not recur.

Service Standard (Customer-Contact Requirements)

A set, measurable level of performance. For example, an objective of an organization might be "prompt customer service." A customer contact requirement or service standard would stipulate how prompt the service should be, such as "Equipment will be repaired within 24 hours," or "The phone will be answered by a person on or before the second ring."

Strategic Objectives

Strategic objectives refer to an organization's major change opportunities and/or the fundamental challenges the organization faces. Strategic objectives are generally externally focused, relating to significant customer, market, product/service, or technological opportunities and challenges. Broadly stated, they are what an organization must change or improve to remain or become competitive. Strategic objectives set an organization's longer-term directions and guide resource allocations and redistributions.

System

A set of well-defined and well-designed processes for meeting the organization's quality and performance requirements.

Systematic

Systematic refers to approaches that are repeatable and and predictable, rather than anecdotal and episodic. *Systematic approaches* use data and information so that improvement and learning are possible. Approaches are systematic if they build in the opportunity for evaluation and learning and permit a gain in maturity. As organizational approaches mature, they become more systematic and reflect cycles of evaluation and learning. A systematic approach also integrates other approaches to ensure high levels of efficiency, effectiveness, and alignment.

Value

Value refers to the degree of worth relative to cost and relative to possible alternatives of a product, service, process, asset, or function.

Organizations frequently use value considerations to determine the benefits of various options relative to their costs, such as the value of various product and service combinations to customers. Organizations seek to deliver value to all their stakeholders. This frequently requires balancing value for customers and other stakeholders, such as stockholders, employees, and the community.

Waste Reduction

Obtained from redesigning a product to require less material or from recycling waste to produce useful products.

Clarifying Confusing Terms

Comparative Information vs. Benchmarking

Comparative information includes benchmarking and competitive comparisons. *Benchmarking* refers to collecting information and data about processes and performance results that represent the best practices and performance for similar activities inside or outside the organization's business or industry. Competitive comparisons refer to collecting information and data on performance relative to direct competitors or similar providers.

For example, a personal computer manufacturer, ABC Micro, must store, retrieve, pack, and ship computers and replacement parts. ABC Micro is concerned about shipping response time, errors in shipping, and damage during shipping. To determine the level of performance of its competitors in these areas and to set reasonable improvement goals, ABC Micro would gather competitive comparison data from similar providers (competitors). However, these performance levels may not reflect best practices for storage, retrieval, packing, and shipping.

Benchmarking would require ABC Micro to find organizations who carry out these processes better than anyone else and examine both their processes and performance levels, such as the catalog company L.L. Bean.

Benchmarking seeks best-practices information. Competitive comparisons look at competitors, whether or not they are the best.

Customer-Contact Employees

Customer-contact employees are any employees who are in direct contact with customers. They may be direct service providers or answer complaint calls. Whenever a customer makes contact with an organization, either in person or by phone or other electronic means, that customer forms an opinion about the organization and its employees. Employees who come in contact with customers are in a critical position to influence customers for the good of the organization, or to its detriment.

Customer Satisfaction vs. Customer Dissatisfaction

One is not the inverse of the other. The lack of complaints does not indicate satisfaction, although the presence of complaints can be a partial indicator of dissatisfaction. Measures of customer dissatisfaction can include direct measures through surveys, as well as complaints, product returns, and warranty claims.

Customer satisfaction and dissatisfaction are complex to assess. Customers are rarely "thoroughly" dissatisfied, although they may dislike a feature of a product or an aspect of service. There are usually degrees of satisfaction and dissatisfaction.

Data vs. Information

Information can be qualitative and quantitative. *Data* are information that lend themselves to quantification and statistical analysis. For example, an incoming inspection might produce a count of the number of units accepted, rejected, and total shipped. This count is considered *data*. These counts add to the base of *information* about supplier quality.

Education vs. Training

Training refers to learning about and acquiring job-specific skills and knowledge. *Education* refers to the general development of individuals. An organization might provide training in equipment maintenance for its workers, as well as support the education of workers through an associate degree program at a local community college.

Empowerment and Involvement

Empowerment generally refers to processes and procedures designed to provide individuals and teams the employee tools, skills, and authority to make decisions that affect their work—decisions traditionally reserved for managers and supervisors.

Empowerment as a concept has been misused in many organizations. For example, managers may pretend to extend decision authority under the guise of chartering teams and individuals to make recommendations about their work, while continuing to reserve decision-making authority for themselves.

This practice has given rise to another term—*involvement*—which describes the role of employees who are asked to become involved in decision making, without necessarily making decisions. Involvement is a practice that many agree is better than not involving employees at all but still does not optimize their contribution to initiative, flexibility, and fast response.

Measures and Indicators

The award Criteria do not make a distinction between *measures* and indicators. However, some users of these terms prefer the term *indicator* (1) when the measurement relates to performance but is not a direct or exclusive measure of such performance, for example, the number of complaints is an indicator of dissatisfaction but not a direct or exclusive measure of it; and (2) when the measurement is a predictor (leading indicator) of some more significant performance, for example, gain in customer satisfaction might be a leading indicator of market share gain.

Operational Performance and Predictors of Customer Satisfaction

Operational performance processes and predictors of customer satisfaction are related but not always the same. Operational performance measures can reflect issues that concern customers, as well as those that do not. Operational performance measures are used by the organization to assess effectiveness and efficiency, as well as predict customer satisfaction.

In the example of the coffee shop, freshness is a key customer requirement. One predictor of customer satisfaction might be the length of time, in minutes, between brewing and serving to guarantee freshness and good aroma. The standard might be 10 minutes or less to ensure satisfaction. Coffee more than 10 minutes old would be discarded.

A measure of operational effectiveness might be how many cups were discarded (waste) because the coffee was too old. The customer does not care if the coffee shop pours out stale coffee, and therefore, that measure is not a predictor of satisfaction. However, pouring out coffee does affect profitability and should be measured and minimized.

Ideally, an organization should be able to identify enough measures of product and service quality to predict customer satisfaction accurately and monitor operating effectiveness and efficiency.

Performance Requirements vs. Performance Measures

Performance requirements are an expression of customer requirements and expectations. Sometimes performance requirements are expressed as design requirements or engineering requirements. They are viewed as a basis for developing measures to enable the organization to determine, generally without asking the customer, whether the customer is likely to be satisfied.

Performance measures can also be used to assess efficiency, effectiveness, and productivity of a work process. Process performance measures might include cycle time, error rate, or throughput.

Support Services

Support services are those services that support the organization's product and service delivery core operating processes. Support services might include finance and accounting, management information services, software support, marketing, public relations, personnel administration (job posting, recruitment, payroll), facilities maintenance and management, research and development, secretarial support, and other administration services.

Of course, if an organization is in business to provide a traditional support service, such as accounting, then accounting services provided to its external customers become its core work/operating process and are no longer considered a support service. Internal accounting services would continue to be considered a support service.

In the human resources area (Category 5), the Criteria require organizations to manage their human resource assets to optimize performance. However, many human resources support services might also exist, such as payroll, travel, position control, recruitment, and employee services. These processes must be designed, delivered, and refined systematically according to the requirements of Item 6.2.

A similar relationship exists in the supplier area. Item 6.3 requires an organization to strengthen supplier and partner performance. This may take place through several measures, including training suppliers and/or building partnerships between operating units in the organization and suppliers.

However, the details of developing work specifications, requests for quotations, and other aspects of procurement process might be assigned to a procurement department. That department would be considered a support service that must design its own products and services to meet the requirements of its internal customer and would be received as a support structure (6.2).

Cross-Functional Work Teams vs. Natural Work Units

Natural work units reflect the people that normally work together because they are a part of a formal work unit. For example, on an assembly line, three or four people naturally work together to install a motor in a new car. Hotel employees who prepare food in the kitchen might constitute another natural work unit.

Teams may be formed of people within a natural work unit or may cross existing (natural) organization boundaries. To improve room service in a hotel, for example, some members of several natural work units, such as the switchboard, kitchen workers, and waiters may form a special team. This team would not be considered a natural work unit. It might be called a *cross-functional* work team because its members come from different functions within the organization.

Appendix A: Global View of Quality

This section describes Quality/Performance awards from around the globe. It describes their purpose, goals, strategies, models, and core values. Much of the research for this section is based on the references at the end of the section. In addition to recognizing the contribution of these organizations and sponsors, phone numbers or e-mails are listed, so our readers may pursue more in-depth research on global awards.

There are about 50 National Quality Organizations around the world:
- Central and Eastern Europe, 18 percent
- Western and Northern Europe, 32 percent
- Southern Europe and Mediterranean, 12 percent
- Central and South America and Caribbean, 18 percent
- North America, 6 percent
- Asia, 10 percent
- Africa, 4 percent

The majority of the previously listed organizations have these common goals:
- To raise the level and quality of management in organizations
- To support the competitiveness of industry in their country
- To share knowledge and best practices
- To increase emphasis on the methods of quality.

Quality awards around the world are based in whole or in part on one of three basic models: The Baldrige model, the Deming model and the European Quality Award model (which in itself, ties to the Baldrige model). The Malcolm Baldrige National Award was funded in 1987 and authorized by the U.S. Congress to recognize service, small business and manufacturing companies. Of the worldwide quality award organizations, 41 percent use the Baldrige model in part or whole as the foundation for their award.

The Deming Prize, the longest standing of the awards, was established in 1951 by a resolution of the Union of Japanese Scientists and Engineers (JUSE) and named after the great leader in quality, W. Edwards Deming. The Deming Prize was and continues to be primarily used in Japan (although several years ago, representatives of the Japanese government benchmarked the Baldrige process and have created a Baldrige-based national quality award). Four percent of the awards (India and Japan's JUSE Award) are based on this model today. Reference: JUSE Tokyo, Japan, +81-3-5379-1227.

The European Quality Award (EQA) was initiated in 1992 to recognize high levels of commitment to quality. It was applied particularly by European organizations and has become increasingly popular. Fifty-five percent of quality award organizations use this Baldrige-based quality award, in whole or part, as the foundation for their award.

Both the European and Malcolm Baldrige Award have common or very similar core values:

EQA Value	Malcolm Baldrige Value
Customer focus	Customer driven
Supplier partnerships	Valuing employees and partners
People development and involvement	Organizational and personal learning
Processes and facts	Management by fact
Continuous improvement and innovation	Managing for innovation
Leadership and consistency of purpose	Visionary leadership
Public responsibility	Public responsibility and citizenship
Results oriented	Focus on results and creating value

The following nine core values were included in over 50 percent of the worldwide awards. The Baldrige value follows in parentheses:

- Customer orientation (Customer driven)
- Continuous improvement (Organizational and personal learning but was formerly called Continuous improvement and learning)
- Participation by everyone (Valuing employees and partners)
- Committed leadership (Visionary leadership)
- Process orientation (Managing for innovation)

- Long-range perspective (Focus on the future)
- Public responsibility (Public responsibility and citizenship)
- Management by facts (Management by fact)
- Prevention (Not clear corresponding value but agility corresponds in part)
- Learn from others (Organizational and personal learning)

Although most awards have review cycles to improve their models, they are not annual as is the Malcolm Baldrige. The EQA, for example, is updating its model in 2000, but it is not yet finalized. Therefore, the following comparison is to its most recent model (1996). Between the two awards, 96 percent of the organizations use one of these models in whole or in part as a basis for their awards.

References on Quality Awards

The Deming Prize Guide for Overseas Companies, 1996. Copyright JUSE, Telephone: +81-3-5379-1227 (Japan) Fax: +81-3-5379-1227.

Quality for Excellence and Prosperity, 1998. Hong Kong Management Association HKMA Quality Award. Telephone: 2774 8569/2766 3303 (Hong Kong).

The European Quality Award, 1996. European Foundation for Quality Management. Telephone: +32 2 775 35 11 (Brussels).

Bases Del Premo Nacional A La Calidad, 1996. Republica Argentina. Telephone/Fax: (541) 326-6104 (Argentina). Private Sector Award.

Australian Business Excellence Framework, 1999. Web site: www.apc.org.au. Telephone 1-800-060-830.

State of the Quality Organisation: A Comparative Review of the Organisations, Their Products and Service and Quality Awards Programs. The report was sponsored by the Swedish International Development Agency, Swedish Institute for Quality and the Xerox Corporation in 1998. E-mail: sari@recomate.se. Telephone: +46 31 53 00 (Sweden).

Comparing the European Quality Award Model with the Baldrige Criteria

European Quality Award Requirements	1.1	1.2	2.1	2.2	3.1	3.2	4.1	4.2	5.1	5.2	5.3	6.1	6.2	6.3	7.1	7.2	7.3	7.4	7.5
Leadership: How the behavior and actions of the executive team and all other leaders inspire, support, and promote a culture of Total Quality Management. Leaders:																			
1a. visibly demonstrate their commitment to a culture of Total Quality Management	●																		
1b. support improvement and involvement by providing appropriate resources and assistance	●							●											
1c. are involved with customers, suppliers, and other external organizations	●																		
1d. recognize and appreciate people's efforts and achievements	●								●										
Policy and Strategy: How the organization formulates, deploys, reviews its policy and strategy, and turns it into plans and actions. Policy and strategy are:																			
2a. based on information which is relevant and comprehensive			●				●	●											
2b. developed			●																
2c. communicated and implemented	●			●															
2d. regularly updated and improved			●	●															
People Management: How the organization releases the full potential of its people. People:																			
3a. resources are planned and improved				●															
3b. capabilities are sustained and developed									●	●	●								
3c. agree on targets and continuously review performance	●			●					●		●				●				
3d. are involved, empowered, and recognized									●										
3e. and the organization have an effective dialogue	●								●										
3f. are cared for										●									
Resources: How the organization manages resources effectively and efficiently. How:																			
4a. financial resources are managed	●							●				●							
4b. information resources are managed				●									●						
4c. supplier relationships and materials are managed				●								●	●					●	
4d. buildings, equipment, and other assets are managed				●								●	●						
4e. technology and intellectual property are managed				●								●	●						
Processes: How the organization identifies, manages, reviews, and improves its processes. Processes:																			
5a. key to the success of the business are identified	●	●					●	●				●							
5b. are systematically managed	●											●	●	●					
5c. are reviewed and targets are set for improvement				●				●				●	●	●					
5d. are improved using innovation and creativity										●		●	●						
5e. are changed and the benefits evaluated										●		●	●						
Customer Satisfaction: What the organization is achieving in relation to the satisfaction of its external customers.																			
6a. the customers' perception of the organization's products, services, and customer relationships					●	●	●	●								●			
6b. additional measurements relating to the satisfaction of the organization's customers					●	●	●	●								●			
People Satisfaction: What the organization is achieving in relation to the satisfaction of its people.																			
7a. the people's perception of the organization							●	●			●						●		
7b. additional measurements relating to people satisfaction				●			●	●			●								
Impact on Society: What the organization is achieving in satisfying the needs and the expectations of the local, national, and international community at large (as appropriate). This includes the perception of the organization's approach to quality of life, the environment, the preservation of global resources, and the organization's own internal measures of effectiveness. It will include its relations with authorities and bodies which affect and regulate its business.																			
8a. society's perception of the organization		●																	
8b. additional measurements of the organization's impact on society		●						●											●
Business Result: What the organization is achieving in relation to its planned business objectives and in satisfying the needs and expectations of everyone with a financial interest or stake in the organization.																			
9a. financial measurements of the organization's performance																●			
9b. additional measurements of the organization's performance																			●

Additional correlations between the Baldrige and European Quality Award criteria might exist, depending on the interpretation of where results of some support areas are reported.

Appendix B: Comparing Baldrige and ISO 9000:2000—A Maturity/Excellence Model versus a Compliance Model

This section compares two different processes that examine business systems. One is based on compliance to very specific standards, and the other is an excellence model based on the extent of effective use of a complex management system. The section addresses first the key similarities and then the fundamental differences in the processes.

The International Organization for Standardization (ISO) has expanded its focus with its ISO 9000 series. This series focuses on quality assurance and management and describes minimum standards for management systems. A major factor in the development and use of ISO 9000 were the European organizations in building a common market. ISO 9000 is intended to be an enabler of global trade. It makes it easier for different countries to establish and communicate minimum standards for processes required to meet customer requirements for products and services. ISO 9000 standards assist users through stages of signing a contract, to designing of products and services through manufacturing and follow-up. They apply to hardware, software, services, and process industries. They are a tool that requires documentation of internal processes to meet customer requirements.

Similarities between ISO 9001:2000 and the Baldrige Criteria for Performance Excellence:
- Purpose is business improvement
- Require some form of improvement cycle
- Have some sort of follow-up review or evaluation
- Valuable to customer

The Baldrige Performance Excellence Criteria are different than compliance programs, such as ISO, in intent, design, and process. While both ISO and Baldrige are designed to enhance quality, ISO is a standards-based, baseline quality assurance program. The aim is to create confidence between suppliers and their clients. ISO has its roots in the objective of setting minimum thresholds of performance. When met or exceeded, ISO certification confers the right to trade internationally and between companies. This is certainly an important purpose since it forces low performers to meet minimally acceptable standards.

The Baldrige Criteria, in contrast, strive to encourage peak performance. Vigorous commitment to improvement by all levels of the organization is pervasive in the Criteria. This encourages companies to raise their performance persistently, from beginning stages of approach and use, to a mature organization where effective approaches are continuously refined and fully integrated and deployed. The objective is ever-improving world-class performance, not compliance with minimum standards for certification.

The seven Baldrige Criteria describe a highly interdependent management system—a system necessary for top performance. Their real power is found in the synergy of their linkages. It is through this integration that the possibility of enterprisewide improvement comes within reach. As organizations commit to more effective approaches, use them fully, and improve them continuously, they move up the maturity scale. ISO, in contrast, has a checklist of individual standards that organizations use to achieve certification.

Using the Baldrige Criteria compels companies to identify strategic and stretch targets. In the case of small businesses and manufacturing, the objective is to continuously improve, to become the industry's benchmark in terms of product and service, and to sustain impressive results as measured by customer and stakeholder satisfaction, market penetration and performance, outcomes, financial performance, and other measures important to your organization.

Summary of Key Differences

Topic	ISO 9001:2000	Baldrige
Value to customer	Generic quality management system to create confidence between suppliers and clients	Provides feedback report to guide organization's senior leaders in setting priorities for Performance Excellence
	Mandated conformity assessment for some organizations	Recognition for excellence
Model includes	All of the planned and systematic activities to meet quality requirements within a quality system	Integrated management system aimed at long-term improvements of all elements of the system.
Assessment	International standards are developed by ISO conformity assessment done by suppliers and clients, not ISO. Certification and Registration done by "third party" assessment services.	Scoring is a complex consensus process where the Malcolm Baldrige Award Office trains and selects evaluators to examine the performance of the entire management system including: effectiveness of approach, extent of deployment, results, and continuous evaluation and improvement. Score from 0 percent (no systems at all) to 100 percent on 1000 (world-class) points in increments of 10 percent.
Goal	Meet baseline standards	Be the best, competitive advantage
Sample Assessment Items	ISO 9001 4.1 Management responsibilities: • Define a quality policy. Your policy should describe your organization's attitude toward quality. • Define the organizational structure that you will need in order to manage your quality system. • Define quality system responsibilities, give quality system personnel the authority to carry out these responsibilities, and ensure that the interactions between these personnel are clearly specified. Also, make sure that all of this is well documented.	Item 1.1: Organizational leadership: Describe how senior leaders guide your organization and review organizational performance. (a) Senior leadership direction (1) How do senior leaders set, communicate and deploy organizational values, performance expectations, and a focus on creating and balancing value for customers? Include communication and deployment through your leadership structure and to all staff.
Geography	Certificates issued in at least 121 countries	U.S.-based companies and organizations

Summary

ISO standards-based assessments and Baldrige assessments are valuable for improving performance. ISO is in the process of revising their 9000 series standards and including more requirements from the Baldrige Criteria to strengthen their minimum standards. ISO is particularly useful in enabling better communication between countries and organizations involved in international trade. The Baldrige Criteria are intended to promote systemwide optimum organizational performance.

Appendix C: 2000 Systems Required for Performance Excellence

The following section is intended for use by leaders of the organization and its units as a management tool. It defines responsibilities and management systems that are drawn from the 2000 Criteria for Performance Excellence. It can be used as a relatively simple way to focus on the Criteria requirements. Some organizations use this type of information to guide the work of management champions. Organizational leaders at various levels can use the following section for setting objectives and requirements rather than having to translate questions into statements. These statements can be used in conjunction with the category champion descriptions to further define the areas of responsibility and focus for each category champion.

1 Leadership

Senior leaders must address values and performance expectations, as well as focus on customers and other stakeholders, empowerment, innovation, learning, and organizational directions. Also, your organization must address its responsibilities to the public and support its key communities.

1.1 Organizational Leadership

Senior leaders must effectively and systematically guide your organization and review organizational performance.

a. Senior Leadership Direction

Senior leaders must clearly set, communicate, and deploy organizational values, performance expectations, and focus on creating and balancing value for customers and other stakeholders through your leadership structure to all employees.

Senior leaders must establish and support employee empowerment and innovation, and organizational and employee learning.

Senior leaders must set clear directions and seek future opportunities for your organization.

b. Organizational Performance Review

Senior leaders must systematically review organizational performance and capabilities to assess organizational health, competitive performance, and progress relative to performance goals and changing organizational needs.

Key performance measures that are regularly reviewed by senior leaders must be defined.

Senior leaders must systematically translate organizational performance review findings into priorities for improvement and opportunities for innovation.

Key recent performance review findings, priorities for improvement, and opportunities for innovation must be known and documented. They must be understood throughout the organization and, as appropriate, by suppliers/partners and key customers to ensure organizational alignment.

Senior leaders must regularly use organizational performance review findings and employee feedback to improve their leadership effectiveness and the effectiveness of management throughout the organization.

1.2 Public Responsibility and Citizenship

Your organization must address its responsibilities to the public and practice good citizenship.

a. Responsibilities to the Public

The organization must systematically examine and address the impacts on society of your products, services, and operations. Key practices, measures, and targets must be identified for meeting or exceeding regulatory and legal requirements and for minimizing risks associated with all products, services, and operations.

The organization must have a system in place to anticipate public concerns with current and future products, services, and operations. It must address these concerns in a proactive manner.

The organization must have a system in place to ensure ethical business practices are followed in all stakeholder transactions and interactions.

b. Support of Key Communities

The organization, its senior leaders, and employees must actively support and strengthen the organization's key communities. A systematic process must be in place to identify key communities and determine appropriate areas of emphasis for organizational involvement and support, consistent with organizational business objectives.

2 Strategic Planning

Your organization must have a clear strategy development process, including a process to develop strategic objectives, action plans, and related human resource plans. Also your organization must deploy the plans and track performance. Strategic objectives define the things your organization must do to be successful in the future.

2.1 Strategy Development

Your organization must have a strategy development process to strengthen your organizational performance and competitive position. Your key strategic objectives need to be clearly defined.

a. Strategy Development Process

A clear strategic planning process must be in place, including key steps and key participants in the process.

The strategic planning process considers relevant data and information for the following key factors as each relates to your organization:
- Customer and market needs/expectations, including new product/service opportunities;
- Competitive environment and capabilities, including use of new technology;
- Financial, societal, and other potential risks;
- Human resource capabilities and needs;
- Operational capabilities and needs, including resource availability; and
- Supplier and/or partner capabilities and needs.

b. Strategic Objectives

Your organization must have a timetable or planned performance trajectory for accomplishing its key strategic objectives. Your organization must assess how well the strategic objectives respond to the bullets in 2.1 that are most important to your success.

2.2 Strategy Deployment

Your organization must make certain all managers and employees understand the strategy and their personal role in carrying it out. Action plans and related performance measures must be clearly defined. Project the performance of these key measures into the future.

a. Action Plan Development and Deployment

Systematically develop action plans to implement key strategic objectives. List key short- and longer-term action plans. Identify key changes, if any, in your products/services and/or your customers/markets and be able to explain the reasons for the changes to employees throughout the organization.

Define key human resource requirements and plans, based on strategic objectives and action plans, the organization must implement to ensure it has the human resources to carry out the plan.

Develop a system to allocate resources throughout the organization to ensure they are aligned with strategic objectives and that your overall action plan is achieved.

Define key performance measures and/or indicators for tracking progress relative to action plans.

Systematically communicate and deploy strategic objectives, action plans, and performance measures/indicators throughout the organization to achieve overall organizational alignment of work and resources.

b. Performance Projection
Define the two- to five-year projections for key performance measures and/or indicators. Include key performance targets and/or goals, as appropriate.

Determine the projected performance of competitors and key benchmarks, as appropriate, for the same time period as your projected goals. The basis for these comparisons must be clear.

3 Customer and Market Focus

Your organization must determine requirements, expectations, and preferences of customers and markets. Also your organization must build relationships with customers and determine their satisfaction.

3.1 Customer and Market Knowledge
Your organization must determine short- and longer-term requirements, expectations, and preferences of customers and markets to ensure the relevance of current products/services and to develop new opportunities.

a. Customer and Market Knowledge
Systematically determine target customers, customer groups, and/or market segments. Specifically consider the requirements of customers of competitors and other potential customers and/or markets in this determination.

Systematically listen and learn from current, former, and potential customers to determine key requirements and drivers of purchase decisions. If determination methods differ for different customers and/or customer groups, define the key differences and show how your techniques for learning about the requirements of these groups vary according to real differences among the customer groups.

Systematically determine and/or project key product/service features and identify their relative importance/value to customers for purposes of current and future marketing, product planning, and other business developments, as appropriate. Use relevant information from current and former customers, including marketing/sales information, customer retention, won/lost analysis, and complaints in this determination.

Evaluate and improve your listening and learning methods to keep them current with changing business needs and directions.

3.2 Customer Satisfaction and Relationships

Your organization must determine the satisfaction of customers and build relationships to retain current business and to develop new opportunities.

a. Customer Relationships

Provide easy access to facilitate the ability of customers to conduct business, seek assistance and information, and complain. Document the key mechanisms used.

Determine key customer-contact requirements and systematically ensure all employees involved in the customer response chain understand and adhere to these contact requirements.

Establish a systematic complaint management process to ensure that complaints are resolved effectively and promptly (ideally at the first point of contact). Ensure that all complaints received are aggregated and analyzed for use in overall organizational improvement.

Systematically build relationships with customers to ensure repeat business and/or positive referral.

Evaluate and improve approaches to provide customer access and build relationships to keep them current with changing business needs and directions.

b. Customer Satisfaction Determination

Implement systematic processes, take measurements, and collect data to determine customer satisfaction and dissatisfaction. Ensure that measurements capture actionable information that reflects customers' future business and/or potential for positive referral. Define any significant differences in processes or methods for different customer groups and/or market segments.

Systematically follow up with customers on products/services and recent transactions so your organization can receive prompt and actionable feedback for use in improving products and services and preventing future problems.

Obtain and use information on customer satisfaction relative to competitors and/or benchmarks, as appropriate, to improve your offerings and support strategic planning.

Evaluate and improve approaches to customer satisfaction determination to keep them current with changing business needs and directions.

4 Information and Analysis

Your organization must have a performance measurement system and a way to analyze performance data and information.

4.1 Measurement of Organizational Performance

Your organization must provide effective performance measurement systems for understanding, aligning, and improving performance at all levels and in all parts of your organization.

a. Measurement of Organizational Performance

Ensure the major components of the organization's performance measurement system, includes the following key factors:

- Select measures/indicators that examine the extent and effectiveness of daily operations;
- Select and integrate measures/indicators to ensure complete data are available to track overall organizational performance in areas key to business success;
- Select key comparative data and information and effectively use the data to set goals and improve work processes throughout the organization;
- Ensure the reliability of data and information used for decision making;
- Use information and data to improve the cost/financial understanding to help set priorities regarding improvement options;
- Use data and information to develop correlations/projections to support planning; and
- Evaluate and improve the performance measurement system to keep it current with changing business needs and directions.

4.2 Analysis of Organizational Performance

Your organization must analyze performance data and information to assess and understand overall organizational performance.

a. Analysis of Organizational Performance

Analyze data that examines the overall health of the organization, including key business results and strategic objectives to support senior executives' organizational performance review and planning.

Systematically ensure that the results of organizational-level analysis are linked to work group and/or functional-level operations to enable effective support for decision making.

Ensure the analysis effectively supports daily operational decision making throughout the organization and ensures that measures align with action plans.

5 Human Resource Focus

Your organization must enable employees to develop and utilize their full potential, aligned with the organization's objectives. Also your organization must build and maintain a work environment and an employee support climate conducive to Performance Excellence, full participation, and personal and organizational growth.

5.1 Work Systems

Your organization's work and job design, compensation, career progression, and related workforce practices must enable employees to achieve high performance in your operations.

a. Work Systems

Design, organize, and manage work and jobs to promote cooperation and collaboration, individual initiative, innovation, and flexibility to keep current with business needs.

Ensure that managers and supervisors encourage and motivate employees to develop and utilize their full potential and encourage and support employees in job- and career-related development/learning objectives.

Ensure that the employee performance management system, including feedback to employees, supports high performance (which is usually defined by the strategic objectives).

Ensure that compensation, recognition, and related reward/incentive practices systematically reinforce high performance.

Ensure effective communication, cooperation, and knowledge/skill sharing across work units, functions, and locations, as appropriate.

Systematically identify characteristics and skills needed by potential employees; and recruit and hire new employees to fill skill gaps consistent with fair workforce practices. When examining key performance requirements to identify needed skills mix, consider diversity within the organization's employee community.

5.2 Employee Education, Training, and Development
Your organization's education and training must support the achievement of your business objectives; build employee knowledge, skills, and capabilities; and contribute to improved employee performance.

a. Employee Education, Training, and Development
Ensure that the organization's system for education and training balances short- and longer-term organizational and employee needs, including development, learning, and career progression.

Design education and training to ensure it keeps current with business and individual needs. Include how job and organizational performance are used in education and training design and evaluation.

Seek and use input from employees and their supervisors/managers to design and set education and training needs and expectations.

Deliver, evaluate, and improve formal and informal education, training, and learning, as appropriate.

Systematically address key developmental and training needs of the entire workforce, including diversity training, management/leadership development, new employee orientation, and safety, as appropriate.

Ensure that training and education address the topics of Performance Excellence, such as ensuring that employees learn to use performance measurements, performance standards, skill standards, performance improvement, quality control methods, and benchmarking, as appropriate.

Systematically reinforce knowledge and skills on the job.

5.3 Employee Well-Being and Satisfaction
Your organization must maintain a work environment and an employee support climate that contribute to the well-being, satisfaction, and motivation of all employees.

a. Work Environment

Systematically assess and improve workplace health, safety, and ergonomics. Ensure employees take part in identifying these factors and in improving workplace safety. Ensure performance measures and/or targets are in place for each key environmental factor. Also identify significant differences in requirements, if any, based on different work environments for employee groups and/or work units.

b. Employee Support Climate

Enhance employees' work climate via services, benefits, and policies. Ensure these enhancements are selected and tailored to meet the needs of different categories and types of employees, and individuals, as appropriate.

Ensure that the work climate considers and supports the needs of a diverse workforce.

c. Employee Satisfaction

Systematically determine the key factors that affect employee well-being, satisfaction, and motivation.

Develop and implement formal and/or informal assessment methods and measures to determine employee well-being, satisfaction, and motivation systematically. Methods and measures should be tailored to examine the needs of a diverse workforce and to different categories and types of employees. In addition, use such indicators as employee turnover, absenteeism, grievances, and productivity to assess and improve employee well-being, satisfaction, and motivation.

Relate employee climate assessment findings to key business results to identify work environment and employee support climate improvement priorities.

6 Process Management

Your organization must have a process management system, including customer-focused design, product and service delivery, support, and supplier and partnering processes that involve all work units.

6.1 Product and Service Processes

Your organization must manage effectively key product and service design and delivery processes.

a. Design Processes

A clear design process for products/services and their related production/delivery processes must be in place.

Design processes must be capable of systematically incorporating changing customer/market requirements into product/service designs and production/delivery systems and processes.

Systematically incorporate new technology into products/services and into production/delivery systems and processes, as appropriate.

Ensure that design processes systematically and thoroughly address design quality and cycle time, transfer of learning from past projects and other parts of the organization, cost control, new design technology, productivity, and other efficiency/effectiveness factors.

Evaluate production/delivery process design to ensure it effectively accommodates all key operational performance requirements.

Systematically evaluate, coordinate, and test design and production/delivery processes to ensure capability for trouble-free and timely introduction of products/services.

b. Production/Delivery Processes
Key production/delivery processes and their key performance requirements are well known and clearly defined.

Day-to-day operation of key production/delivery processes consistently meet key performance requirements.

Key performance measures and/or indicators are used for the control and improvement of key work processes. Real-time customer input is used to improve work processes.

Evaluate and improve production/delivery processes to achieve better process performance and improvements to products/services, as appropriate. Improvements are consistently shared with other organizational units and processes, as appropriate, throughout the organization.

6.2 Support Processes
Your organization must manage effectively its key support processes.

a. Support Processes
A systematic process is in place to determine key support process requirements, incorporating input from internal and/or external customers, as appropriate. Key operational requirements (such as productivity and cycle time) for the processes are clearly defined.

Processes are designed to meet all the key requirements.

The day-to-day operation of key support processes consistently meet key performance requirements. Define and use in-process measures and/or customer feedback in your support processes.

Evaluate and improve support processes to achieve better performance and to keep them current with business needs and directions, as appropriate. Improvements are routinely shared with other organizational units and processes, as appropriate.

6.3 Supplier and Partnering Processes
Your organization must manage effectively its key supplier and/or partnering interactions and processes.

a. Supplier and Partnering Processes
Key performance requirements your suppliers and/or partners must meet to fulfill your overall requirements are clearly defined. Systematically incorporate performance requirements into supplier and/or partner process management.

Develop a system to ensure that performance requirements are met. Systematically provide timely and actionable feedback to suppliers and/or partners to enable them to improve their performance quickly. Define key performance measures and/or indicators and any targets used for supplier and/or partner assessment.

Systematically and proactively minimize overall costs associated with inspections, tests, and process and/or performance audits.

Provide business assistance and/or incentives to suppliers and/or partners to help them improve their overall performance and their ability to contribute to your current and longer-term performance.

Evaluate and improve your supplier and/or partner processes, including processes to help customers and partners keep current with your business needs and directions. Improvements are systematically shared throughout your organization, as appropriate.

7 Business Results

Your organization's performance and improvement in key business areas must include customer satisfaction, product and service performance, financial and marketplace performance, human resource results, supplier and partner results, and operational performance. Also, your organization must track and improve performance levels relative to competitors.

7.1 Customer Focused Results

Your organization's customer focused results must include customer satisfaction and product and service performance results. Your results must be segmented by customer groups and market segments, as appropriate and include appropriate comparative data.

a. Customer Focused Results

Display data regarding current levels and trends in key measures and/or indicators of customer satisfaction, dissatisfaction, and satisfaction relative to competitors.

Display data regarding current levels and trends in key measures and/or indicators of customer loyalty, positive referral, customer-perceived value, and/or customer relationship building, as appropriate.

Display data regarding current levels and trends in key measures and/or indicators of product and service performance.

7.2 Financial and Market Results

Your organization's key financial and marketplace performance results must be segmented by market segments, as appropriate, and include appropriate comparative data.

a. Financial and Market Results

Display data regarding current levels and trends in key measures and/or indicators of financial performance. Include aggregate measures of financial return and/or economic value, as appropriate.

Display data regarding current levels and trends in key measures and/or indicators of marketplace performance. Include market share/position, business growth, and new markets entered, as appropriate.

7.3 Human Resource Results

Your organization's human resource results must include employee well-being, satisfaction, development, and work system performance. Segment your results by types and categories of employees, as appropriate. Include appropriate comparative data.

a. Human Resource Results

Display data regarding current levels and trends in key measures and/or indicators of employee well-being, satisfaction and dissatisfaction, and development.

Display data regarding current levels and trends in key measures and/or indicators of work system performance and effectiveness.

7.4 Supplier and Partner Results

Your organization's key supplier and partner results must include appropriate comparative data.

a. Supplier and Partner Results

Display data regarding current levels and trends in key measures and/or indicators of supplier and partner performance. Display data regarding performance and/or cost improvements resulting from supplier and partner performance and performance management.

7.5 Organizational Effectiveness Results

Your organization's key operational performance results that contribute to the achievement of organizational effectiveness must be tracked and improved. Include appropriate comparative data.

a. Organizational Effectiveness Results

Display data regarding current levels and trends in key measures and/or indicators of key design, production, delivery, and support-process performance. Include productivity, cycle time, and other appropriate measures of effectiveness and efficiency.

Display data regarding results for key measures and/or indicators of regulatory/legal compliance and citizenship. Display data regarding results for key measures and indicators of accomplishment of organizational strategy.

About the Author

Mark L. Blazey, Ed.D.

Mark Blazey is the president of Quantum Performance Group, Inc.—a management consulting and training firm specializing in organization assessment and high-performance systems development. Dr. Blazey has an extensive background in quality systems. He is a member of the Board of Examiners and a fifth year senior examiner for the Malcolm Baldrige National Quality Award. He is also the lead judge for the quality awards for New York State, Vermont, and the nation of Aruba. Dr. Blazey has participated in and led numerous site visit teams for national, state, and company-private quality awards and audits over the past 12 years.

Dr. Blazey trains thousands of quality award examiners and judges for state and national quality programs, including the Florida Sterling Award, Wisconsin Forward Award, Alabama Quality Award, New York State Quality Award, Pennsylvania Quality Leadership Awards, Illinois Lincoln Award for Business Excellence, Minnesota Quality Award, Vermont Quality Award, Nebraska Quality Award, and Aruba National Quality Award, as well as managers and examiners for schools, health-care organizations, major businesses, and government agencies. He has set up numerous Baldrige-based programs to enhance and assess Performance Excellence for all sectors and types of organizations.

Dr. Blazey has written many books and articles on quality, including the Quality Press best-sellers *Insights to Performance Excellence for Health Care* and *Insights to Performance Excellence in Education.* He is a member and Certified Quality Auditor of the American Society for Quality.

Index